T0316656

Film and Fashion amidst the Ruins of Berlin

This book steers attention toward two key aspects of German culture—film and fashion—that shared similar trajectories and multiple connections, looking at them not only in the immediate postwar years but as far back as 1939. They formed spectacular sites of the postwar recovery processes in both East and West Germany. Viewed against the background of the abundant fashion discourses in the Berlin-based press, the films discussed include classics such as *The Murderers Are among Us, Street Acquaintance,* and *Destinies of Women* as well as neglected works such as *And the Heavens above Us, Martina, Modell Bianka,* and *Ingrid.* These films' treatments of fashion during times of crisis offer subtle reflections on the everyday lives, desires, careers, and self-perceptions of the women who made up a large majority of the postwar public. Costume—in films produced both by DEFA and by West German studios—is a productive site to explore the intersections between realism and escapism. With its focus on costumes within the context of the films' production, distribution, and reception, this book opens up wider discussions about the role of the costume designer, the ways film costumes can be read as intertexts, and the impact on audiences' behaviors and looks. The book reveals multiple connections between film and fashion, both across the temporal dividing line of 1945 and the Cold War split between East and West.

Screen Cultures: German Film and the Visual

Series Editors
Gerd Gemünden (*Dartmouth College*)
Johannes von Moltke (*University of Michigan*)

Also in this series

Film and Fashion amidst the Ruins of Berlin

From Nazism to the Cold War

Mila Ganeva

CAMDEN HOUSE

Rochester, New York

First published 2018 by Camden House
Reprinted in paperback 2023

Camden House is an imprint of Boydell & Brewer Inc.
668 Mt. Hope Avenue, Rochester, NY 14620, USA
and of Boydell & Brewer Limited
PO Box 9, Woodbridge, Suffolk IP12 3DF, UK
www.boydellandbrewer.com

Paperback ISBN-13: 978-1-64014-157-5
Hardcover ISBN-13: 978-1-57113-576-6

Library of Congress Cataloging-in-Publication Data

Names: Ganeva, Mila, author.
Title: Film and fashion amidst the ruins of Berlin : from Nazism to the Cold
War / Mila Ganeva.
Description: Rochester : Camden House, 2018. | Series: Screen cultures:
German film and the visual | Includes bibliographical references and
index.
Identifiers: LCCN 2018021689| ISBN 9781571135766 (hardcover : alk.
paper) | ISBN 1571135766 (hardcover : alk. paper)
Subjects: LCSH: Fashion in motion pictures. | Costume—Germany—
History—20th century. | Motion pictures—Germany—History—20th
century. | Motion picture actors and actresses—Clothing—Germany—
History—20th century. | Fashion—Germany—History—20th century.
Classification: LCC PN1995.9.C56 G37 2018 | DDC 791.43026—dc23
LC record available at https://lccn.loc.gov/2018021689

This publication is printed on acid-free paper.

Contents

Illustrations

Acknowledgments

THE IDEA FOR THIS BOOK started forming some years ago, even before my previous project on women in Weimar fashion was fully done. The abundance of archival material I came across was simply too compelling not to pursue a continuation of the fashion theme in the years that followed the Weimar Republic, the postwar period, and into the 1950s. The focus this time shifted exclusively on the connections between the fashion industry and film history.

The grants I received from several institutions in the United States and abroad made it possible for me to complete various parts of the research and writing. The Internationales Forschungszentrum Kulturwissenschaften (IFK) in Vienna, Austria, provided ideal working conditions and opportunities for intellectual exchange for one semester in 2014. In addition, several short research trips to Germany and Austria were funded by the German Academic Exchange Service, the Institut für die Wissenschaften vom Menschen (IWM, Vienna), and the Stiftung Preußischer Kulturbesitz/Staatliche Museen (Berlin). My gratitude goes to Helmut Lethen (IFK), Ivan Krastev (IWM), and Adelheid Rasche (Kunstbibliothek Berlin), whose expertise and kindness contributed immensely to the success of these research trips. I value their feedback, their enthusiasm for my work, their suggestions, and their very concrete logistical help. Renathe Göthe (Film University Babelsberg), Cordula Döhrer (Deutsche Kinemathek, Berlin), Britta Bommert (Kunstbibliothek Berlin), and Heike Remus (Stadtmuseum Berlin) have been wonderful guides in my archival treasure hunts. Dagmar Hahn and Gudrun Drechsler-Reichhardt generously shared with me their time, their photographs, and their families' experiences in the Berlin fashion business. I could not have written the book without the friendship of many in Germany and elsewhere in Europe, especially Julia Bertschik, Werner Kindsmüller, Ulrike Bruckner-Kindsmüller, and Nathalie Huet. Philipp Stiasny always managed to discover yet another valuable film source or historical document that I did not know about and has arranged for numerous opportunities to share my research with interested audiences. I am particularly indebted to Manfred Flügge for his enduring friendship, countless inspiring conversations, and so many good walks in Berlin.

Miami University has supported my research by granting me a sabbatical in 2011–12 as well as travel funds to present parts of my project in progress at national and international conferences. The staff of the interlibrary loan department supplied innumerable hard-to-obtain books, periodicals, and microfilms. Daniel Meyers helped me with digital images and film stills. My wonderful colleagues Mariana Ivanova, Qinna Shen, and Nicole Thesz read various chapters of the book in progress and gave me honest and constructive criticism. The Humanities Center provided grants to two brilliant students, Matthew Armelli and Graham von Carlowitz, who assisted with translations from German and expert editorial work. Despite all the support I have received in compiling the manuscript, I take full responsibility for any mistakes and inaccuracies in the text.

At Camden House, this project was once again embraced by Jim Walker and benefited from his strong and steady guidance. I am grateful to the series editors Johannes von Moltke and Gerd Gemünden for their encouragement, and to the two anonymous reviewers for their detailed and thoughtful feedback, which contributed enormously to the improvement of the manuscript.

I am most grateful to my family. My sister Lora Aroyo, my parents, Marina and Mois, my in-laws, and my children, Iordan and Martin, have been unflagging cheerleaders of my work and have been most patient with me through periods of intensive work. My husband, Venelin, has strongly encouraged me throughout, reading and critiquing multiple drafts and putting up with my various research trips. This book is dedicated to him.

Introduction

I

IN A FICTION FILM that premiered in 1948 and was shown in both West and East Berlin, *Vor uns liegt das Leben* (Life Lies before Us, directed by Günther Rittau), a piece of textile plays a central role in a tragicomical subplot.[1] The wife, Renate Harms, played by Helga Zülch, has stashed away some fine fabric from before the war. She travels to the countryside and trades it to a peasant woman for a goat so that her child will have some milk. The peasant woman wraps herself in the cloth, swirls indulgingly in front of the mirror, and admires the quality of the newly obtained treasure. "Friedensqualität!" (Peacetime quality!) she exclaims and is happy about the shrewd deal that she has just made. At the same time, Captain Harms (Hermann Speelmans), not aware of his wife's trade, arranges to sell his treasured model ship to a black-market dealer in order to buy that same piece of fabric from the peasant woman's husband. It is meant to be a surprise present for Renate, so that she will have a warm winter coat, something she desperately needs.

This small story from a now-forgotten early postwar German film encapsulates the harsh experiences of ordinary civilians in the transition years from 1945 to 1949, experiences marked by hunger and cold, rations and depravity, self-sacrifice and hope, hard physical labor and predatory black-market deals. It complements poignant earlier sequences in the film that feature women with ration cards in their hands, waiting in long lines to obtain sacks of potatoes. The culture of deficits even offers realistic glimpses of the dynamics of postwar relationships within the family as well as the relationship between cities and the countryside. The visual narrative around the piece of fabric also hints at how clothing items and even scraps of textile became extremely necessary for survival within this context: they were seen as valuable barter items to exchange for food, the objects of dreams, nostalgic traces of a lost past, and hopeful signs of a future normalization of life.[2]

If one dares to talk at all about fashion in the immediate aftermath of the war—something the journalist Marietta Riederer considered "grotesque"—then the term "fashion" (*Mode*) inevitably refers to various creative practices of bartering, mending, and making do with what was available.[3] "Everyone put on whatever they had left. We scrambled to find something basic for survival und paid skyrocketing black market prices,"

Riederer recalled of the times when she resumed a successful career in fashion journalism in postwar Germany after working for almost ten years (1929–38) in Paris as a reporter and illustrator for the *Frankfurter Zeitung*.[4] As attested in multiple other sources from the period, it was also common for women to recycle old clothes into new ones. In light of the chronic short supply of all goods, they reworked tablecloths, drapery, bed linens, blankets, upholstery fabrics, old uniforms, and parachutes into new outfits and underwear.[5] Memoirs by contemporaries and newspaper reports are full of detailed accounts of such practices, meant to alleviate an acute shortage of clothing that was ranked next highest in the scale of postwar woes after the chronic scarcity of food.[6]

Actually, the practices of refashioning, repurposing, and reusing old clothes and fabrics didn't differ from how women had dealt with the shortage of clothing and textiles before May 1945: "Aus Alt mach Neu" and "Aus Zwei mach Eins" (Make new out of old and Make one out of two) were familiar slogans from the period of wartime privations under Nazism, when the press had tried to keep spirits at the home front high by urging women to continue to improvise and maintain a stylish appearance despite all hardships. An article in the Berlin edition of *Die Neue Zeitung* from October 1945 is typical of the tone in fashion reporting in the daily press in the immediate postwar months, urging its readers to apply the "fantasy" ("*Phantasie*") as an antidote to the ubiquitous "empty clothes closets" ("leere Kleiderschränke"):

> What about those old blankets from the air-raid shelter? They can now come out into daylight, and with some imagination we can transform them into an elegant coat, a jacket, long pants, a wraparound skirt, or something like that. First dye the blanket, then cut it up, sew it, line it, and there you have a new outfit. A dress may look "hopeless" from a certain point of view, but if you add a pair of new knitted sleeves, a collar or a bodice, using some random pieces of colorful yarn, it will become not only more beautiful but also warmer.[7]

Yet the first postwar months were a time when fashion made also rapid strides beyond fiction and fantasy. As a business sector with its corresponding institutions and media, fashion came back to life amazingly quickly, despite the prevailing scarcity and despair among the civilian urban population. The fashion industry had suffered a direct impact during Nazi rule, for its majority Jewish owners and employees had been forced out, bought out, exiled, arrested, and many killed, while business as a whole continued to thrive under new "Aryan" ownership.[8] Many of these businesses were also destroyed during the wartime air aids. However, within mere weeks after the collapse of the Third Reich, the multiple signs of recovery were visible everywhere, especially in the capital,

Berlin, where the ready-to-wear trade, the *Konfektion* branch, had had its traditional center for almost a century. The surviving members of Berlin's *Konfektion*—mostly non-Jews, but there were also some returning Jews—set up shop again. The fashion journalist Hanne Voelcker reviewed the process in a lengthy 1947 article in which she called the restored businesses "the resurrected" ("die Wiedererstandenen").[9] Designer salons and textile merchants who had been bombed out at the their original location around Hausvogteiplatz in the eastern part of the city, the Soviet Sector after 1945, moved westward and reopened on and around the Kurfürstendamm and elsewhere in Charlottenburg, Wilmersdorf, and Friedenau.[10] Tapping into a pool of home workers (*Heimarbeiterinnen*), a largely female labor force that worked from home, the fashion industry resumed production.[11] Moreover, within only a few months it became a significant part of Berlin's reconstruction boom and the third-strongest sector of the city's economy.[12]

Another sign of this remarkable recovery was the return of the fashion show in Berlin. On September 8, 1945, the first "peacetime fashion tea" ("Friedens-Modentee") took place in the private apartment of the designer Walter Friedrich Schulz in Xantener Straße, where a few of his loyal customers modeled the so-called patchwork dress (*Flickenkleid*), a colorful outfit made out of several dozen leftover pieces of different fabrics found in Schulz's studio.[13] There were numerous and more varied shows to follow in all quarters of the city, both east and west, in the months to come.

Almost simultaneously—during the first postwar months—the Berlin-based fashion press was resurrected and proliferated with licenses from all four occupying forces. The first periodical dedicated entirely to fashion, a monthly called *Berlins Modenblatt*, was published with a Soviet license in October 1945, followed by *Chic, Illustrierte Textilzeitung, Elegante Welt*, and bi-weekly fashion supplements or sections in virtually all daily newspapers—from *Neues Deutschland* to *Neue Zeit*, from *Tagesspiegel* to *Der Kurier*, from *Berliner Zeitung*, to *Telegraf*. Almost all publications featured an editorial on a variation of the contentious question "Are we allowed to talk about fashion today?" quickly followed by a variation of the affirmative answer: "Yes, because it is part of the new life rising from the ruins, a tiny flower with a grotesque stem sprouting from the rubble, that consoles us and makes us smile."[14]

The press regularly dispensed practical advice on reworking old outfits into new ones, but the majority of the space on the pages of the magazines was dedicated to reporting on the beautiful new collections designated primarily for export or for customers drawn from the occupying forces.[15] What the regular domestic consumer could see on the pages of the magazines was, in the words of one Berlin journalist, "fashion without clothes" ("Mode ohne Kleider"), as most of the featured fashionable outfits were out of reach for the majority of German women, who relied mostly on the ration card.[16] Nevertheless, the sumptuous display of new fashions at shows and in the printed press served as an important vehicle for vicarious consumption, for diversion and entertainment, and for the cultivation of future consumer tastes and practices that would come to flourish in the 1950s.

In the months and years following the end of the war, the new trends of production and presentation—from the popular patchwork dress (*Flickenkleid*) and "transformation dresses" (*Verwandlungskleider*) to the triumphal advance of Christian Dior's New Look after 1947; from the improvised fashion shows of the immediate postwar period to the elaborate Cold War competitions during the Leipzig Trade Fair (Leipziger Messe) in the early 1950s—could also be followed closely on the silver screen.[17] Fashion shows and postwar fashion practices were a regular feature in all newly founded newsreels and reached even wider audiences than the print media, as they were shown before each film screening: the Soviet-overseen *Augenzeuge* newsreels, the US- and British-backed *Welt im Film*, and *Blick in die Welt*, supervised by the French authorities. More important, the spectacle of fashion found its way into numerous fiction films produced on both sides of the growing political divide—by DEFA (Deutsche Film-Aktiengesellschaft) in East Berlin and by several small studios based in West Berlin. The revived fashion practices together and their spectacular representations on screen would become some of the most potent visual and symbolic signs of Germans' will to survive and rebuild in the late 1940s and ultimately to prosper in the 1950s.

II

Indeed, film, very much like fashion, constituted a significant aspect of the symbolic and real revitalization and transformation processes that took place in the immediate postwar period. In addition to the renewed production of newsreels under the supervision of the occupying allies, about forty new German feature films in different genres were completed between 1945 and the end of 1948. Film culture, as many have noted, came back to life in the capital with impressive speed after the end of the war. Within a context of prevailing deficits for the civilian population—lack of food, shortages of clothing and housing, and inadequate security—film projection resumed in 17 surviving cinemas as soon as electricity was restored.[18] The situation improved quickly: two years later, 219 cinemas were in operation, which was more than half of the 410 film theaters that existed before the air raids.[19] Not surprisingly, moviegoing, a popular diversionary routine on the home front even through the darkest moments of the war, also increased: archival photos show throngs of people under the marquees of various film theaters.[20] In contrast to

basic necessities of everyday life—movies were readily available again—
and affordable, to boot. After all, a ticket often cost just a tiny fraction of
the cost of a pound of butter on the black market (as little as 1/250), and
the hours spent in the cinema were deemed more pleasurable than those
spent in the unheated homes during the severe postwar winters.[21] What
had been attractive to the audiences at the height of war in 1944—"diversion, entertainment, relaxation, in combination with music, glamour,
flirting, love, beautiful landscapes, decors, and costumes"—continued to
delight the public in the years after the war as well, if not even more.[22]
Also similar to the wartime years, women often made up the majority of
cinema audiences—up to 70 percent.[23] To be sure, this gender misbal-
ance reflected the overall impact of the war on the demographic structure
of German society, but it also reflected the centrality of cinema to women
during the war and in its aftermath, representing the primary leisurely
activity for them in a safe public space.[24]

Initially, the occupying authorities allowed the screening of popular
pre-1945 films with no propaganda content and later on introduced multiple imports from their own countries. Within a year after the end of
the military conflict, Berliners from all four sectors of the city enjoyed
conditions that the contemporary press described as "heavenly" for moviegoers: in no other place in the world one could see in so many American, Russian, French, and English films.[25] Gradually, filmmaking resumed
with licenses from all four occupying powers, as the Soviet authorities
helped found the film studio DEFA, and the Western powers encouraged
decentralized film production by multiple smaller studios. The majority
of German films produced in the immediate postwar period until 1949,
about thirty-five, dealt with contemporary (*zeitnahe*) topics; hence they
were often referred to as *zeitnahe Filme* or *Zeitfilme*. Because of the centrality of war ruins, destruction, and trauma in many of the films' plots,
these works were also called *Trümmerfilme* (rubble films).[26]

The new cinematic production during those early years seemed to
embrace a double, somewhat contradictory purpose. On the one hand,
some German filmmakers, most of whom had started their careers in
UFA during the Third Reich, aimed at a radical break with Nazi aesthetics by presenting a new, bold, clean beginning. "The dismantling of
[Ufa's] dream factory," as director Helmut Käutner referred to this process, was accompanied by an effort to find fresh, new, young, untainted
film faces such as Hildegard Knef to partially replace the old stars, as well
as by a search for a new film language, inflected by the best traditions in
German filmmaking and also, later on, in tune with international developments such as Italian neorealism and French poetic realism.[27] In some
limited ways and largely depending on the professional experience of "old
hands," that ambition was realized in some important early postwar films
that are discussed in this book: *Die Mörder sind unter uns* (The Murderers

Are among Us, 1946, directed by Wolfgang Staudte); . . . *und über uns der Himmel* (And the Heavens above Us, 1947, directed by Josef von Báky); and *Straßenbekanntschaft* (Street Acquaintance, 1948, directed by Peter Pewas).[28]

At the same time there was a realization that films needed to reaffirm among contemporary Germans a sense of normality through diversion and escapism, and with less harsh realism and eschewing bold formal experimentation. In addition, entertainment guaranteed the commercial success of domestic filmmaking. In the words of Helmut Weiß, another director who made the transition from working in Nazi Germany to directing postwar productions, "The entertainment film means stability; the dream factory is still needed."[29] Pushing this tendency for mindless amusement to an extreme, Weiß directed the very first West German postwar film, the light comedy *Sag die Wahrheit* (Tell the Truth; premier in December 1946), based on a script written in 1944, followed by *Herzkönig* (King of Hearts, 1947). Despite the rejection of his films by many critics, Weiß remained steadfast in creating movies aiming to provide pure entertainment and devoid of any political or social criticism.[30]

In trying to achieve this seemingly impossible double goal—to entertain and to enlighten, to amuse and to innovate—German films between 1946 and 1949 produced mixed results. The consensus in current scholarship is that in general, both the contemporaries and critics were dissatisfied by the achievements of early postwar German cinema.[31] In numerous public statements, German moviegoers voiced an aversion to the prevailing rubble films, in particular because they reminded viewers too strongly of their daily misery. At the same time critics, too, rejected many of these films: they were disappointed with insufficient innovation on the level of aesthetics as well as content. Yet in reality and after revisiting the broader context of their reception as reflected in the media, some of the early postwar German films at the center of this book, although significantly less popular than imports or Nazi reprises, were seen and enjoyed by large postwar audiences: *Die Mörder sind unter uns*; . . . *und über uns der Himmel*; *Zwischen gestern und morgen* (Between Yesterday and Tomorrow, 1947, directed by Harald Braun); *Film ohne Titel* (Film without a Title, 1948, directed by Rudolf Jugert); *Wege im Zwielicht* (Paths in the Twilight, 1948, directed by Gustav Fröhlich); *Straßenbekanntschaft*, and *Martina* (1949, directed by Arthur Maria Rabenalt).[32] Judging by the proliferation of reviews and discussions in the mass press, the statistics released by distributors, and the amount of attention these films have received in subsequent scholarship on German postwar cinema, they did strike a chord with their viewership. It seems that these postwar productions of various genres and styles, despite their daunting themes and the prevalence of ruins in the background, contained not only hidden entertainment potential but also an invitation for positive experiences and projections of successful renewal and personal transformation that were visible and understandable to its contemporary audiences. Moreover, as some scholars have argued, it may be precisely the heterogeneity of these early postwar films in terms of their genres and styles that determines their original realism, realism that is not limited to the representation of rubble and destruction, but that offers its characters as well as its viewers an array of positive identification possibilities.[33]

In order to comprehend rubble films' somewhat unusual escapist value for the predominantly female audiences at the time, this study revisits a number of these movies and probes them for their ability to shed light on the immediate postwar situation in terms of clothing, food, other everyday objects, gestures, and habits and the ways in which such representations resonated with the immediate concerns of the contemporaneous public. In particular, the surprising proliferation of images of fashionable clothes and appearances, in films as well as in other popular discourses in the public realm, exposes the importance of escapist pictures for the desired rapid reconstruction and democratic rebuilding of the two soon-to-be postwar German societies. Magdalena Saryusz-Wolska and Anna Labentz call this phenomenon a "visualization of normalization," referring not so much to the images' mimetic qualities to reflect reality but to the process of "negotiation of meaning" ("Sinnaushandlung") in a postwar world.[34]

In that regard, I build on the connections that other scholars have already established between fiction film and historical discourse. Dudley Andrews elucidates well the value of cinema for reconstruction of a past and for extracting a specific sense out of it for those who had lived in that past. "Movies, especially popular ones, comprise a record of the aspirations, obsessions, and frustrations of those who spend time and money making or viewing them."[35] Not only what is seen on the screen adds to film as a "historical source for the micro-operations of every-day life," Andrews writes, but also the ways the subject matter is approached and what is left out.[36] When talking about his own explorations of rubble films, Robert Shandley writes that the study of fiction film as a historical source is inseparable from the inquiry into "the spectatorship that it addresses and the assumptions the film appears to be making about this spectatorship."[37] Keeping in mind that postwar domestic audiences to a large extent were the same as during the war years, one can assume that the transitional films of the late 1940s reminded them of their own viewing habits and histories back then. By revisiting a selected body of films of the immediate postwar years as well as some wartime productions and films from the early 1950s against the background of the abundant fashion discourses of the time and with the women's audience in mind, this book zooms in on the ways these cinematic reflections on clothes and fashion-related activities offer subtle reflections on the everyday lives, desires, the professional engagements, and self-perceptions of the postwar public. Such a reevaluation extracts these films from the narrow confines of the term *Trümmerfilme*, often associated with early postwar cinema, and uses them as a starting point to expose the often obscured lines of continuity and commonality that they establish with both prewar productions and with East and West German cinema in the subsequent decade.

Both fashion and film in the long 1940s seem caught up in the same duality: they vacillate between continuous engagement with social reality and a temporary surrender to the world of fantasy. The parallel productions of film and beautiful fashion images for public presentation were conceived as defiant acts of recovering or maintaining the routines of a "normal" everyday life in the face of serious challenges. The most productive site for analysis of this tension between realism and escapism is at the intersection between the two media: film and costume design. As Sarah Street has emphasized, more than any other element of the mise-en-scène, film costume not only "conforms to notions of realism but also employs notions of cinematic spectacle."[38]

A renewed scrutiny of film costumes in German fiction films of the immediate postwar years within the context of the films' production, distribution, and reception can open up wider discussions about the role of the costume designer, the ways in which film costumes can be read as intertexts, and the impact of such representations on audiences in their everyday behaviors and appearances. Furthermore, a closer look at these films through the lens of their costumes reveals multiple and nuanced connections between the two institutions, film and fashion, in terms of the commonality of audience, the shared escapism, and the continuity of personnel in the production process across both the temporal dividing line of 1945 and the Cold War divide between East and West.

The most obvious connection between the two institutions of entertainment, film and fashion, was the audience: film presentations and fashion displays were directed at the same sector of the public, namely women, and this determined various postwar practices. For example, cinemas, catering to a predominantly female urban public, printed tickets and film programs that featured, very much like the fashion magazines at the time, multiple advertisements oriented toward women that took consideration of regular viewers' demands, desires, and habits. On the film program for December 1947 of the Neue Scala am Nollendorfplatz cinema, the announcement for the premiere of . . . *und über uns der Himmel* is accompanied by advertisements for nearby businesses such as Steinhardt for ladies' and gentlemen's clothes and A.G.B., a fabric and clothing store. There were also numerous ads for hairdressers, beauticians, perfumeries, and stores for trading clothes in the vicinity of the movie theater. Even when the advertisements were for items difficult to procure at regular markets, the companies sought to remind cinema goers that these products still existed and would be accessible once life returned to normal.[39]

Fig. 1. Program for the Neue Scala am Nollendorf Platz,
December 1947. Deutsche Kinemathek Berlin.

There was plenty of sartorial display on the silver screen itself, which presented an aspect not only of cinema's escapism but also of its peculiar realism. Films of the immediate postwar era featured a variety of fashion-related activities as elements of the films' subplots, activities that Berlin women could easily relate to and that served as an antidote to the image of the ruins. We see close-ups on the female protagonists who practice fashion photography, labor on sewing machines, draw illustrations for fashion magazines, try on new dresses even if they are made out of lace curtains or remodeled from old outfits, trade sexual favors for silk stockings and nice clothes, work professionally as models and designers, and run their own dressmaking and hat-making businesses.

The surprising display of elegant or simply cut garments—often against the background of material misery, rubble, and shortage—served also as shaping elements of a distinct mise-en-scène, cinematography, and, most important in the quest for the new female, stardom. The very young actresses discovered and promoted by the postwar German film productions—Hildegard Knef, Heidi Scharf, Gisela Trowe, Jeanette Schultze, and Cornell Borchers—personified a distinctly new, modern, international sense of glamour and beauty that they presented on screen as well as on the pages of fashion and women's magazines. Ultimately, the enthusiastic promotion of these rising female film stars on screen and in the print fashion media made them into symbols of the reinvention of a new, postwar Germany.

A third commonality shared between the film and fashion industries can be traced back to the continuity in personnel from the wartime to the postwar period. A certain stylistic continuity between wartime and postwar film productions in terms of costume, staging, and cinematography is established by the fact that many of the postwar film professionals had a formative experience working for the UFA (originally, Universum Film AG) film studio. For example, the majority of costume designers who outfitted the German film productions after 1945—Getraude/Gertrud Recke, Vera Mügge, Bessie Becker, Hildegard Ordnung, and Manon Hahn—had started their careers in the late 1930s or early 1940s, during the war, when some of them even had the opportunity to design costumes for the first color movies.[40] In postwar times, these film professionals, although working in obscurity, had their fingers firmly on the pulse of fashion, because parallel to being engaged in film, they often were active as fashion journalists as well (for example, Manon Hahn, Gertrud Recke, Hildegard Ordnung) or were running their own designer studios (Bessie Becker). Up until 1953, these women, like other film personnel, could and did work for both East and West German movies, moving freely across Berlin's sector borders. The designers' connections in the capital also helped them purchase or borrow costumes for their star performers from the new fashion salons on the Kurfürstendamm that were quickly gaining in fame and reputation. In the work of the costume designers during the early postwar years, who carefully crafted and intensely constructed the look of many central characters, film and fashion were intertwined to create the perfect mix of playful diversion and realism.

III

This book steers scholarly attention toward two key industries, film and fashion, that in some ways followed similar trajectories and shared multiple connections, not only in the immediate postwar years but also in the "long decade" that includes the Second World War, between 1939 and 1955. This period has been thoroughly examined in terms of the momentous political events that shaped it and that created seemingly unbridgeable ruptures. Scholars have paid ample attention to the Holocaust, the Second World War, the division of Germany among the victorious allies and the conditions of occupation, the black market, the advent of the Cold War with the introduction of the Marshall Plan, the currency reform, the Berlin Blockade, and the founding of two German states that pursued diverging ideological and economic tracks. The study of both film and fashion within this context has thus generated multiple isolated cultural-historical narratives that emphasize the chronological and geopolitical divisions: between the war and postwar period, between the immediate postwar period and the 1950s, as well as between the Soviet-dominated German Democratic Republic in the East and the Federal Republic of Germany in the capitalist West.

This book, in contrast, explores the continuities, the commonality, and the interrelations across historical and ideological dividing lines, as well as the synergistic connections between the fashion and film industries. It sheds light on the multiple contacts between the vibrant fashion and film scenes across Berlin's four sectors, that is, on connections that often have been left out from the master narratives altogether. Such omissions apply especially to the discursive area of fashion, which as a topic may have appeared to many scholars as frivolous and irrelevant against the background of grave historic events.[41]

The vast scholarship on cinema of the long 1940s, for its part, has been shaped by a preoccupation exclusively with the concept of the *Trümmerfilme* of 1946 to 1949 and by interest in the ways the themes of this body of films seek for a new beginning, relate to the troubled past, operate in the contemporary context of occupation and Allied control, and reflect on selected social and political issues.[42] The scholars Erica Carter and Hester Baer have broken new ground by shifting the attention to issues of gender, the representation of women on the screen, and female spectatorship, yet their focus has been almost exclusively on the 1950s and on the West German context. Building on previous studies of the culture and film of the postwar period and relying on findings from extensive archival research, the current study attempts to bridge some of the discontinuities in existing scholarship by looking at filmmaking as inseparable from a broader popular media context in the service of entertainment and diversion. It therefore revisits filmmaking not only in the period between 1946 and 1949 that immediately followed the "zero hour," but in the long decade of the 1940s with its task of offering to the German public some positive identification fantasies, a sense of reemerging normality amidst the prevailing chaos, and a lasting model for consumer behavior. Furthermore, the book exposes the continuities that have structured patterns of visual experience, tastes, and everyday practices of the predominantly female audiences of both films and fashion displays in and outside of films. The analyses of the function of fashion in a selected body of emblematic films demonstrate that in the everyday practices and private experiences reflected upon in the films, the transitions from peace to war, from war to peace, and then to Cold War as well as the tensions generated by different regimes of occupation and diverging ideological agendas may have been less dramatically different and much more continuous than previously assumed.

IV

In outlining the book's argument in the context of revisiting film history, several theoretical and methodological questions need to be addressed that pertain to the choice of the subject matter (fashion and film costume), the central agent (women), and the location (Berlin), and the ways these three aspects come together in the present study.

In her 1950 essay "The Aftermath of Nazi Rule: Report from Germany," Hannah Arendt observed that in the time following the genocide and in the face of ubiquitous destruction, Germans reacted with apathy to the crises surrounding them. "It is difficult to say," Arendt writes, "whether this [apathy] signifies a half-conscious refusal to yield to grief or a genuine inability to feel. Amid the ruins, Germans mail each other picture postcards still showing the cathedrals and market places, the public buildings and bridges that no longer exist."[43] At the same time she notices "the atmosphere of feverish busyness" that characterizes the process of rebuilding and the efforts "to restore a facsimile of pre-war economic conditions."[44] Arendt's description applies particularly well to the paradoxical nature of the intense activities surrounding the revival of the fashion and garment industry in Berlin and elsewhere in Germany. Prior to 1933, this was a branch of the national economy in which Jewish businessmen, owners, and salespeople formed a strong majority. In the process of the Aryanization of those successful businesses, the Jewish owners were to sell out for low prices (in many cases they ended up in exile or in concentration camps, along with many of their Jewish employees). By the end of the 1930s, the ownership of the businesses that made up the fashion industry had changed and so had many of the beloved and renowned labels: Gerson became Horn, Hansen Bang became Hermann Schwichtenberg, and Auerbach & Steinitz became Gehringer & Glupp, to name just a few. Thus the frantic activities accompanying the swift revival of the famous Berlin *Konfektion* to its immediate prewar conditions, rather its pre-1933 conditions, reflects an act of double amnesia: not only were the ruins ignored in an effort to achieve "normality" as quickly as possible, but also in this picture of "normality" the banished Jews were still missing, willfully forgotten.

In a 2006 study, Alon Confino referred to the 1945–49 period in Germany that Arendt had reflected upon as full of "dissonances." Dissonance, in Confino's usage, is when "that which actually happened seems totally incongruent with the conditions of the time," and thus tests our interpretative ability.[45] Confino focuses on Germans' thinking about tourism, but "tourism" in his argument can easily be replaced by "fashion," and similarly challenging questions can be posed: What do we make of Germans—both as producers and consumers—getting involved in fashion in the midst of rubble, hunger, and occupation? Why did fashion revive so quickly after the defeat? How do we explain a fashion revival in a devastated society where overall economic improvement and consumer culture in the immediate postwar years belonged to the realm of fantasy more than to the realm of actuality? Building on Confino's notion of dissonance, this study examines fashion discourses in the long 1940s in the printed press and on the silver screen in their dynamic relation to ostentatious displays as well as everyday practices. These historical dissonances reveal the complicated character of the postwar years but have been ignored in most traditional historical accounts. Often deemed marginal and unimportant, especially in times of crisis, the fashion discourse is fraught with serious implications such as the meaning of "normalcy," "remembering," and "forgetting" in war and postwar situations, and particularly in the wake of the Holocaust. The fashion discourse becomes a place where the tensions between the private and the public spheres, between the traumatic past and uncertain future, between genders, and between Germans and the Allied forces play out.

Nowhere else is this dynamic more interesting than in Berlin, the bombed-out and carved-up city that forms the exclusive focus of this study. Berlin was, and is, a political, economic, and cultural center of historical importance, as the German capital before 1949 and as the frontline of Cold War divisions after the founding of the two German states. Both the film and fashion industries have been heavily concentrated there and flourished since their respective beginnings in late and mid-nineteenth century and even throughout the dark years of Nazi dictatorship. Complementary media outlets—daily newspapers, illustrated magazines, and trade publications—also proliferated in the German capital. The transition from the horror of the Holocaust and wartime destruction to some semblance of normality in the immediate postwar years could not have been more swift or dramatic than in Berlin, as both the film and the fashion industries resumed as soon as the military activities ceased.

Many accounts point to the exceptional status of the occupied and divided German capital after 1945. In her report from Germany, Arendt writes that "the customs, manners, approaches to people are in the smallest details so absolutely different from everything one sees and has to face in the rest of Germany that Berlin is almost like another country" (254). In Arendt's account, there seems to be less resentment in Berlin against the victors, more openness about what happened during the Holocaust. Detailed studies of the "liminal interregnum" of four-power occupation and military government emphasize that Berlin also became a truly international city where—like nowhere else—the four victorious powers convened, as well as refugees, displaced people from all over, and German Jews coming out of hiding.[46] These diverse groups of people who negotiated daily life among the ruins of the city in the period from 1945 to 1949 transformed it, in the words of the film historian Gerd Gemünden, into a "site of unprecedented exchange, openness, and experimentation," where "the return to the time before the descent into barbarism seem[ed] possible."[47]

Berlin remained a place with a special status and unique atmosphere throughout the early 1950s. There is no doubt that the currency reform in June 1948, the ensuing Blockade, and the founding of the two German states affected Berlin in ways that didn't touch other locations. The economic, political, and ideological divisions intensified. Especially under the pressures of the Berlin Blockade (June 24, 1948, to May 12, 1949), some fashion businesses, fashion and women's periodicals, and film companies relocated from Berlin to West Germany, where economic opportunity and everyday life conditions appeared to be more beneficial. Nevertheless, many remained and continued to cater to Berliners, an eager public that more or less defied the imposed divisions and still moved relatively freely across the sector borders until about 1953. Berlin continued to maintain its status as a center of fashion and strived to remain a center of film culture as well, especially with the founding of the Berlin International Film Festival in 1951.[48]

If there is one group of concrete agents at the center of this book's narrative who reappear in all of the chapters in various roles, it is the women of Berlin. There is a widely shared consensus around Elizabeth Heineman's argument that the period from 1942 to 1948 is temporally condensed in German memory as the "the hour of the woman."[49] During this time, women were catapulted to the forefront of historical events, not only by their sheer numbers—Germany experienced then the most pronounced "surplus of women"—but also by the monumental tasks they were forced to assume during the time of wartime destruction and postwar rebuilding. It was the women of Berlin who suffered terrifying mass rapes by the occupiers; it was the women who collaborated, even fraternized, with occupiers in their quest for their own and their families' survival; and it was women who cleared the debris and ensured the community's survival. For a long time, there have been three types, three more or less clichéd images, or three terms that have been widely used in various media accounts as persistent leitmotifs for women's roles in the immediate postwar period: the heroic "rubble women" (*Trümmer-frauen*,) who physically sorted out the mess left behind in the cities after the devastating war; the rape victims who suffered horrid atrocities perpetrated by the occupiers; and the *Fräulein*, known also as *Amiflittchen* and *Veronika*, a designation with largely negative connotations given to young German women who struck up relationships with US soldiers. The cultural stereotype of the *Fräulein* implied youthfulness, promiscuity, and a strong orientation towards consumerism.[50] In the early 1950s, these stereotypical images supposedly gave way to new clichés: in the West, that of the housewife, the woman who had retreated entirely to the domestic sphere in the West; and, in the East, the socialist working woman, who is interested more in building the new social order than in pursuing her own consumerist desires.

Revisiting a selected body of films from the long 1940s against the backdrop of fashion reporting in the daily press and in women's publications allows for the reconstruction of a historic female experience of the period that goes beyond the few clichéd media images as well as beyond the stark division of East German and West German women.[51] In these cinematic fashion projections upon the bodies of women one sees in a new, nuanced, and much more palpable way the effects of war, conflict, ideological clashes, contemporary politics, and the aesthetics of everyday life during this crisis period. By taking a closer look at the presentation of women's clothes and various sartorial practices in films and on the pages of the press, this book delineates a much wider range of subjective positions associated with female characters in both West and East German contexts, and a broader array of attractive professional identities offered to a predominantly female spectatorship across the city of Berlin. As the sole providers for extended families under the conditions of deficits, defeat, and occupation, women moved into a variety of independent professional roles—as seamstresses, designers, graphic artists, models, and journalists—that underscore their mobility and reflect on their sophisticated involvement in imaginary as well as real consumption. Notably, many of these professions are related in one way or another to fashion and fashion media.

In these roles—as fashion professionals and as mass consumers—women participated actively in the postwar economic regeneration, in the transition from a scarcity economy to mass consumption. Some scholars have identified a "consumer-based model of citizenship" that "produced a new sense of national identity," especially in West Germany of the 1950s.[52] Sara Lennox has questioned the axiomatic assumption that women retreated en masse "from public politics to a timeless realm of traditional domesticity" in the early 1950s.[53] In her analyses of fashion spreads in West German magazines such *Film und Frau* and *Constanze*, Erica Carter argues that fashion discourses often mirrored a "reality in which middle-class women had carved out an independent existence as white-collar workers and businesswomen."[54] Similarly, Hester Baer has claimed in her scholarship on the West German illustrated magazine *Film und Frau* that fashion media provided "a space of pleasure and fantasy for women" and a site in which women could envision themselves not just as objects but also as agents.[55] Based on ample archival evidence from the illustrated press, this argument can be extended back to the late 1940s, to the hungry years, when these trends actually originated and spread across the East-West divide, even before the onset of the Marshall Plan and the economic miracle in West Germany. My research suggests that those conclusions apply even more to developments that started much earlier, in the 1940s: the wartime and immediate postwar years. Moreover, despite emerging Cold War divisions and considerable differences in economic models, they are common in both East and West German contexts, if one takes into consideration fashion discourses in the Soviet-occupied sector of Berlin. These put forward, on the visual level, an image of the modern woman as one who, far from rejecting current fashion trends, embraces them and strives to adapt them to her everyday existence.

V

A major idiosyncratic moment in terms of the relationship among film, fashion, and politics was signified by the war years, 1939 to 1945. Chapter 1 of this book is dedicated to tracing the roots of various entertainment-related practices prevalent in the immediate postwar period but with roots in the time before 1945. Despite relentless restrictions on regular consumer behavior, the German fashion industry, with the official support from the Third Reich's Ministries of Propaganda and Economics, thrived and expanded during the war. At the same time, the female readers were encouraged to browse in the countless glossy pages of magazines such as *Die Mode* and *Der Silberspiegel* and enjoy the high-quality photographs, the intricate illustrations, and the verbal descriptions of elegant clothes that they would not be able to purchase anywhere. The representations of the latest production of leading Berlin designer salons (designated mostly for export) were meant to distract from war-related news, to lift the spirits at the home front, and to forge a sense of German superiority in questions of style and aesthetics. Similar tasks were assigned to the Nazi entertainment film. Not only were a number of prominent designers such as Heinz Schulze actively involved in dressing popular UFA's star actresses on and off stage, but also a number of cheerful movies produced between 1939 and 1944 were actually completely or partially set in the fashion milieu. In chapter 1 I analyze *Großstadtmelodie* (Melody of a Great City, 1943, directed by Wolfgang Liebeneiner), *Achtung! Der Feind hört mit!* (Attention! The Enemy Is Listening!, 1940, directed by Arthur Maria Rabenalt), *Das himmelblaue Abendkleid* (The Sky-Blue Evening Gown, 1941, directed by Erich Engels), *Meine Freundin Josefine* (My Friend Josefine, 1942, directed by Hans H. Zerlett), and *Kollege kommt gleich* (The Colleague Will Come Immediately, 1943, directed by Karl Anton), all lighthearted feature films that contained lavish fashion presentations. These works proved to be effective vehicles for providing apolitical diversion and vicarious consumption for wartime audiences and also distraction from the reality of the Jewish genocide by normalizing a daily life, in particular a fashion scene, that was "free of Jews."

Chapter 2 offers a comprehensive panorama of the revival of both the fashion industry and the fashion media in the immediate postwar years, 1945 to 1947. That brisk renewal was not only conspicuous to any foreign visitor in Berlin, from British and American journalists to the Swiss writer Max Frisch, but also intensely debated on the pages of newly founded local magazines, weekly newspapers, and specialized supplements to the daily press that were catering to a large female audience across the four sectors of the divided city. The multitude of publications licensed by the different occupying powers—*Berlins Modenblatt, Chic, sie, Für Dich,* and *Heute*—and other media venues such as the newsreels demonstrated remarkable similarity on the visual and rhetorical level in discussing questions of fashion, despite the growing Cold War divisions. The coverage of new collections and various fashion shows fostered escapism as well as optimism. The fashion media steered Berlin women in both the East and the West toward erasing the painful past from their minds, embracing a fictitious present dominated by pleasant appearances, and evolving into future consumer citizens.

The remaining three chapters of the book have a similar structure. They proceed in a chronological order, each one of them juxtaposing and analyzing representative films, in most cases one DEFA production and one film from the West, against the background of debates in the fashion press that dominate that historical moment. Chapter 3 revisits two early rubble films from 1946 and 1947, DEFA's *Die Mörder sind unter uns*, and the first production with an American license, . . . *und über uns der Himmel*. These films are discussed against the background of the contemporary fashion discourses in order to reconstruct a historic female experience of the immediate postwar period that goes beyond the clichéd images of the German woman as *Trümmerfrau, Amiflittchen, Fräulein*, or a victim of rape. By taking a closer look at the presentations of clothes and various sartorial practices in these two films, this chapter delineates a diverse range of subjective positions associated with female characters and a broader configuration of attractive identities offered to a predominantly female spectatorship.

At the center of the comparative analysis in chapter 4 are DEFA's *Straßenbekanntschaft* (Street Acquaintance, 1948, directed by Peter Pewas) and the West German *Martina* (1949, directed by Arthur Maria Rabenalt), two films that bear striking similarities but have never been looked at in tandem. They both have the same type of female protagonist: a rebellious young woman, eager to live life to the fullest, caught between conventional familial allegiances and a strong sense of independence. Both the eponymous Martina, and Erika, in *Straßenbekanntschaft*, strive to overcome past traumas through achieving a satisfactory level of material comfort in the present. Most important, they are interested in owning and wearing nice clothes. This theme is further emphasized by the fact that the films' costumes were designed with amazing stylistic consistency by the same costume designer, Gertrud Recke. Contrary to audiences' expectations, the fashion display as well as the overall mise-en-scène in these films on contemporary topics bids farewell to the aesthetics determined by ruins and embraces the newest fashion trend of the day: the triumphal ascent of Christian Dior's New Look. Therefore, this chapter discusses the two films in the context of heated debates in the fashion press about the meaning and relevance of the New Look to German women in the immediate postwar period.

The last chapter extends the comparison between East German and West German films featuring prominent fashion themes into the early 1950s, when both states had embarked on separate economic tracks and embraced opposing political agendas. Chapter 5 contains discussions of three films, each of which challenged the prevailing trends in their respective cinematic traditions: DEFA's lighthearted comedy *Modell Bianka* (The "Bianka" Design, 1951, directed by Richard Groschopp), another DEFA production, the dramatic *Frauenschicksale* (Destinies of Women, 1952, directed by Slatan Dudow), and the West German *Ingrid: Die Geschichte eines Fotomodells* (Ingrid: The Story of a Fashion Model, 1955, directed by Géza von Radvanyi). The in-depth look into these three films from the point of view of their involvement with postwar consumer culture in general, and with the business of fashion in particular, leads to some surprising discoveries. *Modell Bianka* is a rare and ambitious attempt in early socialist filmmaking to entertain audiences through an apolitical story set entirely in the GDR's nationalized clothing industry while acknowledging the East German women's desires to dress fashionably and nicely, despite inadequate supply within the state-run economy. *Ingrid: Die Geschichte eines Fotomodells*, on the other hand, is set in an exclusive West German designer salon in which the title character is the top model. What is uncharacteristic for that film, however, is the subtle psychological portrayal of a woman professionally employed in that industry, who is not merely an object and victim in a male-dominated world but is a firm and autonomous player who determines her own destiny. Finally, *Frauenschicksale*, unlike the other two films, engages in a comparison and critical analysis of the two German fashion industries by zooming in on the ways in which they organize their production and cater to women's needs and desires.

Interwoven into the structure of the book are also two "vignettes," two case studies that expand and reflect on the preceding chapters. The first vignette is an exploration of the work of Charlotte Glückstein, a Jewish dressmaker who returned to Berlin after her incarceration in Ravensbrück and opened her own fashion salon, Charlott, near the Kurfürstendamm in 1946. Analyzing a great number of articles in the fashion press that discussed her production, I use Glückstein's story of as a starting point for understanding the complicated dynamic between forgetting and remembering, destruction and recovery, exhibition and repression when it comes to fashion history during and after the Holocaust.

Vignette 2 follows chapter 3 and sheds light on the connection between fashion and film stardom. It revisits several of Hildegard Knef's early films, after her iconic appearance in *Die Mörder sind unter uns*, and analyzes them within the context of her intensive mass media presence, especially in the world of fashion. Knef's celebrity, an evolution from "Germany's favorite *Trümmermädchen*" to a cinematic femme fatale in the course of her work between 1946 and 1953, reveals how cinema addressed the sartorial fantasies and the changing needs of the postwar film audience. Her stardom reflects particularly on the efforts of German women to embrace fashion initially as a visual antidote to the sight of ruins, but subsequently also as an inspiration for unrestrained consumption as well as affirmation of achieved normalization.

This book traces the intertextual connections between film and fashion within three periods: the wartime years, the immediate postwar years, and the initial escalation of the Cold War in the early 1950s. All three periods are shaped by the dynamic between relentless crisis and continuous striving for normalcy. In this book I aim to illuminate both the historical experience of women as producers and consumers of visual spectacles and the role of these spectacles in the shaping of their everyday lives. I do this by focusing on selected representations and projections of fashion on the silver screen in the Third Reich during wartime and in postwar divided Germany, and in addition on the broader context of costume design for the movies, the impact of fashion on stardom, and the coverage of film and fashion events in the popular press.

1. Vicarious Consumption: Wartime Fashion in Film and the Press, 1939–44

In fashion, film is both dictator and captive.
—Review of *Frischer Wind aus Kanada*,
Der Silberspiegel, 1935

WHEN GROSSSTADTMELODIE (Melody of a Great City, 1943, directed by Wolfgang Liebeneiner) premiered on October 4, 1943, in Berlin's Gloria-Palast cinema, at the beginning of the fourth year of war, the German home front was already suffering severely. City dwellers endured heavy bombardments and were getting used to decreasing rations of food and clothing. Berlin itself, the metropolis that is also a character in this film and a subject of cinematic adoration and exploration—the most popular song from the film was "Berlin, ich bin verliebt in dich bei Tag und Nacht"—would soon be destroyed beyond recognition. Yet it seemed that the prevailing wartime difficulties made the film all the more popular with audiences, especially women on the home front, because it was lavishly produced and offered an opportunity for escapist diversion.[1]

Apart from a short sequence in which an enthusiastic Nazi rally is featured, the film's plot consciously transports the viewers back to the carefree prewar years, 1937 to 1939, when Berliners flocked en masse to various sites of entertainment: in-door bicycle races, beaches, ballrooms, and dazzling fashion shows. Reproduced on the screen, partly by means of documentary footage shot previously by Leo de Laforgue and Richard Angst, these spectacles created an almost déjà vu impression of the heyday of the Weimar years, with the only difference that the various venues in the film are reassuringly in Aryan ownership: The publishing house Ullstein has become Deutscher Verlag and the fashion salons, previously the domain of the mostly Jewish-owned Berlin *Konfektion* sector, are now Aryanized and carry bland names such as "Elegante Herren-Moden" (Elegant Men's Fashion) and "Elegante Damen-Moden" (Elegant Ladies' Fashion).

This chapter is a substantially expanded and updated version of Ganeva, "Vicarious Consumption: Fashion in German Media and Film during the War Years 1939–1943," in *The Consumer on the Home Front: Second World War Civilian Consumption in Comparative Perspective*, ed. Felix Römer, Jan Logermann, and Hartmut Berghoff (Oxford, UK: Oxford University Press, 2017), 199–221. Reprinted by permission of the publisher.

Fig. 2. Hilde Krahl as journalist Renate Heiberg in the *Großstadtmelodie* (1943). Murnau-Stiftung, Deutsches Filminstitut, Frankfurt

Rather than being coded as trivial, frivolous, and self-indulgent, the consumption of fashion in this popular 1943 production was actually celebrated within the film. *Großstadtmelodie* foregrounds prominently two visually attractive events. First is the striking sartorial transformation of its magnetic female protagonist, the photographer Renate Heiberg (played by a young Viennese actress, Hilde Krahl, soon the wife of the director, Liebeneiner). Starting as a dirndl-wearing provincial girl from Bavaria, overnight Renate becomes an urbane photo-reporter in Berlin, impeccably dressed for all her professional and personal engagements. In a process that parallels her success as a photographer, Renate's sartorial appearance is gradually liberated from its rural connotations as she replaces the clothes she has brought from home (hand-knit sweaters and dirndl dresses) with a variety of modern outfits that match the urban surroundings.[2] To the delight of the predominantly female audiences, in the course of the film Renate parades more than half a dozen elegant contemporary outfits that both conform to the latest international trends and contain subtle nods to traditional Bavarian costume—for example, a hunting-style hat with a feather in the brim.

Second, one of the film's sequences is a major fashion show in Berlin, which is filmed in a documentary style. In the course of four minutes, models present a whole array of stylish daytime dresses and evening gowns that exemplify the fashion trends of 1939. The show not only serves, within the film's plot, as an auspicious occasion for Renate Heiberg to begin a romantic relationship with the reporter Rolf Bergmann, but the sequence also marks her spectacular comeback as a professional photo-reporter. She chooses to photograph the fashion show from unusual angles and perspectives, in order to create a photo essay entitled "On the sidelines of the fashion show" ("Am Rande der Modenschau") for a popular Berlin illustrated magazine.[3] This extensive fashion show sequence in the film foreshadows the multiple connections between fashion in the wartime and postwar periods. Both the protagonist's costumes for the film and the gowns presented at the lavish fashion show were designed by an up-and-coming couturier working at the UFA studio, Irmgard Becker-Schulte; her work would leave a lasting mark on the mise-en-scène of German cinema before and after 1945.[4] The fashion designer who is a minor character in the film is played by the actress Hilde Weissner.[5] Several years later, in March 1946, Weissner would act as the master of ceremonies during the first major, much publicized, peacetime fashion show in Berlin.[6]

The 1943 film *Großstadtmelodie* is a suitable starting point for examining the multivalent status of wartime luxury consumption through the lenses of the illustrated press and cinema. The mass media discourse on German fashion between 1939 and 1944 contained elements of both rigid ideology and frivolous entertainment, of both realism and escapism, of both actual and imaginary consumption; it reflected the Third Reich's nationalist agenda as well as its internationalist aspirations. On the one hand, popular magazines such as *Die Dame, die neue linie,* and *Der Silberspiegel,* which had presented images of glamorous fashion throughout the 1930s, started dispersing more practical advice for women on how to manage war-related scarcities, refashion outdated attire, and combine random pieces of leftover fabrics into new outfits.

Simultaneously, however, the visual media were also participating in an orchestrated effort to promote Germany's status as the emerging new center of high fashion in Europe. Such were the country's aspirations, particularly in the wake of France's defeat in 1940, when silk, wool, and other luxurious fabrics requisitioned by the Wehrmacht made their way to fashion houses in Berlin, Munich, and Frankfurt, and some new markets for German exports opened up.[7] It was during the war years, too, that both women's magazines and cinema became the primary media for the German companies' bi-annual fashion shows, which exhibited to local audiences out-of-reach products that had been exclusively designed for profitable export to neutral and occupied countries or that were featured in entertaining film productions.[8]

The intensive publicity provided by the fashion shows of designs for export (*Export-Modenschauen*) and other fashion-related coverage affected the wartime consumer in subtle and indirect ways. Even though ordinary German women suffering under war-imposed restrictions had no access to these clothes in real life, fashion in the media provided a welcome occasion for distraction and imaginary consumption. Captivating images of nicely dressed women and commentaries of the latest trends proliferated on the pages of popular magazines, in newsreels, and on the silver screen. In addition to *Großstadtmelodie*, numerous other entertaining movies that contained explicit fashion demonstrations such as *Achtung! Der Feind hört mit!* (Attention! The enemy is listening!, 1940, directed by Arthur Maria Rabenalt), *Das himmelblaue Abendkleid* (The Sky-Blue Evening Gown, 1941, directed by Erich Engels), *Meine Freundin Josefine* (My Friend Josefine, 1942, directed by Hans H. Zerlett) and *Kollege kommt gleich* (The Colleague Will Come Immediately, 1943, directed by Karl Anton) and others proved to be effective vehicles in cultivating apolitical distraction and vicarious consumption for wartime audiences, a sense of enjoyment of fashion "among ourselves."

It was relatively easy for fashion to find its place in Nazi cinema. As a number of film scholars have pointed out, despite the Nazi's fascination with war, very few films were openly propagandistic or dealt directly with the contemporary Second World War experience.[9] The majority of films served as platforms for entertainment that, as Eric Rentschler argues, "maintained the appearance of escapist vehicles" and innocent, cheerful diversion, "while functioning within a larger [political] program."[10] Present-day settings were, for the most part, avoided, but even in films that referred to the contemporary moment, Nazi emblems, Hitler salutes, and party slogans were nowhere to be seen.[11] It was a different, more subtle, form of wartime propaganda. While the film industry relied heavily on its star artists to provide good entertainment and consequently maintained their life of privilege by supplying them with luxury foods, clothes, and fuel, the actors and actresses were advised to limit their fashionable appearance to the silver screen and to refrain from smoking, entertaining, and wearing glamorous clothes in public.[12] The majority of films sought to achieve the "enchantment of reality" and catered to the needs and desires of a mass audience that was craving relief from everyday life.[13] The spectators, it was assumed, very much like the readers of fashion magazines, "wanted to be transported to a world that is far away from rationing and other war-related circumstances" ("fern von allen Bezugscheinen und anderen kriegsbedingten Umständen").[14] Whereas filmmakers in Great Britain and the United States demonstrated somewhat more pronounced preference in their films for presenting everyday types and situations—including food and clothes rationing, blackouts, and other hardships—German filmmakers after 1939 continued to rely on the compensatory function of fantasy and escapism.[15] The heightened "investment in illusionism," as the film scholar Sabine Hake concluded, had become a distinctive trait of Germany's wartime media, yet there have been no focused and systematic investigations of the role of the escapist mise-en-scène and costumes in these light-fare films produced between 1939 and 1944.[16] Such a study would reveal a particularly ambiguous image of women consumers as well as savvy businesswomen in Nazi cinema that is at odds with the propaganda stereotype of the German woman as maternal, homebound, rejecting fashionable attire, luxury items, makeup, and high heels.

In this chapter my interest is in examining cinema's costume display within the larger fashion discourse in the visual media between 1939 and 1944 and in revealing the ways in which the predominantly female consumers were addressed. The strong media presence of fashion during the war was associated with fantasies of normalcy, with an illusory sense of agency and autonomy, and, toward the end of the period, 1943 to 1944, with nostalgic memories of intact cities and intact lives. At the same time, vicarious consumption was, in certain ways, also a forward-looking activity. John Davidson's observation about some of the wartime film productions (including other films by the director and UFA production chief Wolfgang Liebeneiner) applies to the broader visual media landscape during the period as well: the prevalence of enticing fashion images on the magazine pages and silver screen of the Third Reich during the 1940s seems to have "fostered the development of a sophisticated consumer culture that is often assumed not to have entered German visual media until after the war, the 1950s."[17] This continuity between the wartime and postwar periods would be sustained by the remarkable reestablishment of the same directors and costume designers right after 1945 and their continued professional production into the early 1950s.[18]

There were also undeniable dark sides to the wartime fascination with fashion. For one, the public discourses on fashion carefully concealed the fact that wartime for Germans on the home front presented not only suffering and deprivation, but also very real opportunities for material enrichment. As documented by Götz Aly, many of "Hitler's beneficiaries" were German women who were delighted to receive on a regular basis generous packages with plundered goods from their husbands, sons, fiancés, and brothers stationed in France, Belgium and other occupied countries.[19] As they advanced on the continent, the German soldiers "literally emptied the shelves of Europe" and sent millions of packages back home from the front. These packages often included fabrics such as velvet and silk, beautiful pieces of clothing, shoes, stockings, and other luxuries.[20]

A second important aspect of fashion's wartime discourse is that there was a successful cover-up of the Aryanization of all garment businesses, which had occurred in the recent past. All fashion accounts in the public media manifest a willful political amnesia vis-à-vis the exodus of Jewish owners and workers, and the theft of Jews' material possessions, including their clothes. As Pamela Swett argues, the images and messages offered by entertaining feature films in theaters and in commercial advertisements provided not only a means of escape, but also a look at daily life "free of Jews."[21] While these wartime comedies were presenting to their audiences a model image of a whole economic branch, *Konfektion*, that was now restructured around the absence of Jews, they were also promoting an imaginary consumption of luxury during the war with the goal of subtly shaping future discourses. Thus, infatuation with fashion, satisfying a desire for both vicarious consumption and a relegation to shameless oblivion of the Jewish component of the sector, would reemerge with remarkable rhetorical and aesthetic continuity within the media landscape of the immediate postwar years.

Wartime Realities

As one would expect, everyday life during the war was marked mostly by severe shortages, and there is no dearth of well-documented historical accounts on the harshly limited production and consumption of clothes and textiles during the war.[22] On August 28, 1939, as part of the ongoing preparations for war, the government issued vouchers for food, consumer goods, and basic clothes. Initially exempt from this rationing were luxury items such as hand-knit sweaters, dresses, tuxedoes, evening gowns, silk fabrics, and clothes for newborns—leading to a manic hoarding of such items, manipulation of prices, a thriving black market in clothing, and even worse shortages.[23] One year into the war, by September 1940, such luxury goods as well as all kinds of fabrics were also subject to rationing.

About a month after the invasion of Poland the press revealed government plans to overhaul the ineffective system of coupons with the clothing card, the *Reichskleiderkarte*, a measure that sought to alleviate the shortages of textiles, which had been caused in part by the massive redirection of personnel and resources to the military effort. After several weeks of delays, the card became a reality on November 14, 1939.[24] The card allowed each holder 100 points, distributed in smaller increments in the course of one year. Different items were assigned different value in points, and the points were to be used for a purchase in a store.[25]

Initially the card was praised, even internationally, for its cleverness. The American magazine *Business Week* called it "the most ingenuous attempt ever made in the field of rationing," and the British government adopted the model for its own ration card scheme.[26] A new *Reichskleiderkarte* was supposed to be issued each year, but the situation deteriorated quickly: fewer and fewer items could be obtained in exchange for the points and the periods between issues got longer and longer. The second card, issued in the fall of 1940, was for 150 points, but the increase proved meaningless as the point value of clothing items also increased and the supplies in stores kept shrinking. The third card, 120 points, was introduced in the fall of 1941 and was supposed to last until January 1943. The fourth and last card, for 80 points, was intended to last until June 1944, but its use was halted in August 1943 for lack of supplies.[27] Needless to say, for a long time, Germans had been openly grumbling that the clothing card had become practically worthless, because attire and textile items were nowhere to be found in stores.[28]

To add to the exacerbating material predicaments, there were also the relentless clothing campaigns, especially the winter clothing collections (*Wintersachensammlungen*). In January 1942, the readers of the *Berliner Lokal-Anzeiger* were barraged daily with reminders about their duty to donate warm clothes and fur items to one of the 360 centers in Berlin where items were collected for further shipment to the troops on the Eastern Front. It was, according to the newspaper, "a big collection party" ("das große Fest des Sammelns") and the question "Are you in?"("Bist Du auch dabei?") was posed repeatedly under cartoons that meant to entice people to giving.[29] On the pages of the popular illustrated *Der Silberspiegel*, prominent actresses with star appeal such as Käthe Haack, who otherwise served as a model middle-aged, middle-class woman reasonably involved in fashion of the day, were also engaged in the effort to promote the winter clothing drive.[30]

Inevitably a black market in clothing and textiles emerged, and it, too, became part of the wartime reality. Most notorious were the barter deals between people in the countryside and the urban population—clothes played a crucial role in this shadow economy, despite strict punishments imposed on the offenders.[31] The desperate search for food in the aftermath of severe rationing and the intensifying air raids in 1943 forced Berliners and other urban dwellers to trade their nice clothing, silk stockings, stashed-away fine fabrics, and other luxury items with farmers in the surrounding areas in exchange for foodstuffs.[32]

The new situation of scarcity and sartorial rationing had an immediate impact on the official fashion media. Traditional advertisements for designer salons all but disappeared, because their products could no longer be purchased freely.[33] In indirect concession to the new realities for women in the aftermath of the ration card for clothes, the illustrated magazines, the fashion publications, and the women's and fashion additions to daily newspapers dedicated large sections of their coverage to detailed practical advice on how to handle the situation: "Aus Alt mach Neu" and "Modisches aus Resten" (Fashion from scraps) became the new slogans for the war years. Although most department stores had to scale down their advertising drastically due to consumers' purchasing power being severely limited by the points on their clothing cards, some, like Peek & Cloppenburg, launched bold new print ads that provided tips on mixing and matching to create more outfits, and more high-quality outfits.[34] The weekly illustrated magazine *Das Reich* promoted the *Verwandlungskleid* (literally, "transformation dress"), a new dress that could be made out of an existing outfit or a dress design consisting of two of more elements that can be used in different combinations. This was a project that one

Fig. 3. The actress Käthe Haack volunteers in wartime efforts to
collect and remodel clothes. *Der Silberspiegel*, February 1942.
Staatliche Museen zu Berlin, Kunstbibliothek.

could undertake "when there were not too many points left on the clothing card." This idea, the magazine stated, had been "born from the
war" and "saves points, fabric, money, and work."[35] Variations on the
transformation theme, including reworking older dresses into new ones
that were "appropriate for the times," saturated all fashion sections of
magazines alongside drawings and diagrams that showed readers how the
transformations could be done.[36] The theme was persistent throughout
the war and used all possible media, including the newsreels, to reach
the female audience on the home front. For example, in mid-1944 *Die
Deutsche Wochenschau* included in its war-dominated coverage a fashion
show (*Kleiderschau*) that took place in an armaments plant during a lunch
break. Stepping gracefully on an improvised catwalk in the middle of the
factory floor, models paraded to an enthusiastic audience of female workers elegant dresses made out recycled materials: an old tailcoat, a men's
evening suit, or a cutaway.[37]

Accordingly, the emphasis in the rhetoric of the state-controlled press was not on the persistent shortages and ensuing hardships, but on the purported "positive" impact of privations on everyday life. The war and the rationing card, although sparingly mentioned in the magazines, were presented as catalysts of creativity, individuality, and original solutions, or as Maria May, the artist in charge of the Manufaktur (manufacturing) division of the Deutsches Mode-Institut (German Fashion Institute), put it: "The introduction of the clothing card teaches quality; it makes us aware of purposefulness in combination with a critical attitude toward matters of personal taste."[38]

The military defeat of France and the occupation of Paris in June 1940 also had a direct influence on the fashion industry. Although German dressmakers initially panicked, because they had been used to taking their cues from the Paris spring and autumn couture shows that had now been abolished, they quickly rebounded by embracing the chance to assume a leading position in the fashion world.[39] All propaganda outlets, including the fashion magazines, gave the new situation a positive spin: after all, the military defeat of France meant a long-awaited liberation from the hegemony of all things French. As an editorial in the inaugural issue of *Die Mode* put it, this was a beginning of a "fashion free of command" ("Mode ohne Diktat").[40] One immediate consequence of this shift was the abandonment of French terminology in favor of German words to designate colors and styles.[41] Another was a breaking away from the whimsical cycles of Paris fashion: "One is not a subject any more to the temptations of a cheap, sensation- and novelty-driven industry. Paris was the fashion of the past. The fashion of the future is in Greater Germany."[42] Just what this "fashion of the future" was going to be and how radically new it was expected to be forms part of the present study. One particularly striking aspect of it is certain, though: its imaginary quality, its virtual existence on the pages of magazines only, and its inaccessibility to the city's actual consumers.

Wartime Fashion and Vicarious Consumption

Both the expected pragmatic turn of fashion advice and the increasing anti-French propaganda could be observed in all fashion publications by mid-1941. Meanwhile, another trend appeared to be even more predominant in the media landscape of the Third Reich: fostering imaginary consumption. The paradox was that despite relentless restrictions on regular consumer behavior, the German fashion industry, with the official support from the state ministries of propaganda and economics, thrived and expanded. It supplied fashionable attire to a tiny sliver of a very small domestic market—the party elite, prominent movie stars, and the cast of some films—but produced primarily for export. At the same time, the mass female readership of magazines was encouraged to browse in the countless glossy pages and enjoy the high-quality photographs, the intricate illustrations, and the verbal descriptions of clothes that they would not be able to purchase anywhere.

Several institutions formed and actively supported the framework for vicarious consumption. First, during the initial triumphant years of the war and right after France's capitulation, the idea for a new organization emerged. It was supposed to promote Berlin as the new geopolitical center and also as the world capital of fashion. An editorial in the influential weekly *Das Reich*, programmatically entitled "Berliner Modell," issued a directive that Berlin as Germany's traditional center of the women's garment industry ("Damenoberbekleidungs-Industrie") should replace Paris; it should assume a world leadership position in "rationalizing garment production, coming up with creative solutions, and boosting Germany's exports."[43] In fact, around that very same time, in May 1940, Arbeitsgemeinschaft Berliner Modelle GmbH (Society of Berlin Designers), an association of Berlin-based top fashion designers, was founded and held its first combined fashion show.[44] The association included virtually all the big names of the business: Hilda Romatzki, Annemarie Heise, Nina Carell, the firm Schulze & Bibernell, Elise Topell, Aribert Schwabe, and Hanns Bisegger, along with many formerly Jewish-owned salons that after 1938 at the latest were completely in Aryan hands.[45] Producing exclusively for foreign and elite domestic customers and for export, the members of the Berliner Modelle nevertheless presented twice a year their collections to the Berlin public. As the press reported in early 1942, "The spring and autumn shows of new fashion production in Berlin have become two fixtures in the annual cultural offerings of the German capital."[46]

Working closely with Berliner Modelle was a second organization, the Manufacturing Division of the German Fashion Institute, headed by the artist Maria May and charged with creating commercially desirable textile designs and supplying them to fashion salons of members of the association Berliner Modelle. Both the Manufacturing Division and Berliner Modelle were granted exceptional protection and huge privileges by the Nazi state during the war years. They enjoyed free access to otherwise rationed resources, including considerable amounts of requisitioned fabrics from France and other occupied countries.[47] Some of their male employees were initially exempt from military service.[48]

Third, a new monthly magazine, *Die Mode*, was founded in January 1941, a seemingly surprising development within a shrinking market for illustrated magazines. Published by the Otto Beyer Verlag, it was distributed in thirteen countries associated with Germany, and continued appearing until April 1943. It defined itself as—and seemed to become— the "mouthpiece of the new era" ("Sprachrohr der neuen Zeit") and,

Fig. 4. Design by Schulze & Bibernell for Berliner Modelle GmbH.
Die Mode, January 1943. Staatliche Museen zu Berlin, Kunstbibliothek.

Fig. 5. Cover of *Die Mode*, April 1942. Staatliche
Museen zu Berlin, Kunstbibliothek.

more specifically, the official media outlet for coverage of the production of the fashion houses that made up the association Berliner Modelle GmbH. In addition, there were occasional features on the Vienna-based fashion industry and on the two other much smaller fashion centers in Germany, Frankfurt and Munich, with their respective fashion institutes. To be sure, there was no dearth of fashion coverage in sections of general magazines such as *Die Dame, Die Koralle, die neue linie, Die neue Gartenlaube,* and so on. *Die Mode* was supposed to be bigger and better, and it was dedicated exclusively to fashion. The journalist Anneliese Hafkesbrink from the magazine *die neue linie* was recruited to be the editor in chief of *Die Mode,* while her editorial staff featured a number of experienced and also some very young contributors, mostly photographers and graphic designers, who were recruited after highly publicized competitions. *Die Mode* rapidly became the agent of a sophisticated, very refined National Socialist propaganda that targeted female consumers during the war—not with direct sales pitches and primitive propagandistic orders, but with plentiful and elaborate images that suggested an enticing mix of individuality and modernity, of freedom and creativity. Compared to predominant outlets of cruder political propaganda such as the *Völkischer Beobachter* and the everyday reality of deprivation and material hardship, *Die Mode* presented an alternative universe of beauty, harmony, and opulence, with its seventy richly illustrated pages of daytime and evening elegance, attainable—to look at only—for only 1.50 reichsmarks a month.

Throughout its roughly two years of existence, *Die Mode* was consistent in conveying to its readers that fashion is of particular importance for the wartime economy. The industry relied not only on the domestic consumer and "female desire to purchase" ("die weibliche Kauflust"), which under the circumstances was limited, but also, and primarily, on the international market.[49] From the start, *Die Mode* made no secret that the designer production presented at the two major fashion shows in Berlin and covered meticulously in the magazine was destined exclusively for export.[50] The economic benefit of exports of women's garments to neutral states such as Switzerland and Sweden and to other countries in Europe friendly with the Nazi regime, while always emphasized, was never explicitly discussed in detail. According to archival documents, the revenues from fashion exports were said to have financed the purchase of much needed steel for the war industry.[51]

Since *Die Mode* itself as a publication was exported, one of its primary tasks was to popularize abroad images of fashion created by German companies and thus to set the tone for new fashion looks throughout the countries in which the magazine was disseminated. Apart from savoring Paris's demise as the leader of the fashion industry after its military defeat, the magazine continuously emphasized Berlin's symbolic emergence as the "capital of the European clothing industry," as a new fashion center in a geopolitically altered continent.[52] These developments were acknowledged even by Lucien Lelong, the French couturier who had been installed as second in command in the French fashion industry by the Nazi occupiers after the fall of Paris. Summoned to Berlin in the second half of 1940, Lelong returned with the favorable observation of "how much recognition is given to the Berlin couture by the German government. The Party considers it, apparently, as a steam engine which has the power to move many other trades and industries."[53]

In this context, the central events in the German capital's fashion life were the huge biannual *Exportschauen*, shows in Berlin of fashion production for export, which made explicit who the targeted consumers of the elegant production were. In addition there were also *Richtungsschauen* (directional shows), which claimed the leadership position in Europe's fashion industry that Germany aspired to.[54] In addition to setting the trends for the countries that Nazi Germany occupied or maintained friendly relations with, it was noted that Berlin was absorbing stylistic influences and inspiration from places such as Japan, Turkey, Norway, and Hungary. Two years into the war, in the 1942 January–February issue, *Die Mode* reported, "For the first time, the fashion collections feature themes that signify the expanded political borders of Europe."[55] Thus, elements of the Nordic lumberjack, the Hungarian Cossack shirt, the Japanese kimono, and the Turkish turban found their way into the spring designs of the Berlin salons. Interestingly enough, the presence of motifs from Germany's own traditional folk costumes, such as the dirndl, was pronouncedly suppressed in favor of the new war-related fashion influences.

Overall, the German designer houses delivered products that strived to remain worldly in spirit, maintain high quality, and attract customers abroad. The pronounced international flair remained German fashion's dominant feature, even more so after the fall of Paris. Occupation was a springboard for the Germans to increase their hold on the French fashion identity; when they were not trying to plagiarize French couturiers, they were freely borrowing their ideas and designs.[56]

In certain ways, fashion coverage in Nazi Germany during the war did not differ that much from what British and American competitors were doing in the fashion sections of their newspapers and magazines. Fashion publications in all three countries, in strict observance of government guidelines, presented modern elegance to their audiences as a morale booster as well as an uplifting distraction for a war-weary nation, for both women at the home front and men in combat.[57] All three encouraged women to make the most out of scarce resources and to keep up their appearance. And those who shaped the media landscape in all three societies shared the belief that fashion in wartimes, as an editorial for *Die Mode* put it, "is a way for women to look more attractive, more lovable, more gracious to the men who are fighting on the front." That statement or one very similar could have appeared in any of the fashion publications coming out of London or New York.[58]

In fact, contributors to *Die Mode* and other German magazines kept casting a curious eye in the direction of "enemy" publications such as the British and US editions of *Vogue,* not only with the purpose of maintaining an internationally viable profile but also in order to find a unique way, if only rhetorically, to distinguish themselves from the enemy's position on fashion. In February 1941, a regular contributor to *Die Mode,* Ernst Herbert Lehmann, reported in *Der Silberspiegel* about an article that had appeared in the American *Vogue* right after Germany's bombardment of London. In it, the managing editor of British *Vogue,* Audrey Withers, had vowed to continue the magazine's existence and keep on disseminating fashionable looks even after the air raids on London in November 1940 had made working conditions impossible.[59] As a gesture of defiance, *Vogue* had photographed its models amidst the destruction and promised not to get deterred by the temporary chaos. Reviewing this photo reportage for *Der Silberspiegel* and commenting on the multiple photographs from *Vogue* that were reproduced, Lehmann emphasized that German women would find such a staging of fashion among the ruins as insensitive, tasteless, and extravagant.[60]

A few months later, in November 1941, Lehmann reviewed in detail several issues of American *Vogue* again, this time for *Die Mode,* and concluded that the British and American attitudes toward fashion during the war were politicized and unnecessarily manipulative. German women, Lehmann concluded somewhat arrogantly, would be "alienated by the use of fashion as an instrument of political agitation," which was finding expression in the use of motifs from British and American national flags and from military uniforms in the design of fashionable clothes.[61] German women have a "different sensibility toward fashion in wartime," he claimed, and they don't wear their patriotism and political opinions on their sleeves but prefer subtle elegance free of political references.[62]

While browsing in British and US magazines, German reporters detected the tendency in their rivals to turn the military uniform into a fashion statement, to promote the colors of the flag as a sign of patriotism, and to give tips for makeup that would match the greenish and brownish hues of military attire. Those trends, while discussed in detail in the German entertainment press, were for the most part ridiculed and rejected.[63] It seemed that wartime fashion in Germany "did not want any militarization or uniformity," as one commentator put it.[64] Colors and cuts were deliberately chosen so that they did not resemble military attire and did not remind viewers and wearers of war activities.[65] Despite musing often about the expected pressure in times of war ever since the wars against Napoleon, *Die Mode* consistently scorned the viability of the

idea of the nation's embracing "an identical costume" ("eine einheitli-
che Tracht") that combined a uniformed look with a national costume.
For example, an article on the *Gemeinschaftskleid* (literally, "community
dress," a term the Nazis preferred to *Uniform*) argued that "the question of how to dress is much too personal for women to allow the easy
introduction of any uniformity in all areas of life." The identical attire that
serves to designate belonging to a certain professional community, *das
Gemeinschaftskleid*, should be strictly limited to work-related situations,
in a hospital or in a factory, whereas the private sphere should remain the
place where supposedly individual and creative fashionable solutions were
to be embraced. The assumption was that "wearing a uniform does not
spoil the pleasure of wearing a beautiful dress on other occasions. To the
contrary, in her private life, the German woman enjoys elegant and fashionable clothes."[66]

A year later, writing on the same topic, Lehmann reiterated the position that the choice and juxtaposition between the *Einheitskleid* and the
designer dress, the *Modellkleid*, is a wrong one. In an article whose title
provocatively placed the terms next to each other, Lehmann engaged in
a lengthy defense of the *Modellkleid*, that is, he articulated the need for
designer fashion especially in times of crisis.[67] Featured in this article were
fashionable creations by the Berlin salon of Gehringer & Glupp, which,
although produced on a strict limit of two and a half meters of cloth per
outfit, in no way resembled an *Einheitskleid*. These were also "neither
destined for export nor were they created for a certain film or theater
production," as was often the case with designs presented on the pages
of this magazine. The limitations imposed by the war notwithstanding,
Lehmann argued, this was precisely what the consumer needed and what
was made possible by the state support for the fashion industry: "not a
war fashion or uniform fashion, but a beautiful, living fashion that brings
joy to women" ("nicht Kriegs- oder Einheitsmode, sondern eine schöne
lebendige Mode, die den Frauen Freude macht").[68] Indeed, rarely would
uniforms, swastikas, or any war-inspired fashion be seen on the pages of
any of the German fashion magazines. All of the efforts of journalists to
highlight how German wartime fashion was clearly distinguishable from
rival production in the United States and the United Kingdom remained
for the most part a rhetorical exercise that had little to do with reality.

Ultimately, despite the professed desire to deliver practical, wearable everyday solutions to meet German women's fashion needs, the
fashion press remained largely committed to the vicarious consumption
of elegance. Through text and images *Die Mode* created on its pages an
imaginary world in which harmony reigned, everyday hardships were
absent, and destruction was invisible. In it, the German woman appears
distinctly up-to-date with international standards, nonmaternal, apolitical.

Oblivious to rationing and shortages, she inhabits a conflict-free realm where all she has to do is indulge the designers' "creative play with velvets and silk" ("das schöpferische Spiel mit Samt und Seide.")[69]

This fantasy image in the fashion magazines of the German woman as a sophisticated consumer of elegance with distinct taste and individualized preferences that encouraged her participation in imaginary consumption was mirrored in wartime cinema of the Third Reich. Like illustrated magazines, entertainment films served as the site of imaginary consumption.

Wartime Fashion and Entertainment Films

Throughout its existence in the 1940s, *Die Mode* was determined to infuse some high-cultural elements into the Germans' understanding of fashion. It was involved in a sustained effort to conceptualize fashion as an intricate part of German national culture on a par with high-culture art forms such as theater, music, and painting, and to explore the various intersections among the arts under Nazi control. Unsurpassed in that respect was the collaboration between film and fashion that was often evoked on the pages of the magazine. The creations of both industries, film and fashion, were seen as "testimonies to the wide range of our cultural production" ("Zeugnisse für die Spannweite unseres kulturellen Schaffens").[70] In the absence of a real domestic market for fashionable clothes and under the conditions of severe rationing and shortages, film, along with the print press, became a principal venue for the distribution of fashionable images, and vicarious consumption became a main form of participation in culture. That special relationship between fashion and film enjoyed unprecedented protection, endorsement, and institutional encouragement from the highest levels in the Nazi state. For example, Benno von Arent, a longtime stage designer employed by the state (*Reichsbühnenbildner*), was appointed simultaneously Reich's agent for fashion (*Reichsbeauftragter für die Mode*) in 1939. In 1942, he was additionally charged to oversee all *Modeschulen*, schools of fashion and design, in Berlin, Munich, and Frankfurt. On that occasion, when he was interviewed in *Der Silberspiegel*, Arent emphasized his double commitment: to ensure during the hardest years of the war that film productions were supplied with the highest-quality contemporary costumes, and also to ensure that German women's need for exposure to fashion—even if only via the illusory consumption offered by the silver screen—would not be neglected.[71]

Light fare, the entertainment films—comedies, detective mysteries, and adventure films—dominated the market. The typical filmgoing experience, especially among the female viewers, was captured in a 1943 article by Hans Traub, the head of the film institute associated with UFA, the UFA-Lehrschau:

We were coming out of the movies one evening. The film we had just watched was nothing special, one of many of this kind. . . . It was an entertainment film, average fare, although it, too, had been created with great professional skill, effort, and attention to detail. The movie did not offer anything exceptional for the hungry brain nor for the yearning heart. And yet, some stray remarks by two female spectators made the evening worthwhile. "What fabulous fashions they had!" said one of them. "Yes, fantastic costumes in a great setting!" confirmed the other."[72]

This anecdote seems to reflect what home-front audiences took away from watching an entertaining film—delight in beautiful costumes and intact interiors.

The unusually intense attention to matters of fashion and costume on the silver screen is reflected in some of UFA's personnel decisions as well as in discussions in the film trade press. In the middle of the very difficult year 1943, for example, UFA's production director, Wolfgang Liebeneiner, appointed the star designer Heinz Schulze as a costume manager (*Kostümchef*) to oversee a small staff of young and upcoming female costume consultants (*Kostümberaterinnen*).[73] At the same time, throughout 1942 and 1943, *Film-Kurier* became the public forum for a variety of opinions and recommendations regarding the role of fashion and costume designers for films made during the war. Parallel to their appearance in *Die Mode*, Hans Traub's two articles on fashion in film were also published in *Film-Kurier*.[74] Traub's affirmative piece outlined meticulously all the steps in the design of costumes for both historical and contemporary films and raised the prestige of fashion in wartime cinema. He declared that the old times of informal exchanges when the fashion industry lent its outfits to films and film stars in exchange for free publicity are definitely over). UFA now had its own fashion department, staffed by specially trained professional designers that raised the status of film costume to an autonomous art form.[75]

But some strong voices called for toning down the fashion statements in films in light of the fabric shortage and the rather humble clothes seen in the streets of the big cities at the height of the war. In early 1942, *Film-Kurier*'s editor in chief, Günther Schwark, wrote a front-page article appealing for restraint and "more taste in film costume." He emphasized the "educational tasks of film when it comes to fashion":

Millions of women go to the movies every year. Their tastes are shaped by the clothes seen in the films. What kind of impression does the appearance of the well-dressed lady from the big city leave on the girls and young women in small provincial towns? They do not suspect that in reality the Berlin or Viennese woman has no access to such fashion. But what if these show-off clothes from the movies become fashionable and are faithfully imitated far and wide? In that sense, film bears a huge responsibility. This obliges film to be the purveyor of good taste.[76]

Later in 1942, similar concerns about the "Modetorheiten" (fashion foolishness) and "modische Überspanntheiten" (fashion excesses) in contemporary films were voiced in an editorial, "Mode und Film," in *Film-Kurier* by the critic Georg Herzberg. Herzberg warned against irresponsible sartorial excesses and extravagance on display in film productions, yet he devoted most of his article to describing how "even at the beginning of the fourth war year the German woman manages to dress well and with taste. . . . She knows that this is not only as her right, but also as her duty," he wrote in a lengthy explanation of how important women's fashion is for the morale of the soldiers returning home on leave.[77] Herzberg argued that fashion in entertainment film, as in real life, should not be subject to frequent change, but should provide delightful examples of the creative interplay of "taste and fantasy, grace and chic" ("Geschmack und Phantasie, Anmut und Schick") within the limits imposed the ration card and the shrinking wardrobes.

Four of these entertainment films from the early 1940s—*Achtung! Der Feind hört mit!*, a spy thriller with an anti-British propaganda message, and the romantic comedies of errors *Das himmelblaue Abendkleid*, *Meine Freundin Josefine*, and *Kollege kommt gleich*—stand out as arenas for vicarious consumption and shed light on the effort and resources invested in the design of historical and contemporary costumes for UFA's lavish productions, which kept coming out even during the harshest period of the war. They have received almost no scholarly attention in studies dedicated to popular or entertainment cinema of the Third Reich, although their contribution to the visual spectacle of Nazi film achieved through the sumptuous use of contemporary costume is significant. Operating within what Sabine Hake calls "an illusionist framework" that is typical for popular German cinema after 1939, these films incorporate at least one extensive two-to-three-minute sequence of a formal fashion show organized by a fictional fashion salon and interweave a desirable item of clothing, a designer dress, directly into their plots.[78] The gifting, possession, the loss of possession, or simply the desire to own the garment—all of these motivations result in dramatic or comic twists in the plots. During these scenes the home front audience is made privy to an experience that has become definitely obsolete in wartime, namely looking and shopping for elegant clothes. Thus the scenes of fashion display become compensatory cinematic fantasies deemed to be of high importance for the intended audiences.

Finally, all these works feature female protagonists that deviate from the oppressive definitions of femininity that otherwise permeated every aspect of public life in Nazi Germany. The majority of central female characters are neither mothers nor exclusively housewives, but independent professionals (entrepreneurs, fashion salon owners, designers, scientists) who crave meaningful realization at the workplace as well as public recognition. Their prominent presence in these films reflects, as Hake has pointed out, "the contradictory demands on popular cinema to at once recognize and disavow the material difficulties of the home front."[79] By encouraging vicarious visual consumption, the fashionable images of women in the films bear witness both to the growing pressures exerted by the wartime economy and the resultant transformation of femininity into a privileged site for self-expression and aesthetic pleasure.

Achtung! Der Feind hört mit! was one of the first German wartime movies that blended fashion into its overall propagandistic story line. The plot involves industrial espionage that is supposed to warn Germans about the dangers of giving away the country's technological and military inventions, but also to amuse and please the mass audience with suspense and spectacle. The researcher Hellmers (played by Christian Kayßler) and his assistant, Inge Neuhaus (played by Lotte Koch), working for the armaments company Kettwig, have developed a unique wire, extremely light and sturdy, which when attached to balloons will be the most effective anti-aircraft device to date. Although the company is very careful about protecting its sensitive technologies, both Bernd Kettwig, the son of the company's owner, and Inge, the research assistant, inadvertently come very close to giving away the company secrets to a pair of British spies, Lilly and Faerber—the characters who bring fashion into the story. Lilly, the owner of a newly opened fashion salon in Baden-Baden, seduces Bernd with her looks and outfits, while her accomplice, Faerber, manages to get Inge to fall in love with him as he showers her with beautiful designer dresses.[80] As the two couples go out on a double date, they attend a dazzling fashion presentation at the Salon Lilly—thus the audience, too, is treated to an extended fashion show staged by the film's costume designer, Reingard Voigt.[81]

Although the dangers of falling into the traps of the British spies arise from situations related to the fashion, it is significant that fashion in itself is presented in a positive light, as a legitimate place of diversion even during the war, as an international endeavor that is of economic significance on par with the products of the military industry. In addition, the involvement in fashion signals a certain notion of belonging to the cosmopolitan international scene on which Germans now claimed to be major players. Repeatedly throughout the film, Lilly's owner and her employees show off their foreign-language skills speaking English and French and talking about their European travels and their international clients. The design of new fabric patterns and dress models is also presented as a serious, scientific activity very much like the design of new materials for the defense industry. Notably, the opening line of the film refers to the importance of fashion that permeates daily activities and conversations. Chief engineer Hellmers, bent over a microscope to examine the structure of the newly invented wire, calls over to his assistant, "Guck mal, Inge, das wäre ein schönes Muster für ein neues Kleid" (Look here, Inge, that would be a beautiful pattern for a new dress).

In addition to being a reference to Germany's continuing efforts to remain a leader in textile and fashion design, this remark serves to introduce director Rabenalt's recent "discovery," young actress Lotte Koch. In an effort to promote her ascending star status in the course of the plot development, Rabenalt has her attend an elaborate fashion show, then try on some designer clothes, and ultimately transform her appearance. When her new boyfriend, Faerber, sends her as a gift the dress that she had tried at the salon, she gladly accepts it. This supposedly generous gesture seals the relationship and opens the door to the unintentional betrayal of industry secrets. It is remarkable, though, that fashion in itself does not serve as a bribe or payment for the "favor." Inge is willing to help out with analysis of the special wire, not so much because she is smitten by the pretty dress and has fallen into the trap set by Faerber, but more because she is tired of her subordinate position in the research team and being constantly treated as an assistant. She would like to prove her value as an expert on equal footing with the chief engineer, Hellmers, and that leads her to inadvertently reveal the state secret.

The other female star of the film, Kirsten Heiberg, a Norwegian actress who came to Germany in 1939 to play femme fatales and who is here cast as the owner of the newly founded fashion salon Lilly, was a somewhat more established and popular actress, which was reflected in her role of a savvy business woman, in her more mature and dazzling outfits, and in the ease with which she seduces young Kettwig and eavesdrops on his phone conversation in order to obtain the secret formula for the wire.

Das himmelblaue Abendkleid, directed by Erich Engels, is another striking example of the presence of the fashion industry and fashion shows on the film screen during the war years. Unlike Rabenalt's *Achtung! Der Feind hört mit!*, this film does not contain any direct political or ideological message, but is staged as pure entertainment, as a "comedy of human vanity."[82]

The comedy places a sky-blue chiffon designer dress at the center of the plot and even elevates it to the status of a main character: "Die Tobis hat jetzt einen Film herausgebracht, in dessen Hauptrolle ein Kleid steht" (Tobis has produced a film in which the starring role is played by a dress").[83] The costume designer for the film is not identified in the credits. Most likely, the costumes were created in UFA's own ateliers rather than commissioned from one of the Berlin fashion salons, since the film did not feature any big stars.[84] The exceptional luxurious appearance of that dress prompted critics to openly comment that "these days such a product could be only seen on the silver screen."[85] Even the publicity materials for the new Tobis film acknowledged the film's amusing preoccupation with a dress.[86] This "main character" is introduced at a fashion show in Zürich at the Salon Haberland and makes its way to several intended and unintended owners across the border, in Germany. These include a singer, played by Elfie Mayerhofer; a revue dancer, played by Ellen Bang; and the middle-aged wife of a famous writer, played by Käthe Haack. Haack's character receives the dress as a present from an old admirer, a Berlin-based fashion salon owner who had purchased it from his Zurich business partner. In an effort to obscure its real origin she deposits it in an auction house and presents the ticket to her husband, claiming that she has found it. He is supposed to claim it, and he does, but decides that the dress is too fancy for his wife, so he exchanges the fabulous sky-blue gown for something much more ordinary and unexciting, "a simple off-the-rack dress" ("ein einfaches Fähnchen von der Stange") and gives the fancy dress to his "young female friend," who later turns out to be his daughter out of wedlock. Meanwhile, the owner's son pursues the dress for his lover. Ultimately, the multiple misunderstandings, which have caused jealousy and suspicion as well as criminal inquiries and investigations by private detectives, are cleared up, a marriage is saved, and two pairs of young people fall in love with each other and plan to get married. Although in the end the middle-aged female character loses the dress, the film seems to validate and be most sympathetic with her desires. It is not insignificant that the well-known and well-loved star of the stage Käthe Haack was cast in this role.

The overall reception of the film was warm and enthusiastic, because, as the critic Günther Dietrich stated, it gave the audience a break from the "reasonableness of fashion in times of war. . . . There have been times in history," Dietrich continued, "when styles went wild and extravagant. . . . Now Germans have embraced a very sensible fashion and the war has played a regulatory role. With the restrictive points in place, no one could or should be able to afford big fashion extravagance. Yet small doses of luxury can still be enjoyed in film."[87] Since the import of luxury items such as designer dresses has been illegal since the beginning of the war, even the police become involved in a criminal investigation of suspected contraband that adds to suspense and a secondary strand in the plot.[88] But the comically staged criminal investigation is the only, minimal, nod to realism in this film. In general the film remains a light fare whose primary function was to entertain and divert the audience's attention from the unpleasant realities of war.

Perhaps the most unrestrained display of spectacular women's dresses at the height of the war occurs in the 1942 comedy *Meine Freundin Josefine*, whose entire plot is set in the fashion milieu of an unnamed city, presumably contemporary Berlin. Young Hilde Krahl, a new film face in Berlin, was cast in the title role of Josefine Bauer, an orphaned woman from the provinces who lives with her uncle's family and is mercilessly exploited, serving almost like a maid. Her particular talents are in designing and sewing clothes. When she is desperate to find an appropriate dress to attend a dinner reception at the house of her host family, she quickly assembles a glamorous gown out of a shiny black bed spread. This very brief sequence constitutes the film's only, and somewhat oblique, nod to the wartime sartorial practices of making do with what is at hand. In a comic twist, the hastily assembled gown falls apart and slips down her shoulders, leaving Josefine exposed in her underwear and causing enough embarrassment to force her to leave the family.

But the star designer in the film, Herr Milander (played by Paul Hubschmid), is impressed by her skills, hires her on the spot to work in his salon, and soon takes her out for dinner. Josefine rejects his hasty amorous advances, quits her job after only a day of work, and with the help of a friend, the famous singer and dancer Bianka Terry (played by Fita Benkhoff), opens her own designer salon. What neither Milander nor Josefine are aware of is that Bianka Terry has persuaded her friend, the celebrated couturier, to make a huge one-time investment into Salon Josefine, without revealing to him the identity of that business. In due time, as a result of Josefine's creativity and diligent work, her salon prospers and its fame soon surpasses that of Milander. Her designs win various competitions, and she inadvertently "steals" all of her competitor's famous clients. It is only after achieving great triumph on her terms, as an independent businesswoman, that Josefine consents to Milander's persistent courting. The happy end, in line with the other entertainment movies of the time, suggests that the marriage of the characters would also bring about the merger of two very successful businesses.

This amusing, lightweight film is notable for the ways in which Hilde Krahl's character prefigures the actress's future breakthrough only a year later as a star in *Großstadtmelodie*. Similar to Renate in *Großstadtmelodie*, Josefine undergoes an overnight transformation from a humble orphan girl into a confident professional woman. This transformation is most conspicuously signaled in the clothes she wears onscreen. As soon as she takes on a job—first as a seamstress for Milander and soon after as an independent fashion designer with her own establishment—she sheds the plain dark dress that looks like a maid's uniform and dons elegant dresses that seem to have been inspired by the fashions one could see in *Die Mode*.

In fact, in addition to Irmgard Becker-Schulte, who designed the costumes for the dancer and singer Bianka Terry and her stage appearances within the film, the production company Tobis hired Annemarie Heise, a prominent Berlin dressmaker who was a member of the Berliner

Modelle, whose work was featured on the pages of almost every issue of *Die Mode*, and who was known to be a personal couturier to Hitler's girl-friend, Eva Braun. (After the war, Irmgard Becker-Schulte took the name Bessie Becker and became well known under that name.) Heise supplied the not only the dresses for Hilde Krahl's character but also the outfits for the numerous supporting roles and extras—the women are featured as clerks, seamstresses, and models in the spacious salons of Milander and Josefine. The dresses seen on screen seem direct quotes from the pages of the *Die Mode*, where Annemarie Heise is celebrated as the leading figure in designing elegant outfits for professional women ("elegante Arbeitskleidung"). In an article from summer 1942 the journal describes Heise as particularly responsive to the new *Zeitgeist*: "Since women's lives today are dedicated to work to an unprecedented degree, fashion needs to tackle new tasks of political and social importance."[89] The featured models in the article (like the clothes of the working women in the film) are far from uniform or drab; on the contrary, they maintain a balance between functional cuts and eye-grabbing detailing and accessories. Finally, Annemarie Heise is responsible also for the spectacular three-minute fashion-show sequence in the middle of the film, which is meant to serve as a culmination Josefine's work, as she puts it, as both "an independent fashion designer and competitor to Milander." This show, and a subsequent appearance in a fashion competition in Vienna, steal all the prizes and puts Josefine on equal footing with Milander.

Fashion as theme and location continues to find its way into film, even as the war progresses. When the comedy *Kollege kommt gleich* premiered in Munich in December 1943, following a series of heavy air raids in the city throughout the year, the local press received the film with excitement: "This amusing film is coming out at the right time in Munich, because everyone is nostalgic about past things and everyone knows that the beginning of the year can once again be marked with happiness and light-heartedness."[90] A huge part of its appeal lay in its central setting, the fashion salon Hillmer, which combines nostalgia for an idealized, peaceful past and a bright future of unburdened indulgence. The film's female protagonist is the salon owner's daughter, Lilo. Despite its glamorous production, however, Salon Hillmer is threatened by bankruptcy and is saved by the generous loans provided by Robert Wendler, a waiter. This theme—about the fickleness of the fashion business, the extreme competitiveness within the industry, and its dependence on steady investments—was popular in cinema of the 1930s, and *Kollege kommt gleich* seems to resurrect it, borrowing numerous ideas almost literally from another film, *Frischer Wind aus Kanada* (Fresh Wind out of Canada, 1935, directed by Heinz Kenter and Erich Holder).

This earlier UFA production set the tone and established the visual style and the themes that would recur in later Nazi films. It, too, stages the numerous fashion shows at a Berlin salon that serve as the constant background for the plot, which features mismanagement and financial troubles and an unexpected investor-savior who hails from Canada. Implied is also a Jewish-capitalist conspiracy, associated with the figure of the deceptive and scheming Bernetzki, that threatens the survival of the otherwise honest and successful fashion business.[91] In addition, there is the romantic entanglement that ends with a marriage. Similarly, in the 1943 wartime film the financial survival of the salon is also dependent upon the finicky tastes of the customers and, ultimately, the romantic relationship that binds the protagonists, Wendler and Lilo. After a series of dramatic and comic developments prompted by Lilo's initial prejudice against Wendler's lower social standing, she comes around and marries the love of her life. Concurrently, the fashion business is also saved. Throughout the light-fare comedy, Lilo is shown as a professionally active woman in multiple scenes related to her job in the family's designer salon: she serves as its most charming model, she participates in numerous fashion photo shoots, and, more important, she is also shown designing new clothes and plotting business strategies that seem much more successful than those of her father.

The choice for the female protagonist Lilo of Carola Höhn, an actress with "an enchanting appearance" and "fabulous acting style," is particularly appropriate.[92] Höhn had not only acquired star status by the end of the 1930s but also was well known for her exceptional elegance and her longtime association with the fashion industry. Before making her breakthrough on the silver screen in the late 1920s, she had worked as a model for a number of fashion magazines, and the steady earnings from her fashion photographs helped her start an acting career.[93]

Like 1935's fashion-related comedy *Frischer Wind aus Kanada*, *Kollege kommt gleich* features the full spectrum of elegant women's clothes for all occasions, but without the explicit product placement. Whereas in the 1935 film all of the costumes, especially for the fashion shows, were created by a leading designer house, Nicoll (and were reproduced in a number of magazines—good publicity for the Nicoll salon), the costumes in *Kollege kommt gleich* are credited to a relatively young and unknown costume consultant, a *Kostümberaterin*, Hildegard Ordnung, hired specifically by the studio Tobis for this production.[94] In the postwar years, as an editor and illustrator Ordnung emerged as one of the pioneers in the process of resurrecting the fashion press.[95]

All four films discussed here and several other, less prominent, productions such as *Meine Frau Teresa* (My Wife Teresa, 1942, directed by Arthur Maria Rabenalt), *Frau nach Maß* (Made-to-Measure Wife, 1940, directed by Helmut Käutner), and *Mädchen im Vorzimmer* (The Girl in the Lobby, 1940, directed by Gerhard Lamprecht) also exemplify the important shift in function of the presentation of wartime fashion: from direct product placement to a substantive part of the targeted ambience of normality. In most cases, fashion with this new function was created by newcomers to the profession, mostly young women and mostly appointed to these positions vacated by more established male designers, who either had been either forced out after 1933 because they are Jewish or had been mobilized in the war. The new female designers remained for the most part unknown, often unidentified in the credits. Nevertheless their work was discussed in a number of articles in the trade press. For instance, in a 1940 *Film-Kurier* article a Nazi Party functionary, Hans-Martin Cremer, shed light on the complex process of training in the areas of art, art history, drawing, and sewing that was involved in the process of becoming a professional *Kostümberaterin*."[96] He gave as a prime example the work of young Margot Hielscher, who "supervised the artistic process in several UFA films."[97]

If one went by the women's and fashion magazines and the multiple entertainment-film productions of the early 1940s, one would hardly notice that there is a total war going on. Images of fashionably dressed women proliferated, which even though it was at odds with the official Nazi doctrine about the looks of the German woman, was considered important for keeping the home front content and in high spirits. Within the war context, fashion was thus made to maintain a precarious balancing act between not drawing too much the public's attention to the actual unavailability of fashion and being an outlet for escapist visual consumption. Dominique Veillon's observations about France under occupation reflects to a great extent the situation of wartime Germany: "The domain of elegance in the prewar sense had taken refuge on the [silver screen] and gave a public deprived of luxury substance for their dreams."[98] The great attention paid to fashion in the public sphere during the war years as well as the considerable resources invested in that enterprise at least up until early 1944 for richly illustrated publications and lavish film costumes also testify to larger issues of historic continuity. As in other European countries and the United States, the images of sumptuous clothes during wartime not only established a nostalgic and thus comforting link to a peaceful past, but in retrospect can be seen to have prepared the public for future, postwar consumption in an indirect and understated way. The citizen consumer of the 1950s may not have come into being without the preliminary work done by vicarious wartime consumption.

2. "Fashions for Fräuleins": The Rebirth of the Fashion Industry and Media in Berlin after 1945

> *This is what one can see on the streets of Berlin—women who look distinctly chic and fashionable. This is the overall impression, while the clothes themselves are not extravagant. The Berlin woman demonstrates again her sense of fashion, her sense of "what's in the air." She does not reach for the stars, but rather for what is feasible. She looks for and finds the right dress for her type as well as for today's Berlin!*
>
> —"The Fashion Barometer: Rising," *Heute*, June 15, 1947

IN THE CHAOTIC AFTERMATH of Germany's unconditional capitulation in May 1945, the tasks of reconstruction and a new beginning in Berlin were daunting. Alongside the ideological and political objectives of democratization, denazification, and demilitarization was the common goal of restoring some sense of normality, which found expression in sometimes paradoxical reinstatements of routines and rituals of everyday civilian life. Many outside observers in the collapsed city of Berlin were astonished by the look of its inhabitants and their general attitude toward appearances. By the end of 1945, a headline in the British newspaper *Daily Mail* announced "Life Returns to the New Germany" and published a report on the first "after-the-defeat fashions," richly illustrated by the Berlin-based artist Alice Bronsch and labeled "Fashions for Fräuleins."[1] Traveling through the decimated German capital in September of 1945, Isaac Deutscher reported in *The Economist* on the paradoxical presence of elegance against the background of destruction and despair:

> The people give a . . . fallacious impression. The misleading factor is their clothes. In the less damaged suburbs within the British and American districts, and in the centre of the Russian district, suits, hats, dresses and baby clothes seem to have survived the air raids and the battle in surprising quantities. Among ruins, one expects to see beggars; instead . . . the Berliners appear rather better dressed than shoppers in the Edgware Road.[2]

That same autumn, the Swiss writer Max Frisch was visiting the city and gauging its contradictory ambience by observing Berliners in the subway and on the streets. In his journal he noted with some astonishment the attempts of women to at put on a more cheerful look:

> Almost everyone is carrying a bundle, a backpack or a box. Next to faces dark as clay and ash, there are others, perfectly healthy faces, but similarly sealed, impenetrable, and masklike. It takes a while to notice the poverty marked by worn collars and elbows. Berlin is still hanging on to its last suits. Women, even though they are wearing pants, headscarves, and heavy boots, appear smart and dapper, and this is nice. And important. While men attach their pride and self-hatred to a battle flag, women take care of their hair, lips, and fingernails. Thus women, in a way that is hard to describe, embody greater and much more genuine hope.[3]

This surprising contrast between the general state of devastation and resignation and the bright spots of hope and recovery represented especially by women's appearance in the cityscape, by their efforts to take care of "their hair, lips, and fingernails," is mirrored in the relatively quick revival of fashion-related businesses in a city that had always had a reputation as a "magnet for designers" ("Magnet für Modemacher").[4] In his entries from the same stay in Berlin, Max Frisch commented on a rare sight of lively economic activities and pleasure among the ruins: "One can see the display windows on Kurfürstendamm again, small but clean, and tastefully decorated. A delight for the eye. . . . There is the understandable desire to see something that is whole again, something dirt free, something beautiful."[5] As noticed by Deutscher, Frisch, and other visitors, the combination of these two persistent traits of Berliners—their efforts to maintain regular, neat and elegant appearances despite tragedy and destruction and their determination to rebuild some of the city's previous glamour as soon as possible—resulted in the amazing revival of fashion amidst the ruins.

This chapter traces in detail the swift and paradoxical recovery of the fashion industry as well as the various outlets for its publicity (women's and specialized fashion magazines, supplements in daily newspapers, fashion shows in clubs, and newsreels) in the first postwar years, from 1945 till the onset of the next dramatic political crisis, the Berlin Blockade, on June 24, 1948. Berlin had traditionally been Germany's fashion capital since the mid-nineteenth century, and close to 90 percent of the businesses were owned by Jews. In its heyday in the 1920s the *Konfektion* sector comprised 700 businesses and employed about 180,000 people. As a site of economic and symbolic significance for the city before the Nazi's rise to power in 1933, the fashion industry became a focal point of Aryanization, and from the government's point of view remained important, even during the worst war years.

The fashion industry's quick rebirth immediately after the end of war activities raises a host of challenging, sometimes even puzzling, questions of importance for postwar memory and for the sense of continuity and discontinuity between past, present, and future: Who were the players in the business within this new context? Did any of the numerous former Jewish owners return to claim their old businesses? What could possibly be the status and meaning of fashion in a society ravished by the hunger, shortages, and misery in the immediate postwar period? How is fashion presented and discussed in the fashion press that proliferated in these early years after the war as the city lay in ruins? What kind of women's public sphere was shaped by the appearance of these publications that placed an intensive focus on practices of dressmaking, fashion journalism, magazine browsing, and window shopping amidst the ruins and thus revealed little-known dimensions of the everyday lives of Berlin women? Can fashion be considered one of the emerging visual battlefields of the Cold War with a particular importance for women's experiences? The following exposition presents a first attempt to address these questions in both a comprehensive and a panoramic way.

The Comeback of Fashion

Traditionally, most of the clothing and textile businesses were to be found in the eastern part of Berlin, around Hausvogteiplatz, not far from Alexanderplatz; they had been located in this area since the mid-nineteenth century; indeed, it was known as Berlin's clothes-manufacturing district (*Konfektionsviertel*). During the wartime air raids the buildings in this part of the city were reduced to unsalvageable ruins. By the end of the war, Berlin's Jews, who had traditionally formed a majority of owners, employees, and sales personnel within this industry, were also gone. As early as in August 1945, however, many of the companies that had been in existence since the 1930s reopened at new locations, mostly in the western part of the city; reconnected with what was left of former employees, suppliers, and customers; and started producing again, with store fronts reappearing on and around the Kurfürstendamm and numerous complementary businesses located mainly in the city districts of Charlottenburg and to Fehrbelliner Platz in Wilmersdorf.[6] Less than a year later, in July 1946, the newspaper *Der Tagesspiegel* reported of 210 functioning businesses on Kurfürstendamm, 43 of them clothes stores.[7]

In that first year of peace, the textile and clothing sector (*Textilien- und Bekleidungsindustrie*) was repeatedly referred to as one of the five traditional Berlin-based industries that sprang back to life with the encouragement of the Allies, despite heavy bombing, related losses of modern production facilities, and multiple postwar hurdles such as measures of denazification, removal, and dismantling of industrial equipment by the Soviet army.[8] The clothing sector of Berlin's economic life revived quickly in part because it reverted to an earlier system of cost-efficient mass production of garments, from the 1910s and 1920s, that did not rely on heavy capital investment in sophisticated manufacturing facilities or machinery. Instead, in this immediate postwar period as in earlier times, production relied heavily on the work of subcontractors (*Zwischenmeister*) and countless seamstresses who worked at home (*Heimarbeiterinnen*). *Heimarbeiterinnen* worked on commission from their homes, using their own sewing machines; after the war they used machines salvaged somehow during the postwar chaos. Additionally, many Berlin clothing companies obtained contracts for mending and manufacturing services with the Soviet occupation force, which contributed between 35 and 40 percent of their income.[9] According to an official report of the municipal administration of Berlin, the number of clothing-related firms in October 1945 rose to 313 and doubled by March 1946, to 662, while the number of their employees grew in the same period from 5,662 to 15,530.[10] Half a year later, in September 1946, in a lengthy article in the newspaper *Der Nacht-Express* the fashion journalist Emmy Klaß remarked on the "promising new beginning" ("vielversprechender Neuanfang") of the Berlin *Konfektion*, which now counted 1,150 firms, employed 29,000 workers and generated 9.5 million marks in yearly sales.[11] Although it is difficult to verify the figures that were published in the press, the upward trend and the enormous scale of recovery of this economic branch seems undeniable.

The story of Hans W. Claussen's salon, Salon Clausssen-Kleider, founded in 1938, is exemplary in many ways for the developments immediately following the war's end.[12] Like other owners of garment companies, Claussen was exempt from military service during the war years and continued to run his business, as the production of civilian clothes and military uniforms was considered essential to the war effort. After being bombed out twice in 1944 and forced to move, Claussen settled in a new location, Kurfürstendamm 217. According to tax documents he filed at the end of 1945, his business was reestablished on August 9 of the same year, had about fifteen full-time employees, and registered a small profit for the year. Notably, the company's expenses for "fashion teas," fashion shows, and other advertisement for the year 1945, again according to his first postwar tax return, were close to 5,000 reichsmarks, or 10 percent of his average monthly budget of 48,571 reichsmarks.[13] Only a year later, Claussen became one of the few Berlin companies to stage an his own fashion shows, each one of which featuring over 100 designs, which attracted unprecedented publicity from newspapers from all the occupation sectors.[14]

To outside observers in those first months of frenetic postwar activities, the fashion show was the flashiest and most surprising sign of recovery and normalization. Only four months after the battle for Berlin was over, on September 8, 1945, the designer Walter Friedrich Schulz invited loyal customers from better times and organized "the first peace-time fashion tea" in his private apartment in Xantener Straße.[15] In her opening comments to the invitees, the Berlin journalist Pauline Nardi joked that when Berliners first heard the announcement for a fashion show in these times, they probably thought it is some kind of misunderstanding. But it was a real show and twenty-four new designs were presented; instead of professional models, however, Schulz asked four of his loyal female customers to model the dresses. The emphasis was on the creative use of whatever fabrics and materials one could find in this period of scarcity. Nardi drew attention to the highlight of the show, the so-called patchwork dress (*Flickenkleid*), a colorful dress made from several dozens pieces of different fabrics that Schulz could find around his studio.[16] A photograph taken immediately after the show was published in several newspapers the following day: it shows one of Schulz's customers, Gabriele, Gräfin von und zu Trauttmansdorff, dressed in the signature *Flickenkleid* outfit walking proudly down Kurfürstendamm with the ruin of the Kaiser Wilhelm Gedächtniskirche (Memorial Church) in the background. This image became a symbol of the times and of the defiant hope that, in Nardi's words, "beautiful Berlin, which conveyed so much joy, will arise [*wie das schöne Berlin, das so viel Freude vermittelte, wieder entstehen wird*]."[17]

The message of the photograph seems to suggest that the easiest first step was to restore one's own appearance, before undertaking the more onerous task of rebuilding "beautiful Berlin" as its residents remembered it.[18] As it was seen numerous times in fashion illustrations and photographs throughout the press in the first postwar months, the *Flickenkleid* not only reflected a practical way for German women to deal with the current situation but also alluded to the process of refashioning as a kind of selective, piecemeal working through of the past and piecing together a livable present, a patchwork of sorts: partly reconnecting to the glorious prewar traditions of Berlin *Konfektion*, partly dropping the fate of the Jewish couturiers and their employees down the memory hole.

After the first fashion show featuring the *Flickenkleid*, other designers and recently revived professional associations of garment producers such as the Innung des Bekleidungshandwerks (Guild of the Garment Trade) and the Ring Berliner Modeschöpfer (Circle of Berlin Fashion Designers) followed suit in the fall and winter of 1945 and throughout 1946.[19] If newspaper ads and announcements are to be believed, fashion salons were in desperate need of chairs to rent and models to hire for all the shows that were mounted throughout the rest of 1945 and 1946.[20] In its new location on the Kurfürstendamm, the Hans Gehringer Salon organized a show for the winter season featuring "clothes against the cold"—coats made

Fig. 6. The first postwar fashion show in Berlin in the salon of designer Walter Friedrich Schulz, on September 8, 1945, with his customers volunteering as models and presenting the *Flickenkleid*. Staatliche Museen zu Berlin, Kunstbibliothek.

out of US Army blankets and redesigned Soviet uniforms.[21] Just recently returned Soviet imprisonment, thirty-one-year old Heinz Oestergaard, one of the youngest couturiers in Berlin, opened his own salon in his apartment in Grunewald and organized a winter-season show of garments sewn from military uniforms, curtains, and with designs ironically called "Black market," "Shortage," and "Power Outage."[22] An open-air fashion show with "designs utilizing fabric from military tents and blankets presented the culmination" of the summer fest organized by the Kulturbund Charlottenburg (Charlottenburg Cultural Association) near Berlin's radio tower, the Funkturm, in August 1946.[23]

The phenomenon of the fashion show provides a prime example of the paradoxes of postwar developments. In defiance of challenging everyday conditions, German women clung desperately to conventions and practices of prewar times, which lifted their spirits and gave them the illusion of normalcy. Hans Borgelt, a journalist for the *Berliner Zeitung*, recounts in his memoir an assignment to attend fashion show by a designer on the Kurfürstendamm that took place on perhaps the coldest day in the merciless winter of 1946–47: The room is illuminated by candles, due to rationed electric power, but is nevertheless filled to the brim with enthusiastic women—fashion journalists and regular customers. The fashion models, Borgelt writes, "are fabulously beautiful, but as skinny as the rest of us," and parade, shivering with cold, in elegant dresses "that most Berliner women would laugh about, because they could never wear them."[24] At the same time, the illustrated media coverage of the fashion shows offers insights into the process of design, into the women involved in the work behind the scenes, and, most important, into the possibilities for those celebrated designs to be copied by the customers and reproduced with their limited means.[25]

Other accounts of fashion shows, especially those in the Soviet-licensed press, place the emphasis elsewhere: on the importance of that branch of industry as an opportunity for women's meaningful employment and active involvement in civic society as soon as it began to reconstitute itself in the summer 1945. Dressmaking as a field of productive work was at the center of reports about the activities of the antifascist *Frauenausschüße* (antifascist women's committees), or AFAs, associated with the Communist Party's activities in the working-class neighborhoods of the city. Immediately after the end of the war, numerous AFAs, especially in Berlin and in the Soviet Occupation Zone (Sowjetische Besatzungszone, SBZ), were founded. Some were spontaneously formed from below, partly controlled by the Berlin Magistrat (Municipal Council) and the Soviet Military Administration in Germany (SMAD), and channeled the energy and determination of women to provide aid to the weakest among them, refugees and orphans.

Along with running soup kitchens and opening kindergartens and women's shelters, the AFA set up numerous sewing rooms (*Nähstuben*) with the goal of providing clothing for Berlin's orphaned children.[26] The very first issue of the AFA organ, *Die Frau von heute*, in February 1946, issued an appeal to all "antifascist women of Berlin" to join the effort of the *Nähstuben* to collect fabrics and sew much-needed clothing and underwear for needy children.[27] Later in the year, the AFAs organized a day-long summer festival near the Funkturm with two open-air fashion shows forming the high points of the event. The first was a presentation of "extremely elegant" dresses designed by Berlin's designers in the *Bekleidungshandwerk* "that were a pleasure to look at, even if we are probably not able to sew them ourselves. But at least the show was accompanied by practical and convenient suggestions on how to adapt these ideas to our own needs." There were also beautiful dresses for young women and girls made out of bed sheets. The second show featured some one hundred orphans dressed in the clothes provided by the AFAs ("Berliner Waisenkinder umgehen im weiten Kreis das Rund in ihren neuen Kleidern").[28] The detailed report on both shows demonstrates the balancing act that the women's committees were often involved in: denouncing fashion for ideological reasons because of its association with luxury, excess, and capitalist interests, while at the same time embracing fashion's positive social benefits, such as providing meaningful and enjoyable employment for women and much-needed clothes for war orphans.

Much of the reporting from fashion shows is related also to the swift revival of Berlin's famous fashion schools, among them the Textil- und Modeschule in Friedrichshain, Modeschule Wolf, Viktoria Fachschule für Damenschneiderei, and the Lette-Verein, where many young women were studying to become professional designers, pattern draftswomen, illustrators, and dressmakers. As soon as these schools resumed their operation after a wartime hiatus, they staged fashion shows, and the magazines immediately started featuring "the wonders one could create out of scraps of old fabrics."[29] Again, a recurring theme in reporting about these vocational schools and the elaborate fashion shows that they put together is the close connection between fashion and labor, fashion and the opportunity for survival and dignified prosperity in these extraordinary times of hardship: "Fashion meant not only joy, but also bread" ("Mode bedeutet nicht nur Freude, sondern auch Brot"), wrote the journalist for *Der Nacht-Express* in a feature about the Lette-Verein, a vocational school for women that despite massive destruction of its main building resumed classes by late summer 1945, initially offering courses in Russian, English, and dressmaking (*Schneidern*).[30] Not only were preexisting fashion and design schools on the rebound, but new institutions were founded, the *Mannequinschulen*, schools for training models, often also in combination with rigorous foreign language instruction in Russian or English and prepared them for a job market where they were supposedly in high demand.[31] "Women who know how to model clothes can enjoy a decent life," reported *Der Spiegel*. "Today's models are well paid and from time to time they can even receive a free dress as a bonus."[32]

Newsreels, too, produced under American, British, and Soviet licenses, brought the first postwar fashion events closer to a larger audience in Berlin hungry for vicarious thrills. For example, in one of its first editions, the East German newsreels *Der Augenzeuge* (The Eyewitness)—usually stern, dry, and very political in its reporting—produced a playful segment called "Ilse and the Rubble Outfit" ("Ilse und das Ruinenkostüm"), in which Georg, the owner of a newly established fashion salon, runs across an old friend, Ilse, and is immediately outraged at how shabby she looks.[33] He pulls her into his recently established fashion salon and within a few moments on the screen (and with the help of smart film editing) transforms her from a quintessential *Trümmerfrau*, dressed in dark pants, coat, and headscarf, into a stylish lady. Ilse's new outfits are made out of men's shirts, pants, and sweaters and drapery and navy uniforms, but are light and bright-colored and are paraded in front of her by a series of models. "Necessity makes us inventive" ("Not macht erfinderisch") concludes Georg at the end of the mini-fashion show on the screen, encouraging the female spectators to get inspired and rework their wardrobes.

The fashion shows during the first months after the capitulation of Berlin reveal not only Berliners' delight in the attractive spectacle, but also deeper meanings and trends that mark postwar realities in the city, and especially fashion's economic and social significance. On the one hand, they bring into sharp relief the fact that this immediate revival of business and production had little direct practical impact on the regular Berlin woman in terms of what she actually wore. Local women, of course, had neither the time to attend events such as the first fashion shows nor the means to purchase any of the haute couture models presented. For many of them, as one article in the American licensed daily *Die Neue Zeitung* from October 1945 pointed out, the phrase "I have nothing to wear" is not uttered in coquettish desperation in front a full wardrobe as it used to, but is meant literally and is "the bitter truth."[34] This anonymous fashion commentator went on to demand that the leaders in the fashion industry focus on more practical issues and organize a show that would teach German women how to refashion old clothes, scraps of fabric, uniforms and wool blankets into warm and stylish coats for the upcoming winter season.

At the same time, the fashion businesses as a whole did benefit the city through revenues generated by garment sales to foreigners in Berlin and through export. The audience in attendance and the actual customers of the revived Berlin fashion scene's products were associated primarily with the Allied occupying forces. For American, British, French, and Soviet staff members and officers' wives, Berlin's stylish production was on par with Parisian fashion, but much more affordable: they paid for it with cigarettes and coffee and that was a good deal.[35] "When we go back to Philadelphia and Birmingham, everyone admires the lovely clothes that we had custom-made for us in Germany," reported the wives of American and British officers.[36] The foreigners ordered huge amounts of clothes and even arranged for cotton and wool fabrics to be delivered to Berlin.[37] Hans W. Claussen alone counted over thirty Americans, wives of senior officers, among his clients, who could pay the high prices that "no mortal could afford."[38] Foreign customers were now "treated as film stars used to be treated in prewar times," and an unnamed company in the occupied capital used the fact that General Lucius Clay's secretary was ordering clothes from them as a successful marketing device.[39]

The wives of Soviet officers also proved to be fashion-savvy. An extensive illustrated report in *Für Dich* documents the efforts of Berlin's Modehaus Gründt to cater to Russian customers: a fashion show of almost fifty different models was staged specifically for a delegation from the Soviet Union and subsequently a special contract was signed. The Russian customers promised to deliver the necessary fabrics, textiles, and other materials, while the Berlin firm guaranteed to complete the orders, which in turn would increase the personnel of the business from the current 150 to 250 employees.[40] Occasionally, the exclusive catering to the demands and tastes of the Allies was also criticized as blatant neglect of the needs of the local women: "Dealing with foreigners is certainly more pleasant and easier, but the German economy should not forget that its premiere task is to satisfy the needs of Germans. To create haute couture with foreign fabrics is more appealing than to work with the scarcest resources for refugees and rubble women. But by doing this one upsets tomorrow's customers." ("Das Geschäft mit Ausländern ist gewiß angenehmer und leichter, aber die deutsche Wirtschaft darf nicht vergessen, daß sie in erster Linie zur Befriedigung der deutschen Bedürfnisse beizutragen hat. Mit ausländischen Stoffen *Haute-Couture* machen, ist reizvoller, als aus knappsten Mitteln für Flüchtlinge und Trümmerfrauen zu arbeiten. Damit verärgert man die Kunden von morgen.")[41] Overall, however, such criticism was rather rare, and the prevailing tone of the press was affirmative and indulging of the attractive spectacles of fashion however unattainable it was.

The predominance of foreign customers dressed in the uniforms of the Allies was evident also in the April 1946 edition of the newsreel *Welt im Film,* which dedicated a long segment on the first large-scale and quite lavish peacetime fashion show (*Friedensmodenschau*) staged at the Femina Bar on March 26 and 27, 1946.[42] It was a lavish two-day event graced by the presence of various celebrities from the film, theater, and music worlds such as Viktor de Kowa, Hilde Weissner, Werner Neumann, and others.[43] But the club was full of people in military uniforms, "prominent members of the inter-Allied commissions" to whom the show was geared.[44] In her welcoming comments, Hilde Weissner, a well-known actress who had been a familiar face since the 1930s and who was often associated with her role of the fashion designer Frau Hesse in the 1943 film *Großstadt-melodie,* encouraged the audience to admire Berlin designers' ingenuity and purchase the outfits. She drew attention to the fact that the fashion industry, especially in these difficult times, was providing "work and bread" ("Arbeit und Brot") "to close to 50,000 people, mostly women who have been hired again as designers, dressmakers, and seamstresses [*Zuschneiderinnen, Direktricen, Näherinnen*], sales clerks, and models."

Indeed, the importance of fashion as a possible opportunity for employment and thus a source of income and independence, especially for women, is an omnipresent theme in the press. The designer salon of Marie Latz was one of the many looking to fill multiple vacancies in her new West Berlin establishment: chief designer (*Directrice*), assistant designer (*Hilfsdirectrice*), model (*Vorführdame*), a saleswoman "with knowledge of Russian and/or English," and over a dozen more trained seamstresses.[45] Indeed, as early as November 1945, the newspapers and particularly women's and fashion magazines started publishing want ads especially for women workers with skills in designing, sewing, presenting, and selling clothes. They also published announcements for schools for models (*Mannequinschulen*) and specialized trade schools (*Textil- und Modeschulen*) that were being reopened or newly founded in Berlin and offered training courses.

The Fashion Media

We owe most of our knowledge of these developments in the fashion world to the emerging media that covered them extensively: women's and fashion magazines, newspaper reports and supplements, and newsreels. If the newly created postwar styles presented at the first fashion shows were intended primarily for customers among the occupying forces (the only ones who could really afford them), the illustrated media targeted a large wider audience of German women, who were hungry for distraction and vicarious consumption. It is truly astounding how the revival of the illustrated press and the introduction of fashion supplements to daily papers occurred just months after the end of the battle for Berlin and how the presence of fashion themes and illustrations actually helped sell newspapers of all kinds.

By the end of 1945 in Berlin each one of the occupation powers licensed at least one publication with an extensive fashion section. One of the first fashion magazines permitted by the Soviet authorities was a monthly, *Berlins Modenblatt*, published and edited by Chery K. Gessinger; its first issue appeared in October 1945. In the American sector, the premiere women's magazine with an extensive fashion section was a weekly, *sie: Wochenzeitung für Frauenrecht und Menschenrecht*. Founded by Heinz Ullstein, Helmuth Kindler, und Ruth Andreas Friedrich, *sie* was launched in December 1945 and appeared initially in newspaper format, for lack of more appropriate paper.[46] The British-licensed *Illustrierter Telegraf* starting in early 1946 also featured extensive materials on fashion. Later, in the fall of 1946, Ruth Andreas Friedrich founded a new, more radically feminist publication of her own, *Lilith: Die Zeitschrift für junge Mädchen und Frauen*, which also contained an extensive fashion section.[47] It was relatively late, not until 1947, that the French military authorities approved the biweekly magazine *Chic*.

A more general magazine dedicated to the interests of women, called *Neue Berliner Illustrierte*, appeared with the permission of the Soviet military authorities in East Berlin in the fall of 1945 and also carried fashion-related items. A few others followed: *Für Dich: die neue illustrierte Frauenzeitung* (later renamed: *Für Dich: die illustrierte Zeitschrift für die Frau*) and *Die Frau von heute*, both published in the Soviet sector. Even the official organ of the Information Control Division of the US Military

Fig. 7. Cover of *Berlins Modenblatt*, January 1946, designed by Ursula Marquardt-Beckmeier. Staatliche Museen zu Berlin, Kunstbibliothek.

Fig. 8. Classified ads for fashion-related positions in the Berlin weekly *sie*, February 22, 1948. Staatsbibliothek Berlin.

government, the magazine *Heute: Eine neue illustrierte Zeitschrift*, whose main functions were "to open a window on the outside world" and "report any signs of German democratic regeneration and reconstruction," dedicated regular sections on fashion trends and the fashion industry. The reporting was mostly on fashion in the United States, on the independence and ingenuity of American women, and on the postwar production and distribution situation in the United States, but the idea was to encourage German women to create her own style and be inventive: "Create your own fashion!" ("Schaff dir deine Mode!").[48] All of these publications dedicated primarily to women's issues and covering fashion were popular in the period from 1945 to 1950, after which, for the most part, they were discontinued in light of the radically changed political and economic situation after the currency reform and the founding of the two German states.

Eventually, two distinct media landscapes gradually established themselves in the East and the West, but in the months immediately following the end of the military conflict, Berlin was yet not rigidly separated into East and West. Culturally it was an undivided unity permeated by the desire for diversion and amusement. Regardless of the origin of their licenses, the fashion magazines as well as the newspapers to which some of them were supplements were distributed and read avidly in all four sectors of the city and had similar tone and attitudes toward fashion.[49] It was common for journalists to contribute to the fashion sections of several different newspaper or magazines at the same time. The proliferation of these venues, despite hunger and everyday misery in the largely destroyed city, can be seen as part of Berliners' explosive postwar interest in the print press that, in the words of Berlin's correspondent for *Die Neue Zeitung*, had transformed their city within less than a year after the war into an unprecedented paradise for newspapers (*Zeitungsparadies Berlin*)."[50] Less than a year after liberation, there were thirteen daily newspapers with a total circulation of 3 million that catered to a population of about 3 million people and were filling up an acutely felt intellectual and political vacuum left behind by the collapse of the Nazi regime.[51]

Newsreels, too, were part of the postwar mediascape, and in comparison with the printed press they were more tightly controlled by the Allies and were much more explicitly used as tools of reeducation. As early as May 18, 1945, the British-American newsreel *Welt im Film* started its run in the cinemas of the three western sectors of Berlin. And later in the same year, the DEFA-newsreel *Der Augenzeuge* was launched in the Soviet occupation zone. Despite their overall diverging ideological stances, in the early postwar years both newsreel services devoted large portions of their reporting to themes from the world of entertainment, and about one third of that portion was dedicated to themes whose purpose, according to Uta Schwarz, was to spread to the mass film audience "pronounced optimistic attitudes": "Reports about fashion and other pleasurable events created an impression of speedily overcoming the consequences of war and the prospect of the return of social normality."[52]

By closely examining the presence of the fashion theme in the mass media of the period from 1945 to 1947, we will discover, as other scholars have suggested, a more complicated historical narrative that contradicts standard claims that the extreme shortages reduced German women's desires for clothes, food, and shelter to the bare minimum, devoid of all aesthetic considerations.[53] As a whole, the content of fashion reporting outlines mental attitudes shaped by the same forces of selective forgetting and remembering that are found in other spheres of cultural production such as the postwar German film.[54] Most notably, the magazines, newspapers, and newsreels provide a remarkable insight into the dynamic relationship between the explicitly escapist dreams and the staggering practical concerns of a society in ruins.

Several interconnected themes recur as crucial in the postwar discourse on fashion in the wide spectrum of magazines and supplements. The first coalesces around self-reflective discussions of the relevance and even appropriateness of fashion in the contemporary situation of material devastation and moral despair. The second is concerned with maintaining equilibrium between topical and pragmatic solutions to the clothing problem, on the one hand, and the reporting on the unattainable world of high fashion, the production of Berlin's leading firms for export, on the other. And finally, fashion journalism of the second half of the 1940s also raises questions related to historical continuity and discontinuity and thus performs an interesting balancing act between forgetting and remembering when it comes to talking about Germany's past. In addressing these dilemmas, the fashion media placed an emphasis on the specific interests of its female readership and revamped some clichéd notions regarding women's everyday life, their work, entertainment, and aspirations, in the immediate postwar years.

"Muß Mode sein?"
Pipe Dreams and Practical Concerns

All women's and fashion periodicals in one way or another felt the need to justify rhetorically their focus on fashion, which may have appeared frivolous to some in times of hunger, physical hardships, and devastating shortages. In the summer of 1946, *Berlins Modenblatt*, the first magazine dedicated entirely to fashion, posed the question "Should there be fashion?" ("Muß Mode sein?") to its readers and published selected answers, all cheerfully positive, that covered a wide range of reasons for accepting the necessity of fashion even in the worst of times. A female conductor on one of Berlin's newly rebuilt streetcar lines, Angelika Masche, emphasized the pure aesthetic pleasure of observing well-dressed people in contrast to the ubiquitous and depressing signs of destruction: "I am always excited when nicely dressed passengers ride in my streetcar. It seems that they bring sunshine in the often dark streetcar whose broken windows are covered with sheet metal."[55] A student responded that the embrace of new fashions was an expression of individualism, pluralism, and a rejection of the uniform dress (*Einheitskleid*) and the uniform look associated with life under the Nazi regime. The men to whom the question about the necessity of fashion was posed—all officials in Berlin's local government—also affirmed the need of fashion, but justified it differently: in terms of its crucial role in reviving the capital's traditionally powerful textile and garment industry and bringing much-needed revenue, economic opportunity, and jobs to the city.[56]

The weekly women's magazine *sie* was also concerned about the frivolous impression that this otherwise very serious and politically engaged medium intended to create by dedicating a whole page in each number to fashion. In the editorial published in the first issue, the magazine editor concedes: "Yes, it is daring to speak of elegance today, even to show it" ("Ja, es ist ein Wagnis heute von Eleganz zu sprechen, sie gar zu zeigen").[57] Nevertheless, this editor, too, asserts that fashion culture is such an essential part of women's everyday lives that it should not be neglected. Looking at fashion—whether designed locally, in Berlin, or coming from other places in Europe and the United States—was also perceived as the easiest way to feel reconnected with Europe and America, with Western values, with the outside world, from which German women had been cut off during the Nazi period. The rhetorical question "Should such an important area of feminine life be suppressed, because the material conditions are more limited than earlier?" ("Soll ein so wichtiges Gebiet weiblichen Lebens verdrängt sein, weil die materielle Erfüllung beschränkter ist als früher?") is followed by an embrace of distraction and escapism as strategies for surviving hardship, or as the fashion journalist puts it: "Let's just simply be pleased by the pipe dreams" ("Lassen wir uns ganz einfach von den Wunschträumen beglücken"). And these *Wunschträume* remain key to a large part of the textual and visual content of the women's and fashion magazines throughout the 1945–48 period.

Attending fashion shows and the detailed reporting on them also belonged to that sphere of *Wunschträume* that were eagerly embraced also by the journalists of the Soviet-controlled East Berlin tabloid *Der Nacht-Express*. Hannelore Holtz, one of the paper's leading fashion reporters, wrote about the fashion show in the West-Berlin club Tribüne with the participation of Berlin's leading designer salons and organized on the occasion of the first anniversary of the founding of *Berlins Modenblatt*. She characterized it as a two-hour visit "in fairy-tale land, as in 'Cinderella'" ("im Märchenland, wie bei Achenbrödel"). As Holtz reported, after two hours of observing everything that could be sewn out of kitchen towels, drapery, and bed covers, and enjoying the cabaret program with Franz Otto Krüger, Hilde Seipp, and Violetta Rensing, the women in the audience went out in the cold and headed home, discovering with some disappointment that they still living the year 1946.[58]

Despite the slightly derisive and dismissive stance toward the obvious frivolity of fashion shows in the face of enduring hardship for ordinary Berlin women, the diligent descriptive writing and detailed reporting of fashion themes continued persistently in all the magazines that spanned the entire political spectrum of publications, but especially in the organ of the AFAs, *Die Frau von heute*, largely under the control of the Communist Party. In the first half of 1946, the contributors also included journalists of different political convictions who wrote on women's issues. In an essay she contributed to one of the first issues, Annedore Leber, who had been persecuted as an antifascist and Social Democrat during the Nazi years, now expressed an attitude common to many women's publications: she saw the embrace of fashion as a precursor of a better and brighter future, as an embodiment of freedom, optimism, and hopefulness: "Finally free from uniform and constraints, [the modern German woman] searches for ways and possibilities to dress nicely and to her advantage despite the limitations of our times. . . . Today, fashion declares the woman's will to live in a difficult and serious period, that through our efforts should be replaced by an easier and brighter one."[59] A similar affirmative position vis-à-vis fashion that highlighted its special meaning to women in the postwar years in particular was expressed by another leading journalist of the day, Ellie Tschauner, reporting on the first big benefit show (*Leistungsschau*) of the Berlin Garment Trade (*Berliner Bekleidungshandwerk*) organized in April 1946 for a large audience of Germans and members of the Allied forces. The event, which was opened officially by the mayor, Dr. Arthur Werner, showcased the work of some fifty Berlin companies, but in a somewhat unusual way: the clothes were modeled not by professionals but rather by regular Berlin women picked by the designer salons. In answer to the question "What was the deeper meaning of the event?" Tschauner wrote:

> [The meaning] lies not only in showing women that they can also maintain their external appearance in troubled times with whatever means they can find—because it is the mirror of inner culture!— but rather in an economic emergency. Fifty thousand people are employed in the Berlin clothing industry, which is their sole source of income. This should be a path into a peaceful world, as soon as the required raw materials are provided.[60]

The ideological preferences of the women's magazines licensed by the Soviet military administration were still articulated strongly in their texts, but this message was belied by the visuals: fabulous drawings of designer clothing. For example, a series of articles in *Die Frau von heute* from the first half of 1946, notably each one of them featuring the word *Mode* in its headline, were dedicated to persuading its readers that fashion, as an invention of the capitalist thirst for profit, had ended and a new era had been inaugurated. The demise of Berlin's traditional *Konfektionsindustrie* in the aftermath of the war should be seen as a blessing in disguise, because now the fashion industry could no longer exercise "the tyranny of fickle taste" and trigger "a never-ending cycle of change."[61] Instead, these articles repeatedly emphasized, women should see themselves as active and empowered agents, revolting against fashion trends and shaping their own appearance in accordance with the practical possibilities and pragmatic needs of the postwar reality that required them to work in order to survive. "We call for an anarchy in the kingdom of fashion," wrote one fashion reporter. "This year we wear everything that we like and that suits us and that has survived the chaos of war."[62]

These fiery verbal expositions were nevertheless contradicted on the visual level by accompanying illustrations that were very similar to the ones found in any other fashion magazines—fabulous images of designer-made dresses and coats that were equally unattainable. The fact was that despite being the organ of the AFAs, *Die Frau von heute* continued to publish attractive drawings and photographs like all the other women's and fashion publications. The illustrations featured the high-fashion export creations of renowned Berlin designers such as Nina Carell and Corves & Seger as well as haute couture from other European capitals and New York, prompting one reader to write, with a mixture of pleasure and dissatisfaction, "There always seems to be a whiff of Paris about it" ("Es weht darin wohl immer etwas Pariser Luft").[63]

For the first two to three years after the war, in reaction to audience preferences and regardless of whether they originated in the eastern or western sectors of Berlin, the magazines aimed to maintain both levels of fashion discourse: one that delivered pipe dreams (*Wunschträume*), distracting and entertaining, and the other that catered to everyday needs and tackled the more practical aspects of fashion. In their letters, too, readers of the East German *Für Dich* expressed both sentiments in the same breath: appreciation for the inspiring ideas from the world of high fashion as well as an urgent demand to see patterns for sewing and knitting on the pages of their favorite magazine. On reader wrote: "All women are surely thankful to you for the fashionable motivation. But why don't you give any sewing patterns and knitting patterns?"[64] Newspapers and magazines responded quickly. One issue of the fashion press or the daily newspaper might both offer peeks into the latest dreamlike creations by Berlin's fashion designers and also dispense advice on quick pragmatic fixes to the daunting problem of what to wear in times of immeasurable

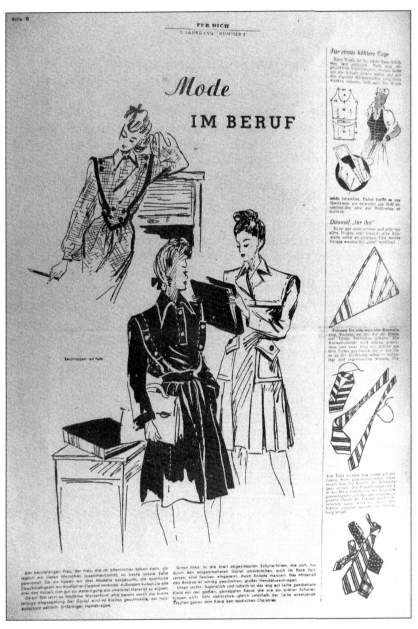

Fig. 9. A page from *Für Dich*, August 1946. Staatsbibliothek Berlin.

misery. Readers were presented with a variety of concrete advice, with sketches in scale headlined by mottos such as "Aus Alt mach Neu," "Aus Zwei mach Ein," "Aus Einfachem Apartes" (An attractive outfit out of simple materials), "Ein Sommeranzug, der nichts kostet" (A summer outfit that costs nothing), "Ein Meter Stoff—ein neues Kleid" (One meter of fabric—a new dress), and "Nachthemden aus Kopfkissen" (Nightgowns from pillows). Despite perpetual shortages of paper, in March 1946 the popular daily tabloid *Der Nacht-Express* added a monthly two-page spread dedicated to patterns, called *Schnittmuster Seiten*, on which sewing patterns were printed in small scale so as to fit as many pattern outlines as possible in the given space. Sewers would then scale these up to the required size.[65] Other publications, such as *Berlins Modenblatt* and *Für Dich*, soon followed suit.

What the magazines actually accomplished in their fashion reporting—both by encouraging pure escapism and by offering sensible suggestions for refashioning old clothes—was addressing directly a wide women's audience that in other ways felt rather neglected by the press, especially in the field of politics. Between 1945 and 1948 the fashion media steered women in both the East and West toward forgetting the past, embracing the present, and evolving into the future "consumer citizen" of the 1950s and 1960s. Tensions between the two diverging economic and political systems intensified with the adoption of the Marshall Plan and the currency reform in the western zones of Germany and the western sectors of Berlin and especially during the Berlin Blockade. The realities and discourses of fashion also started differentiating more strongly than before. However, women played an enormous and active role in the resurrection of both the fashion industry and fashion-related media in the immediate postwar years. They were part of an expanding and ever more confident workforce, as designers, seamstresses, and models as well as fashion journalists, photographers, and illustrators who contributed massively to the fashion mediascape and shaped the terms of the predominantly vicarious consumption that the German female audience was involved in.

Vignette 1. Charlotte Glückstein: Historical Ruptures and Continuities in Postwar Fashion

Lovable fashion. It is so nice, when one can write this about fashion! And this fashion is truly wonderful, as it is presented here in a lovely collection that is as likable as its creator, Charlotte Glückstein. She knows what women like to wear. She does not fall for any extravagance, and the demand that clothes be "pretty and wearable" is her highest standard. At the same time, the spectrum is broadly expanded, every fashion trend comes into its own and is "transposed" so that the appealing note, the graciously inconspicuous become a Leitmotiv and guarantee success.

—Berlins Modenblatt, 1949

A NOVEMBER 1946 ARTICLE in the newly founded weekly newspaper *sie* reported on a small Berlin salon Charlott. It had opened at the beginning of the year amidst enormous material difficulties, but was "already surprising its customers with a collection of ninety new outfits that provide the Berlin woman with stimulating new ideas." The journalist wrote a lengthy praise of the salon's production, ending with a brief mention of the designer's fate during the Holocaust:

> This Salon Charlott presented a lovely demonstration of how tastefully someone can overcome the hardship of our times. . . . These constraints imposed by the shortage of material, however, do not hinder the creative imagination of the designer. If anything, one has the impression that scarcity inspires imagination. The accomplishment of the salon's owner, Miss Charlotte Glückstein, deserves even greater appreciation, since she had spent two difficult years in a concentration camp.[1]

Another fashion magazine, *Berlins Modenblatt*, featured in its April 1947 issue dresses by the same young designer and mentioned in a brief cryptic sentence, "The difficult years in the camp did not destroy Charlotte Glückstein's joy in creating fashion."[2] No further mentions of Glückstein's past appeared anywhere else in the press, even though, judging from the extensive coverage in all postwar fashion publications and the weekly supplements to daily newspapers, Charlotte Glückstein's name and work had become quite well known on the fashion scene in Berlin by 1947.

None of the publications mentioned explicitly that Charlotte Glück-stein was a Jew who returned to her home city to set up business in the immediate aftermath of the expulsion and genocide of Jews and was one of the 6,000 or 7,000 surviving Jews who resided in Berlin in the late 1940s.[3] Her renewed participation in the postwar fashion scene is all the more astounding given the fact that dressmaking and fashion retail, as traditionally Jewish-dominated Berlin-based industries, had been thoroughly purged during the process of Aryanization. Prior to 1933, *Konfektion* was a branch of Berlin's economy that was 80 percent Jew-ish owned. Following the November 1938 pogroms, these businesses were forcefully Aryanized. In some cases the Jewish owners made mutu-ally beneficial arrangements with non-Jewish employees, transferred the business to them and went into exile, while continuing to main-tain friendly relations with the new management. In other cases, they were forced to give up their companies to brutal expropriation or to sell cheaply and flee, while the new Aryan owners thrived by building upon the reputation and success of the formerly Jewish business.[4] Between 1933 and 1938 Jewish owners were forced to sell their establishments at "fire sale" prices or to transfer ownership to non-Jews, and all Jewish employees were fired. Some were forced to operate their businesses as employees of new non-Jewish owners until they were finally deported or found a way to escape. Subsequently, many of the Jewish owners left Germany, were forcibly expatriated, were arrested and detained, were worked to death as slave labor, or were murdered in the concentration and death camps.

Charlotte Glückstein seems to be the only Jewish woman at the helm of a successful fashion business in Berlin in the immediate post-war years. Her case, her career, and her coverage in fashion media are both exceptional and paradigmatic for the spectacular revival of the German fashion scene after 1945. Glückstein is tightly connected to those aspects of postwar recovery revealing not only a pervasive desire to ignore the past but also to embrace a notion of normalization that emphasizes primarily female agency, beauty, and consumption, both real and imaginary. A closer look at the larger context in which Glückstein's star ascended provides a concrete sense of the dynamics and nature of the processes of "recovery" and "normalization" of life that took place in the German capital in the aftermath of the Third Reich's demise, a process that had particular import on the Berlin women. After recov-ering some biographical data about Charlotte Glückstein, I return to the debates in Berlin's fashion press and their complicated relationship to the contemporary political realities, the shameful past, and various related moral conundrums.

Who Was "Charlott"?

Very little biographical information can be found in the fashion and popular women's media of the late 1940s about the successful fashion designer Charlotte Glückstein (1919–83). This is in stark contrast to the ample attention paid to a fellow newcomer to Berlin fashion, Heinz Oestergaard (1916–2003), who was of Glückstein's generation. Oestergaard's wartime ordeals on the Eastern Front and in Soviet imprisonment were the subject of various interviews and features in the Berlin daily and illustrated press at the time.[5] In subsequent decades, historians of fashion dwelled on how his wartime and immediate postwar experiences shaped his work, while they remained silent on Glückstein, who was equally successful and well known on the fashion scene in the late 1940s. Granted, Glückstein herself did not like to talk, publicly or privately, about what she had gone through during the Nazi period, according to her friends and relatives. Nevertheless, her story, uncovered in recent interviews with relatives and survivors of the period as well as in archives, reflects the often paradoxical, controversial nature of the postwar recovery in Berlin, especially in the turbulent years from 1945 to 1949.

Charlotte Glückstein was a Berlin native whose father, a Jewish garment salesman, had died when she was a child. Her mother was Gentile. In early 1939, at the age of twenty, she was hired as a designer and chief dressmaker (*Direktrice*) by the Wolf & Geppert Salon. Despite being a *Mischling ersten Grades* (half Jewish), she was not only able to find employment in an Aryan business but remained on its staff until 1943. The reasons for this remain unclear: possibly she lied on the questionnaire she was supposed to fill out before employment or possibly her employers turned a blind eye to her Jewish status. We don't know. What is known is that in February 1939, Hellmut Wolf and Erich Geppert took over a prosperous fashion salon, Salon Heumann, whose Jewish founder and owner, Siegfried Heumann, had left Germany in 1938. Among their Jewish employees until they were fired in January 1940 were two brothers, Walter and Werner Caro, the sales manager and accountant, who had previously worked for Salon Heumann. Charlotte fell in love with Walter Caro and they were soon engaged.[6]

Glückstein was among Wolf & Geppert's highest paid employees, earning 500 reichsmarks per month, and was one of the most valuable ones with her superb technical skills and creative input. She was involved in all aspects of production—drawing, designing, making patterns, choosing fabrics, and sewing—which continued throughout the early war years despite increasing material difficulties. Glückstein and Walter and Werner Caro were arrested by the Gestapo on September 7, 1943, and were accused of supporting subversive activities, including the falsification of passports for Jews. On a double charge of being both Jewish and a

Fig. 10. Charlotte Glückstein (1919–83). Photograph
courtesy of Gudrun Drechsler-Reichhardt.

political prisoner, Glückstein was held captive in the women's prison in Berlin-Charlottenburg and was subsequently sent to KZ (Konzentrationslager) Ravensbrück, a women's camp where is she was assigned to work as a seamstress in a dressmaking shop that manufactured prisoner uniforms for all the camps. Later on she was moved to KZ Flossenbürg, not far from the current border with the Czech Republic. At the end of April 1945, as the Red Army advanced and the camps were consequently in turmoil, the camp was evacuated, and prisoners were marched to KZ Dachau in multiple columns. Glückstein was able to escape and made her way back to Berlin.[7] Less than a year after her return she opened her own salon near the Kurfürstendamm, in Meinekestraße. Werner Caro survived the camps and opened his own salon. Walter, Charlotte's fiancé, did not survive his numerous transfers from one camp to another and perished upon his arrival in Auschwitz in April 1944.[8]

Soon after the founding of the company in early 1946, designs by "Charlott" were being featured regularly in all fashion magazines highlighting the best fashion Berlin had to offer in the postwar years. Indeed, Glückstein's prolific production became an integral element of the peculiar spirit of renovation of both fashion business and fashion media among the ruins of the devastated city.

Willful Amnesia: Fashion and History

Ordinarily, fashion discourses in the mass media were so affirmative of and preoccupied with an imaginary, possibly normalized present that the experiences of the past were often left untouched. Rarely did an article appear that expressed outrage about aspects of the workings of the fashion industry during the Nazi dictatorship. But one exception was a report in *Der Nacht-Express* on Eva Braun's relationship to a well-known Berlin fashion designer of the 1930s and 1940s, Annemarie Heise.[9] The journalist recounts the tight bond between the designer and her client: Braun had her entire wardrobe made exclusively by the Salon Heise using fabrics that all came from Paris. Allegedly, after the capitulation of France, Braun ordered a festive white gown that she designated optimistically "a peace-time dress" ("Friedenskleid"). As a reward for Heise's dependable service, all of her employees enjoyed considerable privileges, being exempt from military service and mandatory war-related labor service (*Arbeitsdienst*).[10] The article does not mention that Heise, along with other high-profile fashion designers, had joined Berliner Modelle GmbH in 1941 in order to consolidate and enhance "the striking power of German fashion production" ("die Stoßkraft des deutschen Modeschaffens"). After the war, in 1945, the designer moved to Munich and reestablished her salon there, continuing to operate with great success.[11]

Within the women's and fashion press of the postwar period, such a spotlight on the activities of the German fashion designers during the Nazi years was extremely unusual. In their quest to restore an imaginary sense of normalcy, the magazines relied on the readers' long-standing familiarity with brands, styles, and personalities from the fashion world, and stayed away from the political themes of the day. They turned to designer houses, journalists, and illustrators who were recognizable names from the early 1940s, the 1930s, or even earlier. The new fashion press, especially *Berlins Modenblatt, sie,* and *Chic,* featured stylish outfits by Horn, Corves & Seger, H. W. Claussen, Hermann Schwichtenberg, Nina Carell, Elise Topell, Marie Latz, Günter Brosda, Sinaida Rudow, Kuno Scheppach, Wolfgang Nöcker, and Gehringer & Glupp. Initially, fashion photographs were rare (due to shortage of models and poor material conditions), but there were plenty of drawings. Some of the leading fashion illustrators were Gerd Hartung, Marietta Riederer, and Alice Bronsch, and their work was accompanied by competent commentaries by fashion journalists such as Anna Paula Wedekind-Pariselle and Erika Berneburg. Almost all of these illustrators and journalists had established themselves professionally in the early 1930s in Ullstein's *Die Dame* and other big fashion magazines and continued to pursue successful careers in the thriving fashion press during the Nazi period.

The search for personalities who would resonate with the audience and would guarantee success even led occasionally to renewed contributions by Elsa Herzog and Joe Lederer, distinguished fashion journalists and writers from the 1920s and 1930s who as Jews had been forced into exile in London shortly after the Nazis' ascendance to power in 1933.[12] But not a word was written to explain their sudden absence from the pages of the German fashion press for over a decade and for the fact that now they were reporting from London on prominent German-Jewish fashion designers such as Harald Mahrenholz, in British exile since 1937.

Personnel oddities—continuity of some personnel from the prewar to the postwar Berlin fashion world and the recycling of other personnel from prewar to postwar times with a blank spot in between—is just one of the features that all of the fashion press in all four sectors had in common in the 1945–49 period. Another common feature was the provision of escapism, a helpful strategy of cheerful distraction from the painful everyday struggles but one with a dark underside: it disguised a position of pronounced political and historical detachment. Despite the explicit ideological divide in the military occupying forces issuing licenses to publish, all of the fashion press chose to remain completely apolitical. The problematic past concerning women's and their clothiers' lives under the Nazi regime was not addressed in any meaningful way; instead it was repressed in vague metaphors evoking catastrophes and destruction. The fashion press focused only on the most recent positive developments in the fashion business—the successful relocation and resurrection of companies—without veering into any rumination about the fate of the fashion industry and its owners under Nazi rule. There was virtually no attempt to reevaluate the fate of the members of the fashion industry during National Socialism, to remind readers of what had been lost—people and traditions—and to reassess the status of fame and success of the current fashion business leaders, most of whose success had been built at the cost of a previous successful Aryanized Jewish establishment. Behind the names of companies that quickly rebounded after 1945 and whose creations are featured in the pages of the fashion magazines lurked the ghosts of Jewish businesses and their owners. In the wave of forced sales of Jewish businesses to Aryan owners at bargain prizes, the Firma Horn bought up the respectable salons of H. Gerson in 1936 and Kersten & Tuteur in 1937; Auerbach & Steinitz became Gehringer & Glupp; Hansen Bang was Aryanized by Hermann Schwichtenberg, and R. Löwenberg & Dannenbaum became Seger & Corves.[13]

None of these tragic historical developments was a topic of conversation in the present-oriented mass fashion press. Like fashion itself, the discourse on fashion remained firmly anchored in the present moment, cheerfully affirmative, self-celebratory, and oblivious of any thorny political associations. Only in the pages of the specialized weekly industry magazine *ITEX: illustrierte Fachzeitschrift für die gesamte Textil- und Bekleidungswirtschaft*, in an article published on December 5, 1947, were readers reminded of the "organized injustice" perpetrated upon Jewish-owned garment businesses by Nazi-created the Association of German Manufacturers (Arbeitsgemeinschaft deutscher Fabrikanten, ADEFA) in the 1930s and urged to consider "Wiedergutmachung"— restitution.[14] The occasion for this reflection was a decree issued by the American military administration for the restitution of property that had been confiscated during the Nazi regime. But the journal never returned to that topic again and never discussed any results from the implementation of this law.

Another relatively short discussion flared up in *ITEX* that touched upon the historical use of the term *Konfektion*. A common designation for attractive fashion made in Germany for mass consumption, the word *Konfektion* was banned from use during the years of Nazi dictatorship, because of its traditional association with a branch of the economy in which Jewish tailors, store owners, and garment traders had predominated. For the Nazis the problem with the word inhered in their phrase "stark jüdisch durchsetzte Konfektion"—strongly Jewish-controlled Konfektion. Over the 1930s, for ideological reasons the Nazis replaced *Konfektion* with the more neutral *Bekleidungsindustrie*, "clothing industry." It was claimed on the pages of *ITEX* that the continuous avoidance of the term *Konfektion* in favor of *Bekleidungsindustrie*, even in the years after

1945, presents a case of entrenched racism and denial of the Aryanization that took place in the 1930s.[15] However, this assertion was vehemently rejected in a subsequent issue by Max Behling, the director of
the Association of the Berlin Clothing Industry (Gesamtvereinigung der
Berliner Bekleidungsindustrie). He stated that the break with the Nazi
past in matters of fashion is irreversible and supported the use of the term
Bekleidungsindustrie as more inclusive of different technologies of contemporary production.[16]

Thus, *ITEX*, the first Berlin-based postwar trade publication about
fashion, was the only media venue that problematized the fashion industry's tainted history under National Socialism. That may have been
because *ITEX* was founded by a formerly persecuted Jewish textile mer-
chant, Hans Hirschfeld, who had returned to Berlin, received compensation for lost property, and obtained the license for *ITEX* from the French
occupation authorities in December 1947.[17] But such discussions that
touched on problematic political aspects of the fashion industry's recent
past were limited to this specialized publication and were largely absent in
the mass fashion press. Against this blackout of discussion of the past, the
brief references to Charlotte Glückstein's survival after imprisonment in a
concentration camp stand out.[18]

Within the German fashion and media landscape of the early postwar
years, Charlotte Glückstein emerges as a rare link between the troubled
past and the amnesiac postwar present. Very few Jews associated with the
fashion business returned to their home city after the war and established
a successful career. Glückstein appears to be one of those very few.[19]

Glückstein was featured in virtually all fashion publications between
1945 and 1950: in *Berlins Modenblatt*, *sie*, *Chic*, the East Berlin tabloid
Der Nacht-Express, the American-licensed illustrated magazine *Heute*,
and the trade magazine *ITEX*. She was acclaimed as one of the several
most successful Berlin-based couturiers of her generation, which included
Heinz Oestergaard (1916–2003), Melitta Gründt (1919–2010), Helene
Bornholdt (dates unavailable), and Ursula Schewe (1918–?).[20] And in
many ways, Glückstein's professional path was not unlike that of others
in her cohort: all of these young designers began as apprentices in the
1930s in Jewish or formerly Jewish businesses, seized additional professional opportunities during the early years of the war, and started or
resumed successful independent businesses in Berlin right after 1945.
They all achieved their postwar breakthrough with only two or three dedicated employees, by launching bold first collections of eighty to ninety
designs.[21] After spectacular ascent and popularity during the 1950s, most
of the women in that cohort brought their independent careers to a
close; Oestergaard remained the only star designer of his generation who
was still active the 1960s and '70s; ultimately as a professor of design he
became the teacher of a new generation.

Rechts: ein weinrot-grau gestreiftes
Kleid, sehr reizvoll verarbeitet, mit
losem Jäckchen aus dem passenden
Stoff in breiterer Streifenstellung

Unten: aus schwarz-weißem Block-
karo ein Faltenröckchen und dazu
ein origineller, ärmelloser Lumberjack
über einer kirschroten Seidenhemd-
bluse. Dazu der passende Schirm

Daneben: Zu einer weinroten Hose ein
abgestimmter kornblauer Lumberjack
mit großem, rot appliziertem Ornament

Charlott zeigt in ihren schönen Räumen eine
sehr kultivierte Auswahl aparter Modelle.
Schwere Jahre im Lager haben Charlotte
Glückstein nichts von ihrer Freude am modischen Schaffen nehmen können. Zusammen
mit Frau Giesen gibt sie ihrer Kollektion eine
sehr feine, damenhafte Note. Die Lust an der
Farbe merkt man ihr an, aber es sind wun-
derbar abgetönte Farbzusammenstellungen in
subtilster Ausarbeitung, die oft bei Inkrustatio-
nen, Stickereien und Applikationen die künst-
lerische Intuition der Modeschöpferin verrät.

Wieder führte uns unser Rundgang durch die
Berliner „Haute Couture" in Häuser, die
maßgebend für das deutsche Modeschaffen
und damit auch für die Bestrebungen sind,
den Export wieder aufleben zu lassen. Wir
kennen das Interesse großer Fachkreise am
neuzuschaffenden Export — sie werden bestimmt die Modelle erster Häuser sehr inter-
essiert betrachten. Ihnen, aber auch unseren
modeinteressierten Leserinnen, wollten wir
mit diesem Rundgang eine Freude machen.
Wir beenden ihn in dieser Nummer, werden
aber in den nächsten Heften weitere Modelle
unserer ersten Modehäuser bringen, um
jederzeit einen Querschnitt durch das neu auf-
blühende Berliner Modeschaffen zu geben.

Fig. 11. Charlotte Glückstein's salon, featured in "Rundgang durch Berliner Modehäuser II," *Berlins Modenblatt*, May 1947. Glückstein is the figure on the left in the photograph, seen from the back. Staatliche Museen zu Berlin, Kunstbibliothek. Photographic reproduction: Dietmar Katz.

Figs. 12a and 12b. Charlott's collections presented in *Berlins Modenblatt*, October 1948 (left), and *Chic*, November 1947 (right). Staatliche Museen zu Berlin, Kunstbibliothek.

"Charlott's" Fashion Ideas for the Postwar Berlin Woman

A closer look at the numerous illustrated articles in the mass press devoted to Charlotte Glückstein's work in the 1946–50 period offers insight into the distinct spirit of her postwar creations. Glückstein's work seems to pay pronounced attention to the specific aesthetic tastes and practical needs of Berlin's working women in these transitional years between immediate postwar and economic wonder. That concern largely disappeared in the 1950s as the fashion scene came to be dominated by a handful of male star designers and the representation of fashion in the press was increasingly oriented toward both glamour and domesticity.

Most Berlin magazines reproduced and commented on "Charlott's" styles, but the most regular, thorough, and affirmative coverage can be found in *Berlins Modenblatt, sie*, and other magazines. The editor in chief of *Berlins Modenblatt*, Anna Paula Wedekind-Pariselle, appeared to have a particular interest in highlighting Glückstein's line among the many other fashion offerings; and Glückstein's line was often discussed in great detail by Erika Berneburg, writing in *sie*. From her very first public show in the fall of 1946, Glückstein offered an unusually wide range of styles, from the most elegant to the everyday, all with a distinct pragmatic flair. She frequently presented variations on a favorite theme, the concept of the "transformed dress" ("Verwandlungskleid"), "a lovely contemporary illusion of how we can make two dresses out of one without letting either of them disappear."[22] The designer applied that idea to some evening gowns with the glamorous names "Scheherezade," "Barcelona," "Belle Helene," and "Nord-Expreß." But she also introduced some simple, attention-catching dress designs for daily use, which the magazine *sie* labeled "a little austerity dress" ("Sparkleidchen").[23] As a whole, Berneburg concluded, Glückstein's collection presents "convincing solutions for coming to terms with the deficiency of the times."[24]

That ability to couple a sense of elegance with a subtle acknowledgement of the scarcities of the time remained a trademark of Glückstein's work in the postwar years and was mentioned in every article in covering her salon in the late 1940s. *Chic* characterized her dresses as "beautiful and practical for everyday life" ("hübsch und praktisch für den Alltag"), and the journalists who attended the regular fashion shows in the salon on Meineckestraße noticed the moderation and absence of extravagance in her designs.[25] Glückstein was one of the first to offer variations on Dior's New Look, which had been launched in Paris in 1947, and she was one of several Berlin-based designers to actively seek out export opportunities even during the Berlin Blockade.[26] Nevertheless, her shows and their coverage in the press were geared to pleasing her local audience of regular Berlin women,—often vicarious consumers who, if they wanted to copy the designs for their own use, had only limited access to fabric (no more than two meters).[27] Glückstein charmed them with her "skillful adaptations of world fashion . . . translated into wearable designs, . . . free from all exaggeration," and often strictly limited to only two meters of fabric.[28] She focused on a broad variety and variability of the designs. The coverage of her shows for the press was also unlike any other reporting: the journalists repeatedly commented on the atmosphere in her salon, the friendly presence of the designer herself, and on the overall effect of her shows:

> Among the leading designer houses in Berlin, Charlotte Glückstein has created and preserved her own note: every one of her charming dresses—thought–through to the tiniest detail!—is such that all of the guests at the show wanted to have it. There are no sardonic smiles and no resignation to be discerned in the faces of the many, many women present. We sit there happy, in a cheerful mood, and delighted, while the various designs paraded in front of us appear simple and yet reveal so much fantasy and technical skill. They are as life-affirming as their lovely creator! With glowing smiles, Miss Glückstein and her assistants thank their female customers, who keep repeating "One wants to have everything."[29]

Particularly interesting was Charlotte's collaboration with the photographer Charlotte Rohrbach (1902–81) in the late 1940s, which contributed to her media image as Berlin's anti-glamour fashion designer. Whenever Glückstein's work was illustrated with photographs, there were usually either by Norbert Leonhard or by Charlotte Rohrbach, a photographer who started in *Die Dame* in the second half of the 1930s as a photo-reporter about art and architecture and established herself primarily as a fashion photographer in the postwar years, first for *sie* and *Berlins Modenblatt* and then for *ITEX* and *Film und Frau*.[30] While avoiding overt sensationalism, Glückstein and Rohrbach working in a tandem contributed to a signature image of postwar fashion that appealed to both the desire for escapism and the sense of practicality, the combination so characteristic of the Berlin woman's needs. Most of the published fashion photographs by Charlotte Rohrbach of Charlott models are of everyday dresses—not evening dress—and the photos are staged outside the studio. Unlike fashion photographs in *Heute* and *Illustrierter Telegraf*, such as the ones by Regina Relang, which incorporated ruins as a stylized background to the fine fashion creations and were particularly popular with foreign audiences, Rohrbach preferred a Berlin landscape that was cleared of rubble and resembled as much as possible a normal urban environment. All allusions to the destruction caused by the war—shrapnel holes on the walls, broken windows, jagged lines of buildings ruins—were meticulously avoided: Glückstein and Rohrbach felt that the last thing

Vielseitige Mode

Ein großes Programm, aber eines, das ungeteilten Beifall
finden wird, weil die Mode sich so vielgestaltig zeigt, daß jede
Frau sich mit irgendeiner Linie befreunden kann. Zunächst
ein Mantelkleid, verdeckt geschlossen, mit den sehr neuen
und sehr beliebten losen Teilen über einem engen Rock. —
Dann: ein Kostüm mit knappem, seitlich durchgeknöpftem Rock
und einer Homespunjacke, deren Weite sich rückwärts kon-
zentriert, neu auch der hinten in Form geschnittene Leder-
gürtel. — Ein schlichtes Kleid, vorn geknöpft, aber modisch
sehr interessant durch die großen Klappen der Taschen und

10

Fig. 13. Multifunctional fashion by "Charlott" with drawings
by Hildegard Ordnung in *Berlins Modenblatt*, May 1948.
Staatliche Museen zu Berlin, Kunstbibliothek.

that the readers of fashion magazines wanted to be reminded of was the reality in which they lived their regular lives. Instead, the models are hugging an undamaged tree—significant because most of the trees in Berlin had been cut down to be used for heating fuel during the cold postwar winters of 1945 and 1946—or leaning against a straight railing or walking on a perfectly repaired sidewalk. For indoor photographs, the interiors are simple but equally carefully chosen to eliminate traces of war. For example, beautiful curtains gracefully fall behind the models and windowpanes are intact.

Many indoor fashion photographs showed women in their work environment, especially if the work is creative or intellectual, and such pictures displayed a marked contrast to the photographs women of clearing ruins that dominated the media landscape. One of the many such examples by Glückstein and Rohrbach were be the pictures published in *Heute* in 1947 of young architect Ursula H. Thus. She is portrayed wearing a practical ensemble, a blouse and a skirt, and standing next to a drawing table. *ITEX* and *Berlins Modenblatt* regularly showed a multitude of photographs and drawings of women in anti-glamour, "wearable" fashion designed by Glückstein: going to work or moving around the streets of Berlin while wearing the designer's signature "transformation" dresses. Both the representation of fashion and the photographed environment in these first postwar years contribute to a sense of regained control, personal confidence, and rootedness in a professional identity.[31] Captured multiple times on the pages of so many magazines, Glückstein's creations during this period offer a lasting testimony to the fact that fashion represented an important, if often forgotten, facet in the larger postwar discourse of restoration, renewal, and transformation that is associated with lives of Berlin women.

Charlotte Glückstein's career as a designer continued for decades, but she shut down her own salon fairly quickly. Within two years of opening the luxury store in the Meinekestraße in early 1946, Glückstein married Hanjo Drechsler and together they launched a new label, CD, for Charlotte Drechsler, around 1950. The label lasted for nearly a decade and continued to receive some limited media coverage, primarily in local venues such as *Berlins Modenblatt*. Glückstein continued to participate in the most prominent West German fashion fairs such as Berliner Durchreise and the Düsseldorf-based Idego.[32] According to her daughter-in-law, Glückstein did not maintain a retail store in the 1960s and 1970s but worked as an independent contractor who sold her designs to mail-order catalogues such as *Quelle* and department stores. Most of her contracts were with the star designer Heinz Oestergaard for various lines of professional attire and uniforms. Her public presence in fashion and women's magazines gradually disappeared. It's high time to rescue her name from oblivion!

Die junge Innenarchitektin Frau Ursula H.
braucht vor allem einfache Kleider für
ihren Beruf. Dieses ist aus zwei Stoff-
resten (Modell: „Salon Charlott", Berlin.)

Fig. 14. Dress design by Salon Charlott for a "simple dress made out of two pieces of fabric" for the architect Ursula H., *Heute*, June 15, 1947. Photo Charlotte Rohrbach. Staatsbibliothek Berlin.

3. Fashion amidst the Ruins: Revisiting Two Early Rubble Films, . . . *und über uns der Himmel* (1947) and *Die Mörder sind unter uns* (1946)

> *It is nice to look again at nice dresses even if one cannot wear them.*
> —*Welt im Film,* newsreel no. 45/5, February 1946

THE IMMEDIATE POSTWAR YEARS witnessed the rapid rebirth not only of the clothing industry and the related media, but also of German film. Despite the dire historical and material circumstances, women's fashion continued to play a significant and very specific role in German postwar films. This chapter revisits two rubble films that have been rarely brought into dialogue with each other: *Die Mörder sind unter uns* (1946), the first DEFA production with a Soviet license, and its counterpart from the West, the much-anticipated first film produced under an American license *. . . und über uns der Himmel* (1947).[1] The comparison between *Die Mörder* and *Der Himmel* and the critical reevaluation of press accounts from the same period, especially in women's and fashion publications, allow for the reconstruction of a historic female experience of the immediate postwar period that goes beyond the stereotypical media images of the German woman as *Trümmerfrau, Amiflittchen, Fräulein,* or a victim of rape.[2] By taking a closer look at the presentation of women's clothes and various sartorial practices in these two films, this chapter delineates a much wider range of subjective positions associated with female characters and a broader array of attractive identities offered to a predominantly female spectatorship.

Rubble films (*Trümmerfilme*) have often been discussed in terms of their troubled reception by contemporaries. The approximately forty *Trümmerfilme* produced in the 1946–49 period often featured ruined cities, especially Berlin, as the backdrop and offered narratives of physical and psychological reconstruction after the demise of the Third Reich. Usually

This chapter is a substantially expanded and altered version of Ganeva, "Fashion amidst the Ruins: Revisiting the Early Rubble Films *And the Heavens Above* (1947) and *The Murderers Are among Us* (1946)," *German Studies Review* 37, no. 1 (2014): 61–85. Reprinted by permission of the publisher.

they disappointed contemporary critics. For example, the critic Friedrich Luft opined that some of the films failed to address adequately the moral conundrums of the postwar period, even though they were "bending under the lead weight of their political content." Another irritant for some critics was the "forced symbolism" and everything that looked like a continuation of UFA style from the 1930s.[3] Particularly outspoken in his repeated disparagement of postwar film productions was Wolfdietrich Schnurre, who claimed that most German films "did not seem able to free themselves from cliché-ridden pompousness und demonstrative righteousness," especially when they tackled issues of the immediate past, and that they missed the opportunity for a "bold aesthetic renewal."[4]

Regular moviegoers were not happy about the *Trümmerfilme* either, but for different reasons. As Tim Bergfelder maintains in his summary of viewers' reactions, there was "too much 'rubble' in the rubble films to the taste of urban dwellers who had to deal with material hardships on a daily basis and were constantly confronted with their moral guilt in the ongoing Allied re-education programs."[5] In January 1947, an article in the new weekly newsmagazine *Der Spiegel* explained why Germans chose distraction and entertainment over the sight of their daily experiences on the screen: "Real life, especially for women these days, is particularly sad. When people go to the movies, they want to relax, 'forget,' and not be reminded of the misery of everyday life. People aren't willing to look at ruins and returning soldiers in rags [*zerlumpte Heimkehrer*]"[6] In the first comprehensive scholarly study of postwar films, Peter Pleyer concluded, similarly, that for many Germans "the mere sight of poorly dressed [*ärmlich gekleidete*] people on a poster or a promotional photograph displayed in front of a theater would prompt them to label the film 'Trümmerfilm' and walk away."[7] Thus, the designation *Trümmerfilm*, coined by audiences initially in acknowledgement of the works' addressing everyday problems in the destroyed urban areas, quickly became a term of rejection.[8]

There was a pronounced aversion to the drabness of life displayed in films on contemporary topics and a general preference for politically innocuous Nazi-era melodramas, entertaining US and British imports, and outright silly contemporary comedies, yet some signature productions of the immediate postwar years did enjoy comparatively great popular or critical success. Cases in point are the first two postwar films produced in the East and the West: *Die Mörder sind unter uns* and *. . . und über uns der Himmel*, respectively. *Die Mörder* was seen by over 5 million people in Germany between 1946 and 1950 and had a positive international reception as well.[9] *Der Himmel*, viewed by 2.3 million in the western zones of Germany and in the western sectors of Berlin, was the first West German film designated for export in 1948.[10] Despite disparaging press critiques, the film became popular particularly with the local Berlin audience, who immediately took to the movie's catchy lead song and made it "the hit of the year 1948."[11] These discrepancies in perception invited the questions: What bright spots did these films' contemporary spectators, especially the disproportionately large number of women and young people, see onscreen that made them look away from the "ruins and the returning soldiers in tatters" to find pleasure and diversion?[12] What sights provided a needed, albeit brief and illusory, reprieve from the "misery of the everyday," as audiences watched the first postwar German films?

To answer these questions, I turn to the cinematic representation of fashion. The surprising yet spectacular images of intact and beautiful clothes against the background of horrific ruins present the works' often overlooked visual aspect to a destitute contemporary audience tired of hunger and perpetual shortages. Fashion was most frequently (although not exclusively) associated with the appearances of female characters in these early postwar films such as Edith Schröder in *Der Himmel*, played by the already well-known Lotte Koch, Susanne Wallner in *Die Mörder*, and Mizzi Burghardt in *Der Himmel*. Two recently discovered young actresses named Hildegard Knef and Heidi Scharf were cast in their first major film roles as Susanne and Mizzi, respectively. Although both films' narratives deliberately prefer to focus on the psychological dramas, dilemmas, and transformations of the male protagonists, the female characters in supporting roles still manage to attract significant attention with their looks, poise, and visual self-presentation. In her analysis of *Die Mörder*, for example, Ulrike Weckel points to the effect of Susanne Wallner's "varying functional clothing" ("wechselnde zweckdienliche Kleidung").[13] Indeed, Wallner parades throughout this first postwar film in an amazing variety of tidy, clean, and well-fitting clothes that are always appropriate for the occasion: behind the easel she wears an artist's protective white coat, and when running errands she is dressed in a simple dark skirt and freshly pressed white shirt, sensible shoes, and stockings with a fashionable dark seam visible along the back of her legs.[14] When she sweeps the apartment and removes the dirt, she is casually outfitted in baggy men's pants, a sweater, and a dark headscarf; even the colorfully striped apron on top seems to add a note of stylish elegance to the typical *Trümmerfrau* image.[15]

Die Mörder emphasizes a rich palette of fashionable clothes appropriate for different everyday situations, without revealing to the viewer how they actually have been obtained in these difficult times. In several scenes in *Der Himmel*, however, the audience is made privy with realistic exactness not only to the public display of attractive attire but also to the specific process of designing, sewing, and refashioning of clothes under postwar conditions of privation and shortages. These scenes repeatedly feature the young female protagonist, Mizzi, trying out new dresses and the war widow, Edith Schröder, working at her sewing machine. In addition, and more explicitly than in any other works, *Der Himmel* attributes importance to fashionable transformations as sure signs of achieved normalization and the successful overcoming of material troubles, even if it involves some shady wheeling and dealing. Although morally questionable and ultimately rejected by the end of the film, the participation in the black market of both men and women—as Hans Albers's and Heidi Scharf's characters in *Der Himmel* demonstrate—leads to their quick and undeniably quite pleasing sartorial makeover.[16] At the same time, *Der Himmel,* through the undeniably narcissistic, self-absorbed character of Mizzi, presents the dangerous double edge of fashion and its less favorable images within the context of postwar renewal.

This chapter builds on renewed recent scholarly interest in *Trümmerfilme* in order to revisit two iconic postwar productions, one from the East and one from the West, against the background of the rapidly revitalizing fashion industry and fashion media in postwar Berlin. Previous separate scholarly analyses of both works reflected traditional approaches to studying cinema in the postwar period. The two films have rarely been considered together as two examples that in a complementary way touch on the specifically female experience of late-1940s material conditions. Here I reconsider the films as constitutive to the emerging postwar visual media that were eager to capture the attention of war-weary female audiences and shape their aesthetic tastes, and appealed to women's consumer desires that may have been temporarily hampered by shortages but nevertheless endured throughout the postwar years. Such an approach is warranted by the abundant newspaper, magazine, and newsreel reports that testify to the period's obsession with fashion and to the prominent social position of women as journalists, designers, artists, and entrepreneurs within this discursive landscape.[17]

Robert Shandley's most comprehensive study of *Trümmerfilme* focuses predominantly on the ways these works record the period's affective responses to the Nazi past. I am revisiting *Die Mörder* and *Der Himmel* with an eye for the films' affective responses to the postwar *present,* a present that imposed on women material deprivations of all kinds but also seemed to offer unexpected opportunities for work, creativity, and independence. In other words, this is a move toward an analysis that, in the words of Brad Prager, pursues a "trail of fading traces" and considers the films primarily as "treasure chests of resemblances" to actual occurrences, attitudes and experiences of the time.[18] In looking at that filmic present, however, the focus of this chapter's argument shifts from the loaded and ubiquitous image of rubble in the landscape of the postwar years, a view thoroughly considered in a recent article by Eric Rentschler "on the place of rubble in *Trümmerfilm.*" Instead, I examine the ruins' paradoxical and often overlooked opposite, namely, alluring images of fashion, intact wholeness, and undamaged beauty.[19] Finally, such an analysis will shed light on how these popular films, as Dudley Andrews suggests, "comprise a record of the aspirations, obsessions, and frustrations of those . . . viewing them."[20]

The present project uses the notion that films and other mass media from the immediate postwar period were speaking, more consciously and more directly than previously assumed, to the contemporary female audience. In her groundbreaking study on gender and postwar German cinema, Hester Baer has argued that this attempt to address female experience "arose from an effort to create a commercial appeal to the largely female viewing public" in the late 1940s and 1950s, while creating at the same time compelling figures of positive identification transcending the clichés of the fully domesticated wife or the female victim.[21] Building on Baer's idea of female agency, I explore often ignored but widely prevalent images of fashionable women in postwar films. These images resonate most of all with numerous representations in fashion magazines and the regular fashion supplements in the immediate postwar years. Like the rubble films, the illustrated media assumed the task of shaping female spectators' modes of self-perception, along with training postwar consumer behavior. Moreover, as Baer has claimed in her scholarship on the West German magazine *Film und Frau* during the 1950s, fashion media provided "a space of pleasure and fantasy for women" and a site in which women could envision themselves not just as objects but also as agents. This argument that can be extended back to the late 1940s, to the hungry years, when these trends actually originated and spread across the East-West divide, even before the initiation of the Marshall Plan and the economic miracle in West Germany.[22]

Fashion and Fashion Design in *Die Mörder*

One of the main protagonists in *Die Mörder*, Susan Wallner (played by Hildegard Knef) is about to return home after being incarcerated in a concentration camp. We catch a glimpse of her clothes before we see her—even before she enters her home. The camera lingers over the relative abundance of fine outfits and silk underwear, as the male protagonist Mertens rummages through her surprisingly intact dresser and closet in search of valuable items to barter for booze. Undoubtedly, the sight of her clothes hanging in the closet along with Wallner's subsequent fashionable look in the film were a shocking contrast to the grave material shortages that Berlin women experienced in those first peacetime months and years. Many had lost their entire wardrobes along with everything else they had possessed in bombings and multiple displacements. Clothing and fabrics could only be purchased on the black market, bartered for food or cigarettes, or in some cases exchanged for rags.[23] Often women were reduced to wearing just one or two dresses in all seasons and were desperate to find warm winter coats and shoes for themselves and their children.[24] Sadly, they had grown accustomed to a reality of extreme scarcity and crisis ever since the ration card for garments (*Kleiderkarte*) had been introduced in 1939 and mandatory clothing drives to aid the war effort had been organized throughout the early 1940s.[25] After May 1945, as during the war years, women continued to apply with ingenuity and imagination the principles "From two make one" and "New clothes from old," battling shortages by creatively reusing remainder pieces of fabric, old clothing, men's attire, military uniforms, blankets, curtains, table cloths and kitchen towels when sewing their own garments.[26]

At the same time, immediately after May 1945, Germans, and especially the citizens of Berlin, were determined to restore some sense of normality in their lives. This effort found expression in a sometimes paradoxical reinstatement of routines and rituals of everyday civilian life that seemed incongruous alongside the rubble piles that constituted most of the city—such as opening fashion salons, organizing fashion shows, and launching a variety of magazines featuring fashion as their main theme. As noted previously, the limited fashion production catered primarily to the occupying forces and their families, who could afford designer clothing, while German women were involved in vicarious consumption, primarily as readers of the burgeoning fashion press. Most popular on the pages of the magazines were the reports of the first fashion shows, undoubtedly the flashiest and most surprising sign of recovery and normalization.

Contemporary female audiences' reception of *Die Mörder*, of its charming protagonist, Susanne Wallner, and of its young star, Hildegard Knef, should be reevaluated against this background. *Die Mörder* traces the painful readjustment to postwar realities of two people, a man and a woman, who come home to Berlin after the war. Hans Mertens (played by Ernst Wilhelm Borchert) has returned from the Eastern Front, where while serving as a military physician he had witnessed the massacre of innocent civilians. This psychological trauma of the past is torturing him and he can't find a way back to his profession. The horrific recollections haunt him all the more as he finds out that the person responsible for the murders, Captain Brückner (Arno Paulsen), is not only still alive but also is quite a successful family man and owner of a factory that now produces pots and pans made from helmets. Meanwhile, from the gossip of neighbors we learn that Susanne Wallner is returning home to Berlin after several years of internment in a concentration camp. Mertens's and Wallner's paths intersect in the ruined apartment that belonged to Susanne before she was detained, and now has been taken over by Mertens. Negotiating how these two strangers could share the place as they deal with their postwar lives is a starting point for their melodramatic relationship in the film.

There is no dearth of analyses focusing on the male *Heimkehrer* (returnee) Hans Mertens with his distressing memories of the Eastern

Front, crises, and struggles. Yet little critical light has been shed on the female *Heimkehrerin* figure, Susanne Wallner. Scholars have relegated her to being an antipode of Mertens: the grounded, focused, hard-working domestic opposite to his spiritual restlessness, his "savior" and the safe haven after a self-destructive, guilt-ridden, and potentially murderous odyssey through the rubble landscape of Berlin. Cinematically, too, she is represented in stark contrast to Mertens, whose shabbily dressed figure often appears in the frame tilted, off-center, with deep shadows crossing his unshaven face. Wallner, on the other hand, comes into view from the very beginning flooded in light, dressed in a variety of light-colored, generally neat clothes and captured in frequent close-ups that illuminate her immaculate, young, and beautifully made-up face. While Mertens is associated with the serious themes of guilt, shame, collaboration, memories of atrocity, feelings of vengeance and post-traumatic paralysis, Susanne Wallner is vital and energetic, immersed in mundane activities such as sweeping, cleaning, and setting the dinner table. Indeed, she is reduced to the image of a typical heroic rubble woman, fulfilling both domestic and maternal roles.

Critics have repeatedly called attention to Susanne Wallner's "undeveloped" nature as a film character.[27] References to both her past and future are either deliberately omitted or oblique. She returns to her bombed-out apartment in Berlin, but little is revealed about the years spent in a concentration camp and the reasons for her detention: Was she sent there because of her own political convictions or those of her father? Wallner's almost flawless appearance at the train station among the crowd of refugees and displaced people carries no marks of past suffering, torture, or hunger. Equally little is conveyed about her professional prospects. In her recently cleaned apartment, we see her behind an easel, working on a poster for the antifascist women's committees' Save the Children campaign, but are given no additional clues about a possible career as a graphic artist or a social worker.[28] While there are some significant hints that Mertens will eventually return to his work as a physician—we see him save a suffocating child—the female protagonist's plans are not part of the main plot line's melodramatic trajectory. In short, as Anke Pinkert points out, Wallner exists "in a historical vacuum, a survivor without story, past or history," and, one may add, without a future.[29]

Yet it is the cinematic *present* of the character of Wallner that has been inadequately explored and yields some intriguing insights. This character is only minimally defined by her emotions, beliefs, or thoughts, yet plenty is revealed visually through her actions and looks. With her character that the film achieves a certain "optical excellence," a quality considered by the critic Friedrich Luft to be key to a film otherwise deemed "a bit slow moving and unoriginal."[30] A closer look at Susanne Wallner's exceptional elegance and the activities in which she is involved (beyond cleaning and setting the dinner table) points to the escapism inherent in this first post-war film, despite the overwhelming presence of rubble and devastation on the screen.

Such a tendency toward diversion was not unique to Germany, as Jackie Stacey has demonstrated in her extensive study on female spectatorship. Stacey investigates the British discourse of escapism at the movies in the 1940s and 1950s, and ties it to two aspects. First, she claims that the heightened desire to find mental refuge in another, more beautiful world had specific significance for women because they, as the ones principally responsible for other family members' material well-being, were disproportionately affected by shortages and rationing during and after the Second World War. Second, she emphasizes that it is important to investigate "the particular pleasurable feelings they were escaping *into*," not only what the audiences were escaping from (fear, loss, anxiety, deprivation).[31] In many instances, as Stacey has argued, this elegant world of pleasure audiences were escaping into was determined by the appealing looks of the movie's brightest shining star.

One particular sequence in *Die Mörder* is exceptionally effective in associating the character of Wallner with the world of beauty and glamour. In so doing, it also associates Hildegard Knef, apart from the character, with that same world. This sequence opens with a shot of a clock neatly perched on a shelf that shows the time as 10:15, followed by a cut and a close-up of Wallner, in profile, impeccably made up and with shiny blond hair freely falling on the side, bent over a drawing board and engrossed in drawing, holding a piece of charcoal in her ringed hand. In the next shot the camera zooms out, Mertens enters the room, and the camera is aligned with his point of view. Now it becomes apparent that Susanne Wallner is at work in her newly transformed space, the room that she had previously swapped with Mertens declaring that she "needs it for work." It resembles an artist's studio, with an easel in the center and large windows on the side that now are covered by long, clean, light-colored curtains. It is night, so Wallner relies on the light lavishly dispensed by a fixture hanging from above and another standing lamp bent over the left side of the drawing. In the other scenes in the film, Wallner appears absorbed in domestic duties—washing clothes, fixing the wreckage within the apartment, carrying water, and serving dinner on a neatly set table. But here she exudes the confidence of an artist wrapped up in her creative work. The white protective smock she wears over her street clothes signals her professionalism. Everything within this frame—from the furnishing of the room to the smiling, friendly appearance of the female character—carries the signs of successful recovery and harmony between work and happiness. Even the spot of peeling plaster on one side of the wall seems to be there for contrast, implying the overall triumph of rebuilding over postwar chaos. In a reverse shot, the background behind Mertens

Figs. 15a and 15b. Stills from *Die Mörder sind unter uns* (1946), showing
the studio of Susanne Wallner (played by Hildegard Knef).

reveals a picture—possibly a reproduction of a portrait by an old master
such as Dürer or Cranach—hanging on the wall. This setup is juxtaposed
to earlier scenes with only Mertens in the room when he is surrounded
by objects in complete disarray, including this same picture and another
painting, a modern-looking portrait of a woman—scattered on the floor
or leaning against the wall.

This scene of Wallner at work on a drawing is remarkable in the way
it suggests an alternative image of the German woman in the immediate
postwar period. This is not the typical, determined, and hardworking yet
desolate and drab *Trümmerfrau*, of whom we have caught glimpses in
passing as Mertens walks through the streets of Berlin. Nor does this character have anything in common with the glamorous divas we will encounter in later films produced in 1947, for example, the singer Yvonne from
DEFA's film *Razzia*. Susanne Wallner bears no similarity to the dancers
and entertainers in the bar often frequented by Mertens, nor does she
resemble Bruckner's wife, who is entirely steeped in domestic and maternal duties, but is also assisted by household help. Instead, this relatively
short sequence in *Die Mörder* hints at the professional possibilities open
for women at the end of the war. In this sequence it is hard to say what
Wallner is drawing. But pinned to the wall behind her are two pictures,
presumably her own creations, which give an indication of the type of
work she is involved in. The images on the peeling wall, one of a woman
in a glamorous evening gown and one of a man in elegant attire and a hat,
appear very much like the illustrations one would encounter at the time
in fashion magazines. This makes us think that the area in which Susanne
Wallner is now professionally involved is the fashion press. Additional
clues are provided by the reference to the Save the Children campaign
elsewhere in the film: as reported in the *Berliner Zeitung* and *Neue Zeit*,
this organization repeatedly relied on fashion shows for fundraising.[32]

Wallner's possible association with the city's fashion industry as
a graphic artist and/or designer has been recognized, albeit somewhat

dismissively, by at least one contemporary commentator. In a rather disapproving tone, Wolfdietrich Schnurre wrote: "Girls [in today's film] still cannot be anything else but fashion illustrators . . . or designers. . . . They return from the concentration camps and only two days later they are at the drawing board full of enthusiasm? Also, how is it that after years in the camps one finds two or three neatly ironed outfits in the wardrobe?"[33] What Schnurre saw as a flaw of the film was most likely appreciated by contemporary audiences, which places it in a long-standing tradition of filmic escapism, harking back to Nazi cinema, but also foreshadowing the visual pleasures of *Heimatfilme*, 1950s films that celebrated Germany's regions, traditional culture, and folklore. Considered within the concrete media context of the second half of the 1940s, however, Wallner's involvement in the fashion business does not appear so unrealistic. More than anything else, the images pinned on the wall next to Wallner's drawing board evoke references to the fashion industry and media of the time, paradoxically popular and thriving despite the extreme material deprivation of Berliners.

As noted, the revival of the illustrated press and the proliferation of fashion publications that took place just months after May 1945 was truly astounding. But the inadequate production conditions for magazines and newspapers and the low quality of the paper available forced many of these publications to forgo photographic reproductions in their pages. Instead, the pages of these periodicals featured elaborate drawings by artists and evocative text descriptions by fashion journalists, with names either familiar from war and prewar times or entirely new to the profession. Within the multitude of recurring names we find trusted veterans such as Anna Paula Wedekind-Pariselle, well known from her work for *Die Dame* and other Ullstein publications throughout the 1920s and 1930s, Elly Lemke-Czerwinsky, Marietta Riederer, Erika Berneburg, Alice Bronsch, Manon Hahn, and Lilo Kittel. There were also newcomers, among them Gusti Kämmerling, Issi Puth, Hildegard Ordnung, Jo Lemke, Ann Mary Sigrist, Emmy Klaß, Renate Scholz-Peters, Ruth Doering, Babette Dievers, and Ursula Marquardt. Many contributed to more than one periodical, moving freely across the borders of all four sectors in Berlin.[34] Indeed, the discourse on fashion in the press was continuously pointing out how both the industry and the media covering it were providing women with ways to earn money as dressmakers, designer-illustrators, sales assistants, and models. Judging also from the abundance of ads in the newspapers and the articles on Berlin's reopening fashion and design schools, female workers were wanted in the fashion industry; new schools for designers, illustrators, and models opened, responding to the need for a trained workforce.

Particularly interesting are the self-referential features on the careers of the professional illustrator-designer for fashion publications

(*Modezeichnerin*) and the fashion journalist, which pointed to new professional opportunities for women in the postwar years and resonated in subtle ways with the screen presence of Knef's fascinating character, Susanne Wallner. Such practices hark back to the 1920s, when female fashion journalists were held in high regard in the public sphere. After the war, magazines such as *Mosaik, Frau von heute,* and *Berlins Modenblatt* not only consistently credited the fashion illustrations on their pages but also ran short biographical features on the illustrators and touted professional involvement in fashion as a possible career that would be available to young women in Berlin. A feature in *Berlins Modenblatt,* entitled "Our Colleagues in Their Own Words" ("Unsere Mitarbeiterinnen stellen sich vor") presented in lavish text, photographs, and drawings the personalities behind the "subtle interpretations of today's fashions": Gusti Otto-Kämmerling, Elly Lemke-Czerwinsky, and Ursula Marquardt-Beckmeier.[35] Marquardt-Beckmeier was also featured in a photo essay in which she shared insights about her everyday life at home and her professional work as a fashion illustrator: "Family Album of a Fashion Designer from the year 1946: The New Dress, from Sketch to Design" (Aus dem Familienalbum einer Modezeichnerin, 1946: das neue Kleid, von der Skizze zum Modell." In this piece she describes and illustrates her balancing act between giving a free rein to her artistic imagination and the limitations of reality (available fabrics), between family life (care for a small child) and work obligations (meeting editorial deadlines, working with designers).[36]

Other publications featured similar essays proudly presenting the magazine's all-female staff of graphic designers, models, photographers, secretaries, and reporters and their work for the fashion department.[37] Such features were often linked to direct advertising for training opportunities for those women wanting to become fashion designers. A long article in *Berlins Modenblatt* made the point that to participate in fashion one needs not plenty of fancy fabrics but "skills, imagination and sure instincts," some of which could be acquired and cultivated in Berlin's School for Fine Arts in Elly Lemke-Czerwinsky's course.[38] Testimonials of successful young professionals and employers also garnered publicity for the career of the *Modezeichnerin.*[39]

Hildegard Knef's extrafilmic appearances complement her persistent public associations with both the *Modezeichnerin* and the emerging film star, the very person onto whom women spectators projected their desires for beauty, distraction, and fashion. Certain expectations about Knef's charismatic appeal were cultivated even before the premiere of *Die Mörder* in mid-October 1946, as the media published numerous materials preparing the Berlin audiences for her screen debut. In June, the tabloid *Der Nacht-Express* dedicated a full page to the making of the first German postwar film, describing the exact locations of filming and reporting about the "patient onlookers," predominantly women, who were curious to see the young, previously unknown Hildegard Knef, and hoping to catch a glimpse of the "romantic, beautiful world of the actress that is not unrelated to the realities and hardships of our own daily professional lives."[40] The tabloid also included a review of Knef's previous career aspirations as a graphic artist, a commentary on her parallel appearances on Berlin's theater stages, and a still of Knef from the film, in which she is shown in her studio dressed in the signature white coat and bent over her drawings.[41]

Knef's association with the world of fashion was reinforced by the media in various ways. On the one-year anniversary of the founding of *Berlins Modenblatt*, which coincided with the premiere of *Die Mörder*, she joined other, more established and prominent actors such as Käthe Haack, Käthe Dorsch, Hilde Seipp, and Viktor de Kowa in congratulating the magazine and supporting its efforts to "promote elegance and beauty" as "a bit of diversion and inspiration amid rough, hard everyday life."[42] Subsequent reviews of *Die Mörder* attributed her persuasive and charming acting to the fact that she played herself: a girl who came "from fashion to film" and who evolved from an "illustrator and designer in UFA's fashion workshops" to an actress.[43] The press also spotlighted her stage appearances in the heavily damaged Renaissance Theater and later in the Schlosspark Theater during the first postwar year in terms of her ingenious, self-designed costumes, often made, in the spirit of the hard times, from a bed sheet or from different pieces of fabric "sewn together in a patchwork dress."[44]

The premiere of *Die Mörder* on October 15, 1946, in the State Opera House presented an opportunity for Knef herself to be cast as a main attraction. Although Wilhelm Borchert played the central role in the plot, Knef was listed first in the opening credits and also was seated in the first row, between the director, Wolfgang Staudte, and the producer, Erich Pommer. All the film posters featured her name in a position reserved for a star, above the film title: "Hildegard Knef in *Die Mörder sind unter uns*." The photo collage printed on the invitation for the premiere features Knef's face five times while Borchert's rather small likeness appears only once, near the edge of the page. This extraordinary treatment of the young actress as the true star of the first postwar film partially resulted from an unanticipated chance occurrence: several weeks before the premiere, Borchert had been arrested by the American military police for failing to disclose his joining the National Socialist German Workers Party in May 1933.[45]

Throughout Knef's initial ascendance into stardom, the media unrelentingly foregrounded those extrafilmic circumstances that not only highlighted her professional association with fashion but also promoted a hybrid public image blending her on-screen appearance as a young, attractive, and elegant *Trümmerfrau* with her offscreen status as a GI-*Fräulein*, the girlfriend of an influential American officer. In the fall of 1945, Knef made the acquaintance of a top ranking film official, the American Kurt Hirsch. In her own accounts and in interviews for the press, their first encounter is stylized as a typical Berlin scene of the time: as she was running in the rain for a rehearsal at the theater, a military jeep stopped, as the driver called "Hallo, Fräulein!" and offered her a ride. In fact, it is more likely that she had met him earlier in the US military headquarters, not on the street.[46] Knef liked to refer to Hirsch, a Jewish émigré from Czechoslovakia to the United States, as a regular, German-speaking GI, one of the many stationed in Berlin. In reality, however, he commanded some power and influence: Hirsch succeeded Billy Wilder as the leading film officer in the Film Control Branch of the Information Control Division and was in charge of overseeing the rebuilding of Germany's film industry. Hirsch turned out to be one of the most important people in Knef's early career, helping her extraordinarily fast professional advancement and assuring her spectacular public exposure outside cinema.[47] This boost undermines the idea of an independent female-oriented film and fashion star: her rise was helped by a powerful male of an occupying army. Knef was entertaining audiences in two sectors of the city, on the stages of the American sector and in DEFA's film *Die Mörder*. Simultaneously she was also charming the Berlin public with her famously fashionable off-screen appearances, in large part attributable to her boyfriend's ostentatious generosity. Not only was Hirsch driving her in a military jeep to stage rehearsals and the set of *Die Mörder*, he was also showering her with dresses and fur coats that she did not hesitate to parade in war-ravaged Berlin. Multiple contemporary accounts attributed this misstep to her youthful artlessness.[48] In any event, however, these public navigations of the offscreen sartorial world reflected and reinforced the star status that she was rapidly acquiring and the standards for postwar stardom that she was creating.

Another young actress, Maria Milde, remembers being told by the director Peter Pewas, when he saw her dressed in an old winter jacket and a coarse sweater she had knitted herself, "Look at how you are walking around! You should follow the example of your friend Knef. I ran into her in the [officers' club], with the Americans. You should have seen her! How she was dressed! Such a beautiful fur cape and sooooo long! And white! And how it swooshed as she went down the stairs!"[49] Other anecdotes involving Knef's clothes circulated. Ilse Werner, the star of the 1940 UFA blockbuster *Das Wunschkonzert*, was stunned to run into Knef at a social gathering in the home of the actor Victor de Kowa. The cause for Werner's surprise was Knef's outfit: it was the dress Werner had worn as a costume in *Das Wunschkonzert*. Knef explained, "Shortly before the Russians took over, I managed to take one or two dresses from UFA's costume storehouse. Yours was one of them."[50] While other Berliners were trudging around exhausted in tattered clothes, Knef was not shy to show off her new luxurious threads. By mid-1947 she had become the brightest film attraction in postwar Germany: with two more films in the making and numerous features and glamour pictures of her proliferating in the press, Knef was the film and fashion star who most firmly commanded the public's attention.[51]

The Role of Fashion in *Der Himmel* (1947)

In depicting postwar realities and especially in its presentation of fashion, the first US-licensed *Trümmerfilm*, *Der Himmel*, has many strategies in common with its counterpart from the East, *Die Mörder*. Both works focused on the presentation of the quotidian in the destroyed city of Berlin by featuring traumatized men returning from the front alongside beautiful women displaying neat clothes against a stark background dominated by ruins. However, the insights into the everyday fashion practices of designing, remodeling, and displaying clothes in postwar Berlin are much more explicit in *Der Himmel*. The film connects them to several figures, the characters Hans Richter (Hans Albers), Mizzi (Heidi Scharf), and Edith Schröder (Lotte Koch), and more concretely embeds them in the social context of the time.

The plot combines optimistic reflections on the restoration of the German family, glimpses into the workings of the black market, and some *Heimkehrer* themes already familiar from *Die Mörder*. The main protagonist, Hans, played by Hans Albers, returns from the war to his destroyed apartment. Bursting with energy, he slips easily into the new Berlin lifestyle, swinging between material crisis and con artistry, which quickly gets him involved in the black market. He uses the proceeds from his illegal deals to fix up his living quarters and to generously help out his neighbors. Hans's son also returns from the front, temporarily blinded, and as he regains his sight he is appalled by his father's imminent transformation into a crook. The son rebels against the father's corruption, leaves the paternal home, and begins working on a construction site. In the redemptive ending of the film, the son leads his father out of his entanglement in the black market and back to an honest life.

The character played by Albers represents a *Heimkehrer* distinctly different from Mertens in *Die Mörder*, one whose recollections are not of war and trauma but of better prewar times: leisurely boat rides on a lake, sipping beer in an outdoor café, pushing a stroller, and fun visits with his son to the zoo. In all of these nostalgic scenes reproduced at the beginning of the film as flashbacks representing the character's happy memories, Albers's character is a sharp dresser, in strong contrast to his shabby appearance after returning from the war. These flashbacks remind the audience of Hans Albers's star persona, whose allure in the past was often associated with fashion: throughout the 1930s and early 1940s Albers was known onscreen and off for his impeccably elegant suits, hats, and scarves.[52] Albers's fashionable image reemerges in his memories as he lies in bed at night, and they become the impetus for the character's subsequent postwar recovery. As if gaining inspiration from these happy memories, he wakes up the next morning and immerses himself immediately in an attempt to rebuild his home and life.

It is remarkable how quickly Hans's downtrodden look is transformed in the process of his adjustment to the postwar realities in Berlin: he sheds the threadbare leather jacket and starts wearing an elegant three-piece suit, a tie, and a light-colored raincoat—all outward signs of his newly acquired prosperity. The gain in material stability, however, comes at a cost. Although he is generous in helping all his neighbors with food and other basic items, Hans is clearly involved with criminals, smugglers, and black-market dealers, who hold him in their grip. When confronted by his son, he decides to break his ties with the black market. In a final symbolic gesture of contrition, Hans dumps his fancy attire—the whole collection, which he describes as "a silken vest, pants with a crease, and wool jacket, all those rotten rags,"—into the garbage.

Although the film dwells extensively on the star power of Hans Albers, it also demonstrates an unusual interest in the female characters, especially in their day-to-day dealings with clothes and their involvement in the fashion scene. The central narrative of rapid material ascent, moral compromise, and a redemptive turnaround accompanies the sartorial transformation of principal male character. However, the stories of the two female characters, Hans's neighbors Edith and Mizzi, provide insights as well. Often ignored in previous analyses of the film, the appearance of these two characters sheds light on the postwar status of fashion in ways that are complex and often contradictory and that resonate primarily with prevailing women's practices of the time.

As Hans is getting reacquainted with his old neighborhood, he is greeted by a little girl who believes that this returnee from the front is her long-lost father. She drags him into her apartment, and we are introduced to her mother, Edith, a widow who lost her husband in the war and is now Hans's neighbor. The establishing shot in Edith's apartment—just as Hans comments, "You have put your place together very nicely"—prominently features a shiny sewing machine. For this sewing machine Hans volunteers to procure a new belt on the black market, so that Edith can use it again. Subsequent scenes in the apartment show the sewing machine and Edith seated next to it, which explains her consistently neat, attractive appearance, in at least three different dresses, and also suggesting that sewing is a career, not a hobby.

Dressmaking helps Edith earn money and maintain a comfortable, somewhat normal domestic life. In this she is one of thousands of Berlin

Fig. 16. Edith (Lotte Koch) in the film *. . . und über uns der Himmel* (1947).

women who earned a living as *Heimarbeiterinnen* for the thriving fashion industry; they became a more elegant version of the *Trümmerfrau* within a domestic setting. Admittedly, Edith's is not a luxurious lifestyle, and she earns very little. Hans later juxtaposes her labor to his smarter way of making money on the black market, commenting, "You work night and day, you toil behind the sewing machine for only a few cents." Her subdued role supports the central male character and the much more exuberant, fashionable Mizzi (played by Heidi Scharf), another neighbor in the same building.

Edith's secondary status echoes the hidden but indispensable presence of women who were employed as *Heimarbeiterinnen*, and this character must have found much sympathy among the audience, as the seamstress who works at home was a widespread occupation for Berlin women. According to a special December 1946 issue of the illustrated women's magazine *Für Dich* dedicated to the topic of *Heimarbeit*, there were more than 12,000 *Heimarbeiterinnen* in Berlin. *Für Dich* noted that their work was regulated by an ordinance of the Berlin magistrate: "Today, our home workers are not the pariahs of our society," although still relatively meagerly paid.[53] The photographs of about half a dozen women at work designing, sewing, and embroidering clothes in this and other illustrated periodicals bear uncanny resemblance to Edith's onscreen character. The unglamorous but honest, professional, and hard work that Edith stands for ultimately prevails in the film: Hans gives up his

Figs. 17a and 17b. Mizzi (Heidi Scharf)
in . . . *und über uns der Himmel* (1947).

involvement in the black market and returns to the neighborhood as a
regular construction worker.

The character who exemplifies the most controversial yet common
aspects of postwar infatuation with fashion is Mizzi, another neighbor
in the same building. A rebellious teenager exasperated by the miserable
existence in her bombed-out apartment, Mizzi is first introduced to viewers when she tells her boyfriend, Walter, her dreams of fleeing to a nicer
place: "I want out. Out and away to a place where I can breathe freely,
where we can be who we are: young and happy." Mizzi's desire for an
escape from the gloominess of everyday life accompanies her spectacular sartorial transformations, forming an attractive subplot of the film. As
many of the contemporary critics noted, Mizzi's "hunger for life" ("Lebenshunger") and her irreverent "aspirations for beauty and elegance"
not only presented a type that many young people could identify with,
but also endowed this none-too-successful postwar film with "powerful
color" and a sense of authenticity.[54]

The trajectory of Mizzi's aspirations is framed by two similar scenes
set among the rubble of the bombed-out apartment building. Both feature the young woman looking at herself in a mirror and talking to her
boyfriend, Walter, who has been traumatized by war, has been displaced,
and cannot adjust to the new conditions. In the first scene the viewers are
cued by Hans's musical theme and expect to see him appear in the frame,
but instead the camera focuses on Mizzi sitting in a lawn chair, sunbath-
ing and combing her hair amidst the ruins. "My new dress will be ready
soon," she tells Walter, explaining that she will then go out dancing in
this new outfit. Walter responds that he cannot think about such trivial
things given the worries on his mind. Although not averse to sympathy,

Mizzi is shown looking intently into a broken piece of mirror throughout the conversation, engrossed with her own perfectly groomed image. This is her preferred mode of coping with the wreck of war: by focusing on her clothes, her external appearance, and her desire to escape. The next scene in the same location—a former living room whose external walls and ceiling have been blown away by a bomb and whose interiors are now exposed to the elements—shows Mizzi wearing the already finished dress and holding a small elegant pocket mirror (not simply a jagged shard). Both objects—the dress and the mirror—signal her progress in the postwar world as well as within her own system of values.

From the beginning of the film, Mizzi's new dress becomes the symbolic vehicle of this escape from the ruins. Her friendly neighbor, Edith Schröder, volunteers to make it out of drapery, a common practice during the scarcity of the early postwar years that reflected the pragmatic advice and encouragement consistently given in the fashion pages.[55] An early scene in Edith's apartment opens on a close up of the sewing machine. As the camera zooms out, we see the two women: Mizzi is trying on a new dress that Edith is sewing for her. Mizzi swirls around excitedly in her not-quite-finished dress, while Hans, who has just entered the room, agrees to take her to one of these places where she can, as she puts it, "dance, listen to music, sit at a nicely set table and forget everything." Inspired by the promise, she breaks into a happy dance in front of the camera in her unfinished dress; she keeps spinning around despite the loud protests of her mother, heard from somewhere offscreen, that she has ruined the only fine curtains in the house for this dress and despite Frau Schröder's complaint that without a new belt for the sewing machine she can't go on sewing. In her subsequent appearance in the now-finished dress, in a medium close-up shot of her full body, Mizzi looks as though she is posing for a fashion photograph: she is seated cross-legged on a table in the center of the room, displaying an unobstructed view of the new dress for the audience to inspect for a few seconds. She is also carrying an elegant self-made purse, similar to the ones that could be created following the practical instructions in women's magazines.[56]

Just a few seconds into the fashion demonstration, it becomes clear that Mizzi's modeling of the finished dress for Hans, who soon enters the scene, is not accidental. She wants to remind him of his promise to take her out. As Jaimey Fisher has pointed out, Mizzi's obsession with nice looks and a glamorous lifestyle is symptomatic of a mode of coping with postwar hardship that resembles Hans's. They share energy, optimism, individualism, and perceived exceptionalness, which in the first half of the film makes them think that they can successfully rebel against the precarious social order. Soon Mizzi does indeed escape with Hans's help: her refuge from the drabness of everyday life and the ruins is the Haiti Bar, a hotbed for black-market activities. Mizzi is quickly engulfed into the vortex of criminality and illegal trade deals done the bar, acquiring new and more dazzling outfits along the way, until she realizes the unacceptable risks and consequences of this lifestyle, which include the tragic death of her boyfriend, Walter.[57]

Mizzi and her association with both Edith (who designs and sews her dresses) and Hans (who takes her to the nightclub) introduces the fashion theme as an important subplot in postwar stories, fully integrating it into the complicated, often paradoxical picture of material life at the time. Fashion signifies both hopeful recovery and longing for normality but also narcissistic indulgence, in sharp contrast to hard and honest work; it is associated with honest daily industriousness but also connotes the flair of dubious morals, crime, black market deals and an empty life of leisure. In fact, in the character of Mizzi and her narcissistic obsession with clothes and appearances, postwar fashion cannot be read merely as means of escape from the drudgery of everyday life, but could also represent a possibility diametrically opposed to that of Susanne Wallner in *Die Mörder*: a dangerous form of abandonment of women's obligation to restore shattered masculinity and keep the home fires burning.

Mizzi is played by the young actress Heidi Scharf, who is can be compared with the star persona of Hildegard Knef, because of her own initial success—but the two starlets had divergent professional trajectories. The character of Mizzi had all the prerequisites for catapulting the actress into star status: in many ways the film coded Mizzi as a narcissistic and rebellious female parallel to Hans's recalcitrant individualistic male. This suggested that in addition to her beauty and charm she shares some of his star aspects.[58] Eventually, however, Mizzi finds out that she has inadvertently aided in criminal acts that cost the life of her boyfriend, and her character is left without a clear resolution and is somewhat forgotten by the end of the film. She is shaken by the tragic developments and returns the ring that Walter has procured in a shady deal, but will she return to her bombed-out apartment? Will she give up on glamour? What will become of her? The film refuses to give a clear answer to these questions, and Mizzi becomes simply another young and charismatic female figure, missing a past, deprived of a clear future, and suspended in the eternal cinematic present tense of the *Trümmerfilm*.

Similar to the character Mizzi, who is forever bound to the present moment, Heidi Scharf remained associated with her spectacular appearance in this film only. She did not manage to replicate her promising success in *Der Himmel* in other works and vanished from the film world's horizon as quickly as she had appeared. Nevertheless, for some time she did attempt to follow the same pattern of offscreen conduct that had assured Hildergard Knef some of her fame. Like Knef, Heidi Scharf had been a newcomer, a coveted young face in Germany's postwar film industry, which linked its prospects for a breakthrough in the East or the West to the miraculous discovery of unknown female actresses. Like Knef, Scharf seemed to be headed for a successful international career validated by the American media. The hype around her started even before the premiere of *Der Himmel* in February 1948. An issue of *Der Spiegel* from June 1947 featured a glamour photograph of Scharf on its cover and included an article describing in detail how she had been discovered the previous summer on the Kurfürstendamm by an American *Life* photographer: "She was headed down the street to buy lipstick, as a Citroën stopped right next to her. The driver, sporting a 'war correspondent' badge on his lapel, spoke with an American accent, 'Are you an actress? You have high cheekbones and are very photogenic.'"[59] Soon after, a photographic series appeared in *Life* with Scharf "performing interpretative dance among ruined buildings," and, an avalanche of fan mail and Hollywood offers allegedly came her way in the following weeks.[60] According to *Der Spiegel*, she resisted the offers from Hollywood and was convinced by Josef von Báky to work in the new Hans Albers film.

In the following months, photographs of Scharf appeared regularly in the popular press, often illustrating fashion trends. In the fan magazine *Die neue Filmwoche* she was featured in a large-format photo in which she took a coquettish pose in order to reveal the details of her signature "dress made from curtains." The photograph was meant to serve also as an advertisement for the upcoming release of *Der Himmel*.[61] At the premiere, February 2, 1948, Scharf surprised the public by stealing the limelight from Hans Albers, causing the critic Christa Rotzoll to enthuse, "She was magnificently dressed, like for a fashion show, and together with great-looking Lotte Koch, they outshone everyone in the hall."[62] After the premiere, the women's magazines were eager to promote her status as a fashion expert and trendsetter on the basis purely of her film appearance in *Der Himmel*.

In 1949, *Lilith* featured Scharf in the company of five popular and more established film and theater actresses who were asked, "What do you like to wear?" She confessed her preference for "simple girlish dresses" that she "often sews herself."[63] But after this brief foray into the fashion and illustrated media of the late 1940s, and after one additional appearance in a supporting role in Rudolf Jugert's *Hello, Fräulein!* (1949), Scharf slipped into oblivion. Unlike Hildegard Knef, who remained a lifelong fashion icon, Heidi Scharf's starlet status faded after her first spectacular role.

Judging from the numerous film reviews and the public reception in women's and fashion magazines, Knef's subtly elegant character in *Die Mörder*, Lotte Koch's neat outfits and diligent work as a seamstress, and Heidi Scharf's youthful extravagance were greeted positively by a female public exhausted by cold, hunger, and shortages. Far from antagonizing their audience, the fictional characters, by consistently showing off an intact working woman's well-fitting wardrobe of clothes originating in better times and adapted to the present moment, presented appealing and escapist images of normalcy and hope.

The actresses' appearance resonates with the upbeat iconography found in the mass media of the immediate postwar years, the illustrated magazines and the women's sections in daily newspapers. The image the characters projected was very much in tune with the plentiful fashion advice dispersed by the illustrated press, women's publications, and newsreels, which showed how to balance the innate desire for beauty with the lack of quality clothing. Thus, the meaning of these female protagonists is paradoxical, determined by the contrastive visual juxtaposition of ruin and fashion. If rubble symbolized the failures and catastrophes of a past that had brought unimaginable suffering to the whole nation, the beauty of fashion on the silver screen and pages of magazines communicated the optimistic spirit of rebuilding. This rebuilding began on a small scale, starting with oneself, in the hope of gradually achieving some sense of normalcy and reconnecting through the fashion media with the world from which Germans had been cut off during the war years. Thus, the presence of Susanne Wallner, Mizzi Burkhardt, and Edith Schröder on the postwar screen signaled peacetime optimism and renewal and fed into the (sometimes problematic) desire for escapist pleasures, a desire that found expression across the visual and printed media of the period.

Vignette 2. Hildegard Knef: Star Appeal from Fashion to Film

IN LESS THAN A YEAR after her public cinematic debut in *Die Mörder sind unter uns*, Hildegard Knef became the brightest film attraction in the immediate postwar period, enjoying popular success and media attention like no other German actress. The film press as well as women's periodicals followed closely Knef's professional and personal moves, her work, her friendships, her varied hairstyles, and her wardrobe.[1] In the assessment of most film scholars of the period, she quickly became the "emblem of postwar femininity," a star whose on- and offscreen appearances merged into a single projection surface for the viewers' desires.[2] It has become customary to think that within the relatively short period during which Knef's star appeal was at its peak, from 1946 till the mid-to-late 1950s, her celebrity image did change, keeping pace with the dynamically changing aspirations of her female fandom. Many critical studies have examined the early trajectory of the actress's fame and tied it to the popularity of her roles as well as compelling aspects of her biography, but little attention has been paid to Knef's deep and continuous involvement with the world of fashion, with questions of style and beauty, with patterns of real and imagined consumption and lifestyle, all issues that were of vital interest to the female German public in the postwar years. Knef staged these issues visibly, in both her film roles and her offstage appearances.

This vignette offers close readings of selected scenes in three of Knef's early films against the background of her intensive mass media presence, in order to trace the interplay between film stardom and consistent fashion iconography during the late 1940s and early 1950s, an interplay that places Hildegard Knef at the center of Germany's postwar visual history. Most explorations of Knef's star image assume that she transformed from a *Trümmermädchen* to a femme fatale over the course of the early postwar years. I propose to show that these opposing stereotypical images were always present in Knef's stardom from the very beginning of her film career. Indeed, her association with fashion trends would continue long after she stopped filming.[3] Thus, the designation for Knef proposed by Johannes von Moltke and Hans-J. Wulff, *Trümmer-Diva*, seems very appropriate, as it embraces the notion that "Knef-images refer to the symbolic practices of [her] contemporaries" ("Die Knef-Bilder verweisen auf die symbolische Praxis von Zeitgenossen").[4] The dynamics of Hildegard

Knef's celebrity brings together the worlds of film and fashion and thus sheds light on the rapid societal reorientation in the immediate postwar years and reveals how film filled the spectatorial fantasies and the evolving needs of the postwar female audience during this brief period. Knef's fame between 1946 and 1953 reflects particularly on the efforts of German women to embrace fashion initially as a visual antidote to the sight of postwar ruins, but subsequently also as a goal of unrestrained consumption as well as an affirmation of achieved normalization.

Fashion figured prominently in all of the publicity surrounding Knef. In mid-1947, when Knef made it to the cover of the *Der Spiegel* magazine and was also featured in a long article in a leading film journal, her connection to fashion seemed inseparable from her star identity. The caption under the glamour photograph on *Der Spiegel*'s cover read "A Fräulein comes from fashion" ("Ein Fräulein kommt aus der Mode"); the article in *Die neue Filmwoche* was entitled "From Fashion to Film" ("Von der Mode zum Film").[5] That connection referred only partially to an earlier chapter of her biography, when the seventeen-year-old started a training program at the UFA studios in 1942 to become a graphic designer and fashion illustrator (*Modezeichnerin*), before moving on with acting classes in 1943.[6]

In her first three film roles shot after the war she does not appear as a glamorous star at all but instead wears a variety of nice yet simple and practical clothes fitting her screen persona as "Germany's favorite *Trümmermädchen*."[7] Yet at the same time, on the cover of magazines such as *Der Spiegel* she is portrayed rather as a *Trümmer-Diva*, in the pose of a major film star: head thrown backward, a luxurious fur around her shoulders, and a cigarette in her languid hand. Her face is made up, her hair is smooth and straight. She wears dark lipstick and false eye lashes.[8] Inside the magazine is a review of Knef's participation in *Zwischen gestern und morgen* (Between Yesterday and Tomorrow, 1947, directed by Harald Braun), her second postwar film and the first US-licensed production in the American occupation zone—it was filmed in the Geiselgasteig studio, near Munich.[9] While one part of the review extols the natural fit of the actress for the role of endearing *Trümmermädchen* Kat, the glamour photograph and the second part of the text serve as a mini-fashion feature, discussing the outfit that she was wearing during the interview—a description that seems a bit at odds with the modesty and simplicity of the character she supposedly plays in the film: "Her long legs are clad in plaid trousers that are rolled up at mid-calf length beneath the knee. Her top is a red sports blazer; her face is nicely made-up, surrounded by softly falling blond hair."[10]

Other high-profile articles in the popular press that followed in detail Knef's brief career to this point and even her life in faraway Hollywood reveal a similar dichotomy. A close up of Knef's perfectly made-up face

Fig. 18. Hildegard Knef on the cover of *Der Spiegel*,
May 10, 1947. Staatsbibliothek Berlin.

with downcast eyes was featured on the cover of *Der Stern*'s inaugural
issue, on August 1, 1948, right after the success of Knef's third film role,
Film ohne Titel (Film without a Title, 1948, directed by Rudolf Jugert),
but the caption emphasized, surprisingly, her "natural grace" and her lack
of glamour: "The star of our times is not extravagant. We admire Hildegard Knef's natural grace."[11]

Perhaps most telling of the idiosyncrasy of Knef's star image, which
combined stereotypical images of both simplicity and sophistication,

is a 1948 feature dedicated to the actress in the trade journal *Berliner Filmblätter*. Embedded in the article are two images. The caption "fully Americanized" ("voll amerikanisiert") is under a photo in which confident and elegant-looking Knef poses as a reader of *Life* magazine and invites the audience, with her direct and insisting glance, to become a reader as well. Her long hair flows freely around her face and in her left hand she coquettishly holds a cigarette. Another caption, "truly German" ("treu-deutsch") explains a still from *Film ohne Titel*, in which Knef's peasant-girl character wears her hair in braids wrapped around her head and her dreamy eyes are directed away from the viewer, toward the sky. The author resolves the apparent contrast between the images in the consolatory conclusion: "The main thing is, Hilde remains herself. Our dear Hilde, a girl of our times: the profile of a Madonna, golden blond hair stubbornly flapping in her face. She finds long pants chic and prefers an exotic cocktail to a chocolate milk."[12]

This divergence between the glamorous media presentations of the actress and her first roles in postwar cinema as the typical young German woman does not seem to have bothered the audiences. On the contrary, these two sides of Knef's public persona fuse into one, and, according to contemporary critics, "hundreds of thousands [of German women] recognize themselves in her."[13] Through the stories that circulated publicly about her private life, she projected an image mixing factual biographical references and fictional traits of the characters she played, and it was with this hybrid star image that contemporary female viewers wished to identify, even if contradicted the reality: Knef was charming, yet relied on hard work and honesty; well-dressed and resourceful, but not excessive and extravagant; hungry for life as the spoiled girlfriend of a Jewish-American officer stationed in Berlin, but not morally corrupt; blond and good-looking, yet natural and distinctly different from the stylized beauty of UFA stars of the past; she was an ideal German, forward-looking, but had also some international, even American, flair about her. As *Der Spiegel* wrote approvingly: "She could have come straight out of an American magazine."[14]

The years of Knef's career following her 1946 screen debut are remarkable in terms of her ability to combine the film stardom with the magnetism of the fashion icon. In films made in Germany before as well after her brief Hollywood engagement—and as different in genre and style as *Film ohne Titel* (1948), *Zwischen gestern und morgen* (1947), *Nachts auf den Strassen* (1952), *Illusion in Moll* (1952), *The Man Between/Ein gefährlicher Urlaub* (1953), and *Die Sünderin* (1954)—she maintained a consistency of appearance and fashion presence that made the audience believe that she was playing variations of the same role over and over again as a young, contemporary German woman, fluctuating between the same inevitable opposites in the films' narratives: innocence and forgivable sin, light youthful charm and glamorous elegance, fierce independence and romantic reconciliation. Eventually, this consistency of appearance would lead to stagnation in Knef's cinematic career in the mid-1950s. Even after she decided to abandon film altogether, however, her status as a fashion icon persisted.

Zwischen Gestern und Morgen

In her second screen role after the end of the war, Knef was cast as "the young girl Kat" in *Zwischen Gestern und Morgen* (Between Yesterday and Tomorrow, 1947), a film set amid the ruins of postwar Munich. Kat is often seen skillfully scavenging among the ruins of a once luxurious hotel. There she meets Michael Rott (played by Victor de Kowa), an artist and a former guest at the hotel who escaped to Switzerland during the war and has now returned to his hometown. A series of flashbacks reveals that a precious necklace that belonged to a Jewish actress, Nelly Dreyfuss, disappeared on the night that Rott fled from the hotel; in the same hotel Dreyfuss (played by Sybille Schmitz) committed suicide. Kat has recently found the valuable necklace in the rubble and intends to sell it on the black market. However, when Rott is wrongly accused of the theft, Kat produces the necklace as evidence of his innocence, which brings the two characters closer together. The film ends with Rott's public rehabilitation and his romantic union with Kat: it is clear that the two of them have fallen in love. With Kat's active help, the male protagonist's reputation in the present is saved, his troublesome past is redeemed, and his future happiness is secured.

Zwischen gestern und morgen confirms and complements Knef's already established allure as "Germany's most beloved rubble girl" (*Trümmermädchen*), who may have had a traumatic past, but has moved on and is firmly anchored in the present. Like her character in *Die Mörder*, here, too, Knef's young character is working tirelessly, with determination and optimism, to seek out an existence within the postwar chaos. In this film, too, the female protagonist is seen most frequently against the background of present-day destruction and demise, but this time she is scavenging among the rubble in search of valuable goods that she can reuse or resell. She is also caring with motherly devotion for her younger brother, and this justifies her involvement in some shady black-market deals using cigarettes as the common currency. Here, the emphasis on the German woman's day-to-day struggles about procuring food, clothes, and shoes for the family, even at the cost of illegal activities, is much more explicit than in the first DEFA production. Throughout the scenes of her daily activities, Kat is dressed in her signature black turtleneck and men's style pants, already familiar from some scenes in *Die Mörder*—a costume in which she was often photographed for contemporary magazines as if featuring the most fashionable attire of the time. An additional visual nod to the mores of the postwar times is the cigarette often tucked behind Kat's ear, the cigarette that she uses as the currency in her various transactions.

That practical dressing style of the young *Trümmermädchen*, along with her age and youthful acting style, formed a strong contrast to the other female characters in the cast of *Zwischen gestern und morgen*, Winnie Markus and Sybille Schmitz, well-established and glamorous former UFA stars. The Munich designer Bessie Becker—who as Irmgard Becker-Schulte started her involvement with UFA in 1941 and was responsible for the designs in the 1943 hit *Großstadtmelodie* (see chapter 1)—also provided the costumes for *Zwischen gestern und morgen*. Becker's costumes shaped a marked stylistic contrast between Kat's and everyone else's appearance in this early postwar film. Although the film was strongly criticized by the contemporary press for looking a lot like "the standard entertainment fare of the UFA system," primarily because of its camera work, costumes, and mise-en-scène, Knef's character was celebrated for being refreshingly different from past models: she was lively, simple, but also more "multi-dimensional, practical, hard-working and bold, just as women are in real life."[15] As Ursula Bessen summarized the responses to the actress's stardom, with her second postwar film, Hildegard Knef reestablished herself not so much as "a type but as an anti-type, embodying everything that the divas from the Third Reich could not be."[16]

With the development of the relationship between the returning artist Rott and the *Trümmermädchen* Kat, Harald Braun's film pushes the sartorial contrast even further and perhaps in a new direction. Most significant is Knef's transformation in terms of costume toward the end of the film, starting when Michael Rott visits Kat in her cozy little place, which she proudly displays ("Gemütlich, nicht?") and which epitomizes her embrace of everyday normality and vitality. "Life must go on. There is no other way"—she repeatedly utters this phrase, which could have been uttered by Susanne Wallner. The sequence then proceeds as Rott and Kat reminisce about the past. Rott confesses his nostalgic longing for his *Heimat* throughout his time as émigré: "As a foreigner in Switzerland, one is nostalgic. I was yearning not only for the people from the past, but also for the land and the air." Kat then delivers an elegiac account of her family's forced flight from their Silesian homeland in Stettin to Munich four years earlier, and her loss of family, home, and work during the bombing of Munich. The two stories about nostalgia for and loss of the *Heimat* are matched visually by the camera's intense focus for most of the sequence on Kat's upper body. Now she is dressed in an elaborate variation of a folkloric dirndl outfit consisting of a white embroidered blouse and a darker dirndl skirt, which in itself is a nostalgic embodiment of national tradition.

It may be surprising for us to see this costume validated on the screen so soon after the demise of National Socialism, which, in its official ideology, embraced the traditional costume (*Tracht*) as the foundation for a genuine German fashion, but it may not have been particularly shocking for the contemporary audiences. In the peculiar apolitical and amnesiac world of fashion in the early postwar years, the dirndl actually made a remarkable comeback in Europe as a hot German haute-couture item and one of the few styles that, according to numerous reports in the press, were successfully presented not only at regional events but also at international fashion shows abroad and were a coveted export item.[17] By wearing a dirndl in the final scenes of *Zwischen gestern und morgen*, Knef seems to be pointing in the direction of the normalization of the upcoming affluent 1950s in which *Heimatfilms* will reign.

Film ohne Titel

The third film that Hildegard Knef starred in before leaving Germany for the United States in January 1948 was *Film ohne Titel* (Film without a Title 1948, directed by Rudolf Jugert), which proved to be the most successful commercial production of 1948. It won the 1949 Bambi Award for best film of the previous year, and Knef received the award for best actress at the Locarno International Film Festival. Film historians and the contemporaneous public applauded this self-reflexive work written by Helmut Käutner and directed by Rudolf Jugert as a fresh and welcome departure from the traditions of UFA and from the heavy symbolism of the *Trümmerfilm* or *Heimkehrerfilm*.

It is a film about the process of conceiving a film that ends up telling the story of Martin and Christine unfolding during and after the war. Martin is an urbane, middle-aged man from Hannover who hires Christine as a maid for the bourgeois household that he is sharing with his widowed sister, Viktoria. Christine is portrayed as the girl from the country who is often lost in her new surroundings. Nevertheless, a romance develops between the two during the height of the war. The two lovers separate, as Christine leaves the city to return to the family farm and Martin is conscripted in the homeland defense initiative, the *Volkssturm*. After the war they meet again when Martin, after imprisonment and loss of all of his material belongings, seeks refuge on Christine's family's farm. This time it is his turn to feel out of place. After overcoming a series of hurdles—including Christine's father's refusal to let her marry Martin and Martin's failure at his previous career as an antique dealer—the prospects for the two of them to get married eventually become clearer and a happy ending appears possible.

In Robert Shandley's reading of this seminal postwar work, *Film ohne Titel* marks of the "end of the rubble film discourse" by moving away

from the ruins of the metropolis toward the idyll of the countryside.[18]
Similarly, Johannes von Moltke sees this film as a pronounced departure
from the *Trümmerfilm*, but also as a premonition of developments in
the 1950s that pave the way for the *Heimatfilm*.[19] This important transition can be mapped out, in very concrete terms, onto the figure of
Christine, played by Knef. Her figure, and especially her costume, both
embodies the stylistic indebtedness to the rubble film and anticipates
the *Heimatfilm*, with all of the contradictory features of that transition.
The pronounced change of costume in the course of the film parallels
the transformation of Christine's character and demonstrates the effective
ways in which the film, as Hester Baer points out, "caters to spectatorial
fantasies and desires" of postwar female audiences.[20]

As in *Zwischen gestern und morgen*, the young postwar star Knef is
cast contrastively opposite some of the most popular UFA stars from the
Third Reich: Hans Söhnker in the role of Martin and Irene von Meyen-
dorff in the role of Angelika Rösch, Martin's business partner during the
war years. The juxtaposition is best visible in the costuming of the female
characters, whose screen wardrobes were designed by Bessie Becker (in
the credits as Irmgard Becker). Even in the middle of war and deprivation, Angelika projects a consistently luxurious, refined, and glamorous
look. As she leaves a notably paltry dinner in which there is almost no
food on the table and which is under the constant fear of an imminent air
raid, she actually takes the time to stop in front of a mirror and don an
elegant, broad-brimmed black hat. The camera lingers in a long medium
shot on the hat and the torso of Angelika's matching black dress.

Knef's character, on the other hand, is presented during her introduction to the family as the new maid in a full-body long shot that allows
for a full assessment of her distinctly different elegance. She is dressed in
a light-colored plaid coat that while not unfashionable seems much more
practical than Angelika's. As Christine starts working for Martin Delius's
household, the narrative and iconographic references to Susanne from
Die Mörder are hard to miss: the character is outfitted in the same spectrum of neat but down-to-earth outfits, suitable for everyday use, and
she is also engaged in similar array of domestic activities such as cleaning,
straightening up, sweeping, serving food, and so forth. The difference to
Susanne Wallner is emphasized in the altered relationship to art and drawing; instead of creating art, Christine is presented with an art historical
catalogue and asked to consume the images of the Madonna passively,
with little understanding.

A first major turning point in both the story told by the "film without title" and the appearance of Knef's character occurs when Christine
and Martin return to the destroyed villa after the chance encounter in
the air raid shelter. As a sign of the increasing closeness between them

during the evening and as allusion of the breakdown of social differences between them, Marin lets Christine wrap herself up in his sister's fine, shiny silk robe. As she puts it on and confirms that she really likes it, Martin suggests generously, "Dann lassen Sie sich ein Kleid daraus machen" (Have a dress made for yourself out of it), which seems not only a prelude to the sexual affair but also a premonition of Christine's ultimate acceptance into fine bourgeois society.

The second sartorial and narrative turning point occurs soon after Christine leaves Martin's home, after being intimidated by his sister, Viktoria. She first stays in Berlin, where she finds work in a garment manufacturing company (*in der Massenkonfektion*) and then, along with her new employers, joins the stream of Germans escaping the cities and the heavy bombardments. That part of the story told by the film director opens on a row of naked clothes dummies arrayed on the truck on which Christine and her female boss are fleeing Berlin. Upon returning home to her family in the countryside, especially after Martin moves in with them following his ordeals on the front and in the POW camps, Christine displays quite an altered appearance. She is conspicuously well-dressed again, but radiates a different, traditional, rustic charm: her hair is braided; she wears an embroidered peasant shirt and a wide colorful skirt. Her demeanor is no longer shy or awkward. Going back to her roots in the countryside seems to instill in her a clear sense of self-worth and self-assurance. It is not accidental that the magazine *Stern* chose a still from *Film ohne Titel* with Christine leaning against a haystack for the cover of its inaugural issue in August 1948, emphasizing Knef's shift in star image from the "city girl" to the natural "country girl."[21]

Yet during this idyllic time at the farm, Christine is actually being prepared for yet another phase in her life. When she is leaning against the haystacks symbolizing some sort of a rustic arcadia, her hair is not braided anymore around her head, but flowing freely around her face. On Sunday, as soon as she notices that Martin is about to ask her father for her hand in marriage, she is overcome with joy, elatedly runs toward the house, and quickly changes into her most urbane dress so far: a stylish contemporary outfit that seems to be designed specifically for her and that has not been shown on screen before. "Wie siehst du denn aus?" (How good you look!) exclaims her brother, dazzled by her appearance. This final sartorial transformation completes the line of development of the young female character that can be traced by her appearance and wardrobe: she is stylized initially as coming straight out of the rubble film, then she gradually gains confidence, refinement, and independence in order to become, eventually, an elegantly dressed woman ready and eager to enter into a stable, comfortable bourgeois marriage with Martin and embrace the pleasures of the *Wirtschaftswunder*.

Nachts auf den Straßen

Upon her return from a brief and disappointing stay in Hollywood in 1950, Knef starred in the sensationalist film *Die Sünderin*, a work whose immense negative publicity she strove to forget as quickly as possible. Adding to the undesirable publicity was her recent divorce from Kurt Hirsch and rumors about her affairs with the directors Anatol Litvak and Willi Forst. Thus, when the producer Erich Pommer realized a long-standing plan to cast her and Hans Albers in the leading roles of a new film, Knef was elated.[22] Produced by Pommer as Knef's true Germany-comeback and drawing on her newly acquired femme fatale image after *Die Sünderin*, this often forgotten and now rarely discussed film, *Nachts auf den Straßen* (released in 1952 in the UK as *Nights on the Road* and in the United States in 1957 as *The Mistress*), proved hugely important for maintaining her status as both the beloved postwar German star and a leading fashion icon.

After *Film ohne Titel*, *Nachts auf den Straßen* is another product of Knef's successful pre-Hollywood collaboration with the director Rudolf Jugert and the costume designer Bessie Becker.[23] Despite premiering during the height of *Heimatfilm* popularity, this post-rubble film on a contemporary topic did not seem to have any trouble enchanting the audiences; in 1953 it won the German Film Prize for the best film, best director, and best script.[24] It helped Knef reaffirm her own star appeal and also served as a vehicle for Hans Albers, now an aging star, to make a strong comeback in what turned out to be one of his best postwar roles. Most of all, contemporary critics saw this work as harking back to Knef's earlier, unsurpassed triumph in *Film ohne Titel*, where, per *Der Spiegel*, she "could be cool, young and erotic, without appearing frigid, perverse or sentimental/sugary." In *Nachts auf den Straßen*," the *Spiegel* critic wrote, "she returns a bit to her old type."[25] There were even plans to screen the film during the second annual Berlin International Film Festival, in 1952, in the Waldbühne, an outdoor amphitheater in Berlin, with a promise of personal appearances of the two big stars. Festival officials felt that this would draw large number of spectators from the East and West and "unite a divided population even for just a few hours."[26]

Filmed partly in the Bavaria Studios in Munich, partly on location on the Autobahn between Stuttgart and Frankfurt, the plot features the sixty-year-old Hans Albers as a seasoned truck driver, Heinrich Schlüter, with a solid family and impeccable professional reputation, who inadvertently gets involved in some black-market deals and becomes entangled in a romantic relationship with a young woman, Inge Hoffmann (played by Knef), whom he meets on the road. Inge serves initially as a bait to lure Schlüter into the criminal scheme as she catches a ride with him, but subsequently she falls in love with the married man and carries on a lengthy affair with him.

In *Nachts auf den Straßen*, Knef's character appears to have left some of the star's association with the rubble years behind: she is more mature in demeanor and appearance, she has adapted to the new, more prosperous times by working alongside her boyfriend on shady deals, and she cunningly entices Schlüter into going out and spending money on her. If there are some vestiges of her innocent *Trümmermädchen* charm, they may be represented by her signature white raincoat, simple and unpretentious, almost identical to the one that she wears in *Die Mörder*. That is how she is dressed when Schlüter first sets eyes on her and during their first few rides between Stuttgart and Frankfurt. Unlike in any of her earlier films, she is actually shown carefully fixing her appearance, applying makeup in front of a mirror and responding to Schlüter's compliments: "I tried to make myself more beautiful for you." When Schlüter scolds her for being dressed too lightly ("zu dünn angezogen"), she replies, "I only have the old raincoat, and it is too ugly to put over the beautiful frock." After hearing this, Schlüter declares resolutely that he will buy her a new coat. After a cut, the next sequence opens on the two of them strolling through a busy shopping street in Frankfurt am Main. The camera follows the shiny row of store windows, one more attractive than the other, and featuring mannequins with elegant clothes. The plenty and the shopping frenzy of the miracle years are on full display. As if to leave no doubts about Albert and Knef's characters' active participation in that consumption paradise, the subsequent frame zooms in on their reflection in the shop windows as they happily smile while carrying several shopping boxes and bags. Inge is now sporting a new winter jacket with a cap in a matching color; she coquettishly rejects the idea of receiving any more presents, insisting instead on buying Schlüter a new tie.

In a later sequence, in Inge's apartment, Knef's magnificent fashionable transformation is used as a powerful visual parallel to the quickly developing love affair. At the end of the shopping spree, the young woman convinces Schlüter to come upstairs and meet her "brother" (actually her boyfriend). After the boyfriend leaves to go to his regular musician's job at the bar, Inge takes off the housewife's apron that she had on while serving dinner to the two men and proceeds to give her guest a little fashion show, presenting the newly purchased outfits. Knef strides across the room with the ease and poise of a professional model, slightly shifting her hips at every step, pausing, half turning or swirling, taking off the jacket to let the "audience" admire the top underneath, putting it on again, disappearing behind the door in order to reappear shortly in a shiny robe. To her contemporary viewers, this performance must have looked unsurprising and very natural, since by this point, in addition to being a film star, Knef was omnipresent in the West German media as the face of many advertising campaigns for consumer products such as clothes, soap, stockings and even illustrated magazines.[27] In November 1950 she was featured on the cover of *Constanze*, perhaps the most influential magazine among middle-brow female readers.[28] In the November 21 issue of the newsreel *Die neue deutsche Wochenschau* she was featured modeling designs by the Hamburg-based artist Helle Brüns: "Die schöne Sünderin zeigt modische Attraktionen für den Weihnachtstisch" (The beautiful sinner shows fashionable looks appropriate for the Christmas table).

With *Nachts auf den Straßen* Hildegard Knef played her last major starring role on the German screen in a contemporary drama. By now she has matured into a charming, pleasure-loving seducer carrying on some of the femme fatale charm she displayed in *Die Sünderin*. But her melodramatic situation carries the traditional traits of "in-between-ness" so typical for her previous works. Her character is still caught "between yesterday and tomorrow": On the one hand, she is loyal to and cares tenderly for Kurt, her cynical, bitter boyfriend who is mentally stuck in the past because of a traumatizing war wound in his shoulder and is deeply entangled in the criminal world of drugs and smuggling. On the other, she is sincerely attracted to and naïvely infatuated with the older, more settled married man, the long-distance driver Heinrich Schlüter, who is well adapted to the contemporary realities and has embraced a future marked by honest commerce and hard work. At the end, when Kurt is sent to jail and Schlüter returns to his wife, Knef's character Inge seems condemned to be eternally suspended in the present moment, not unlike Suzanne in *Die Mörder*, lacking both a meaningful past and a predictable future. It is not clear what will happen to her after the end of the affair. Nevertheless, Knef's appearance in *Nachts auf den Straßen* seems to be a welcome return to the role of a contemporary postwar woman, who is by now more mature and more experienced and manages to combine and synthesize in her image traits of several previous filmic characters, in which the star has been very successful: Susanne (*Die Mörder*), Kat (*Zwischen gestern und morgen*), and Christine (*Film ohne Titel*).

Throughout the early 1950s Knef continued her career in German cinema with relatively small roles that still capitalized on her appeal as a contemporary German fashion icon. Onstage and off she reaffirmed her reputation as a fashion trendsetter, while displaying her strong relationship to various high-profile fashion designers in West Berlin (Heinz Oestergaard), Munich (Schulze-Varell and Bessie Becker), and Vienna (Fred Adlmüller). Her costumes were crafted by couturiers who used her appearance on the silver screen to shape a lasting impression of exclusive West German elegance, style, and newly gained affluence only a few years after the end of the war, an impression that did not go unnoticed by audiences of different generations.

Oftentimes Knef had a rather minor role, yet her fashionable presence combined with her signature acting style of the early postwar years "stole the show," making her inadvertently a center of visual attention and contributing to the overall success of an otherwise unexceptional film production. Such is the case in *Illusion in Moll* (Illusion in a Minor Key, 1952, directed by Rudolf Jugert), where once again she is cast opposite Sybille Schmitz, deemed at that time to be the much bigger star. Knef plays a young fashion illustrator (*eine junge Modezeichnerin*), Lydia, who is introduced to the audience as she passionately sketches, draws, and works on her designs—another image reminiscent of Susanne in *Die Mörder.* Although Lydia is terminally ill, she manages to intervene successfully in a family tragedy that involves the owner of a luxurious hotel, Maria Alsbacher (Sybille Schmitz), who is to be deceived by a much younger lover. "The content is as thin as the silk of Knef's marvelous dresses," wrote one reviewer, who pointed out that overall the film is saved by "this one and only German actress after 1945 who displays world class."[29] Knef dazzled both critics and the general audience with her superb acting, but especially with her contemporary outfits paraded quite conspicuously onscreen, which she had had specially designed for her by a famous Vienna designer, Fred Adlmüller (the rest of the costumes were credited to a less-known costume designer, Charlotte Fleming).[30] Reviewing the film for Berlin-based *Der Kurier*, Rita Pesserl declared that Knef was the actual "acting motor of this second Pommer production, [performing] without the sinner mannerisms, completely without vamp allure, and without any erotic tricks" ("der . . . schauspielerische Motor dieser zweiten Pommer-Produktion, ganz ohne Sünderinnen-Habit, ganz ohne Vamp-Allüren, ganz ohne erotischen Trick und Tick.").[31] In fact, a major portion of most discussions of the film were dedicated to Hildegard Knef: "She is a typical representative of the modern young woman: uncomplicated, confident, and observing the world with a healthy dose of skepticism," wrote Pesserl, without making clear whether she was talking about the actress herself or her fictional film character.[32] Indeed, for a long time the two had been indistinguishable components of Knef's star status.

Even smaller, yet visually memorable, was Knef's supporting role in another 1953 film, the Cold War drama *The Man Between* (1953), a British production directed by Carol Reed, the director of *The Third Man* (1949).[33] In this political thriller set in Berlin in 1948, Knef plays Bettina, the German wife of a British army doctor, who finds herself in the midst of a complicated scheme to kidnap westerners into the eastern sector. Despite her relatively short presence on screen—she more or less vanishes from the plot after about fifteen minutes—Knef's stands out most of all as the personification of "the elegant and spectacularly clad Berlin woman," emblematic of a city that defiantly projects a glamorous image against the evocative backdrop of vacant lots and bombed-out buildings.[34] In this film, as was her habit in other productions, Knef had outfits supplied especially for her by the legendary salon of Schulze-Varell, whose recognizable and original style had been familiar to audiences since the 1930s

Fig. 19. Advertisement for Luxor soap featuring Hildegard Knef, *Constanze*, June 2, 1951. Staatliche Museen zu Berlin, Kunstbibliothek.

(the other costumes were the responsibility of the British designer Bridget Sellers).[35] In fact, according to critics at the time, Knef's supporting role became memorable primarily because of her acting as "a model for the haute couture designer Schulze-Varell."[36]

By the early 1950s, when Knef performed in these two films, Knef's on- and offstage appearances had become very similar: she had shed the *Trümmermädchen* charm and became the glamorous fashion diva through and through. Both on screen and in the pages of magazines, she unapologetically advertised a variety of consumer products. Knef regularly modeled fashions for magazines such as *Film und Frau*, *Brigitte*, and *Constanze* and was featured in advertisements for Ergee nylon stockings, lipstick, and Luxor soap.[37]

None other than the master fashion photographer F. C. Gundlach staged her in exquisite fashion photographs. Gundlach later commented that Knef was the perfect model for dresses she had labeled "Hildegard" and "Ninotschka," which magazine readers could sew on their own using the patterns published in a special edition of *Constanze*.[38] In the 1990s she even designed her own line of clothing, for working women over forty, in collaboration with costume designer Cordula Stummeyer.[39]

The brief trajectory of Knef's stardom demonstrates how her fashion and her films are caught up in the same duality: they vacillate between continuous engagement with social reality and temporary surrender to the world of fantasy. Her onscreen presence and offscreen appearances complemented each other auspiciously. Her stardom combined groomed glamour and natural beauty and derived its success from a mix of kind treatment by the media and the public's genuine fondness for her. It relied on the right proportion of facts concealed from the fans and the right myths perpetuated by friendly publicity. If initially the fashion practices displayed in her first postwar roles bore the markers of modest normality and were pronouncedly anti-glamorous, by 1950 and beyond, Knef's conspicuous elegance onstage and on the page pointed unabashedly to the aspired-to affluence and materialism of the new decade.

4. Farewell to the Rubble and Welcome to the New Look: *Straßenbekanntschaft* (1948) and *Martina* (1949)

> *It feels good to encounter new faces and not old stars costumed and gotten up as rubble women.*
>
> —P.E., *"Martina,"* review, *Weltbühne*, no. 17, 1949

> *Fashion in Berlin today is the way we don't dress.*
>
> —"Sommer in Berlin," *Mosaik*, July–August 1948

SOME OF THE THEMES ANNOUNCED in the first two postwar rubble films from the East and the West cast a long shadow over the films produced in subsequent years, especially in works that predominantly reflect the lives and struggles of young women. At the same time, films from the end of the 1940s show signs of departure from the aesthetics of the ruins and turn their interests in slightly new directions, toward depicting in detail the pleasures of material comfort and consumption. Whereas *Die Mörder sind unter uns* and . . . *und über uns der Himmel* feature women in supporting roles, highlighting their primary function of assisting—or sabotaging—men's traumatic return from the front to postwar normality, some later films, such as DEFA's *Straßenbekanntschaft* (1948, directed by Peter Pewas) and the West German *Martina* (1949, directed by Arthur Maria Rabenalt) focus exclusively on rebellious girls "hungry for life" ("lebenshungrige Mädchen") as protagonists, caught between conventional familial allegiances and a strong eagerness to live independent lives. In both films, the young heroines at the center of the plot follow similar trajectories: Initially, the precarious postwar circumstances have pushed them into exploitative and criminal schemes; they end up providing sexual favors in exchange for food, fancy clothes, shelter, and security. Gradually, however, through a series of dramatic personal and institutional interventions, these young women's fates are turned around and their psychic and physical wounds are healed as they prepare for a much more stable life within a secure, domestic setting.

As has been common in the bifurcated German postwar film history, *Straßenbekanntschaft* and the lesser-known *Martina* have always been looked at separately. The primary focus has always been on how both works present somewhat predictable narrative paths of downfall and redemption and how their content is sometimes overtly didactic. It seems also that it was quite common at the time for critics in both East and West to issue off-hand rejection of productions from the other side of the divide on a strong ideological bias. The all-too-quickly assigned labels (*Trümmerfilm, Fraulein-Film, Sittenfilm*) and the reference to familiar topics addressed by the script ("Hunger, Heimkehrer, Pappfenster, Hunger, Schieber, Frauenarbeit, Hunger") create the impression that both films were met with little understanding and minimal analysis from many critics on the either side of the political divide.[1]

Missing from the existing approaches to these thematically related works from the East and the West is an attempt to recognize them as interventions into a shared social context, addressing a common female audience as much through the films' narratives as through their settings, costumes, visual aesthetic, and acting styles. A careful consideration of these films' mise-en-scène sheds light on their relationship to various extrafilmic aspects toward the end of the decade: the rising public status of their stars—Gisela Trowe, Ursula Voß, Jeanette Schultze, and Cornell Borchers—and the growth of consumer culture; the elimination of the black market; and the advance of new international fashions, such as Christian Dior's New Look in Germany, coupled with the ascent of a new image of the modern woman. Seen from such a vantage point, the heroines' self-assertiveness and desire for independence appear to be related not so much to their sheer rebelliousness but to a pattern of emerging consumer behavior, to unabashed endorsement of material stability, and to young women's strong need for establishing postwar "normality" on their own terms. All of these are features of both the West and East German societies that began to assert themselves toward the end of the 1940s and gained momentum throughout the 1950s, especially in the West.

A critical reevaluation of these two late-forties films reveals a shared aesthetic in flux, fluctuating between the two more clearly pronounced ideologies and transitioning from the visual dominance of the ruins to the lure of future material abundance. Although originating on either side of the increasingly rigid political divide, the two works exhibit remarkable similarity in their approach to the representation of female crises, in their reexamination of women's material needs and sexual desires, and in their critical attitudes toward key postwar institutions such as the family, press, the police and courts, and the medical establishments. The films also attest to a period in German postwar film history in which professional and political allegiances were not yet fixed, and film professionals—directors, actors, camera people, and even costume designers—still worked in both the East and the West.

The two films' release dates are significant, as they frame a short but crucial phase of tumultuous political and cultural developments that determined the course of the next decade. *Straßenbekanntschaft*, a production of DEFA, was filmed in the renowned Babelsberg Studio (the world's first large film studio) in Potsdam during the second half of 1947 and premiered on April 13, 1948, in East Berlin, at the end of a relatively liberal period for the now-Soviet-controlled film studio. This was just few months prior to the East German government's decree that only party members with sound ideological credentials could occupy leading positions at DEFA, a decree that was followed by a radical personnel reorganization and severe limitation of formal experimentation in film.[2] *Straßenbekanntschaft* was also among a handful of DEFA productions that were distributed in the West as part of an exchange agreement that was in place during 1947 and 1948—it was soon to be superseded by an escalation of East-West tensions in late 1948 and 1949.[3] Its release preceded the currency reform introduced in the Western zones by a week and the year-long Berlin Blockade imposed by the Soviet Union on the Western sectors of Berlin by a good month. Between June 24, 1948, and May 12, 1949, West Berlin was supplied with food, fuel, and virtually anything else needed through the Air Lift, the *Luftbrücke*. *Martina* was produced in West Berlin under those conditions; it opened there on August 19, 1949, shortly after the founding of the Federal Republic of Germany and just before the establishment of the German Democratic Republic.

Thus, during the year and a half that separated the premieres of the films, the foundations were laid for the sharper political divisions of the Cold War. At the same time, the visual media in both East and West Berlin—magazines, newspapers, and newsreels—quickly were transformed and became open toward new international trends and fashions in similar ways. The most prominent change was the open embrace of the New Look and the beginnings of public debates that would determine women's appearance and dress during the upcoming decade. These developments formed the dense intermedial context from which the production and receptions of both *Straßenbekanntschaft* and *Martina* cannot be separated.

The two works feature very similar protagonists, played in both cases by newly discovered and very young actresses: Gisela Trowe plays Erika in *Straßenbekanntschaft*; Jeanette Schultze plays the title role in *Martina*. The criminal scene of Berlin, with its despicable black-market dealers, pimps, and other crooks, forms the background for both films' plots. Further commonalties include the prominent medical discourse, seen in both works as symptomatic for an afflicted society in urgent need of cure. The films reflect extensively on the pervasive experience of hunger and homelessness as well as the counteracting, normalizing pull of prosperity, harmonious heterogeneous relationships, and a cozy bourgeois home.

Curiously, another relative film novice, the actor Siegmar Schneider, makes an appearance in both films, in both cases cast as an idealist journalist on a mission to save the young women in trouble. Finally, costumes for both *Straßenbekanntschaft* and *Martina* were designed by Gertrud Recke. She contributed to the special elegance prominently on display in both films, elegance that took its cues from Christian Dior's New Look, which was advancing internationally. Recke's contribution to both films explains why the two films, despite their diverging political provenance, seem to engage, through their similar mise-en-scène, with the tastes and expectations of their shared postwar, female audience.

Straßenbekanntschaft (1948)

This film takes a special place in DEFA's productions of the immediate postwar years: it was the only film made on explicit commission by the East German public health authorities with the goal of educating the wider public about the hazards of promiscuous behavior and sexually transmitted diseases; it was the director Peter Pewas's only DEFA feature before he left for work in West Germany; and it was one of the few DEFA films of the 1940s that drew big audiences (it was definitely the most profitable film of the year).[4] Despite escalating political confrontations, *Straßenbekanntschaft* was also distributed in West Germany, too. In September and October of 1948, it was released with considerable success in Hamburg and different cities in Niedersachsen, and in late 1949 and the early 1950s it made its way to theaters in Frankfurt, Wiesbaden, and Munich.[5] By 1950 it had reached almost 5.3 million viewers in both parts of Germany.[6]

Part of the reason for its warm reception by postwar audiences was the director's ambition to transform the moralistic material into a truly poetic tale, retold in a sophisticated cinematographic language, replete with convincing characters and stories that the audience could sympathize and identify with. Although he had relatively little control over Arthur Pohl's didactic script with its somewhat stiff and awkward dialogues, Peter Pewas, who had training in art and design at the Bauhaus, transformed the visual appearance of the film by positioning the characters within wide frames and sophisticated interior settings and equipping them with carefully selected costumes. Believing that "the surrounding world should always be present" ("Die Nebenwelt sollte immer präsent werden"), he engaged the cameraman Georg Bruckbauer, who at that time was experimenting with a wide-angle lens.[7] In *Straßenbekanntschaft*, Pewas and Bruckbauer ultimately recreated a cinematic atmosphere of the city that reminded critics of the poetic realism in French cinema of the 1930s or of the neorealist grittiness of later Berlin films from the 1950s by the DEFA duo Gerhard Klein and Wolfgang Kohlhaase.[8] In addition, the filmmakers created a type of female character that made a rare appearance in DEFA cinema, namely, "sensual and full of hunger for life, without negative connotations" ("sinnlich und voller Lebensgier, ohne gleich negativ belastet zu sein").[9]

At the center of the story is a young working-class girl, Erika, who works at a laundry ironing clothes and looks for ways to escape the misery of her postwar life. Blaming her parents' belief in the war for her current desolate situation, she runs away from home. After failing to rent a room of her own, Erika is taken in by her altruistic admirer, Walter (played by Siegmar Schneider), with whom she has a platonic relationship. Walter is relatively poor himself and is dedicated to his work as a local newspaper reporter. Everything that he can't provide her with—real and abundant food, American cigarettes, silk stockings—Erika finds at her friend Annemie's wild parties, where all of these goods are readily available in exchange for sex.

The story of Marion and Herbert is partly parallel to and partly interconnected with that of Erika and Walter. After his release from a POW camp in Bavaria, Herbert returns to Berlin to his wife, Marion, who in the meantime has found work as a conductor on a streetcar and lives in a new apartment in Prenzlauer Berg. Soon after his arrival, he learns by accident that Marion has had an affair with another man during his absence. Herbert runs away from the family home and ends up at Annemie's apartment and, ultimately, in bed with Erika. Shortly thereafter, Marion discovers that she has a sexually transmitted gonorrhea infection and that she has likely passed it on to her husband, who in turn has infected Erika.

After Erika is arrested with a group of single women during a police raid in a city café, she is diagnosed with gonorrhea and sent to the hospital. Terrified and not fully comprehending the consequences of the untreated ailment, Erika escapes from the hospital and runs back to Walter's apartment. However, Walter promises to turn her in to the police if she does not go back to the hospital for treatment. Erika runs away again, this time to Annemie's, where she discovers that Annemie herself had succumbed to the same disease some time ago, has left it untreated, and is now hopelessly ill. Shocked by the discovery and persuaded by the sight of Annemie's physical deformity, usually hidden under her fancy gowns, Erika now returns to the hospital, where she is welcomed by a caring nurse. The happy end is ushered in by a final scene in which Erika leaves the clinic, cured, runs into Walter's passionate embrace, and, we assume, remains reunited with him.

The film crosscuts between the intertwined stories of the married couple, Marion and Herbert, and of the couple-to-be, Erika and Walter. The narrative connection between the two couples is meant to exemplify the ways in which sexually transmitted diseases can spread and affect anyone. The film's real cinematic interest, however, is in the experiences of women. Although men are afflicted to a similar degree as women and are spreading the infection further, it is the female characters who are front and center and who are presented as the true victims within the postwar context, as the disease affects them in the most immediate, visceral ways: they are the ones whose bodies show deformities (Annemie), who experience such a severity of symptoms that they become bed-ridden (Marion), or whose freedom is severely limited as they are rounded up in raids and forced into a hospital (Erika). Infected men, on the other hand, are not targets of any raids, they are not forced to get treatment, and it is not clear how the disease affects their bodies at all.

Most effective in shifting the cinematic focus from the dramas of war-traumatized men to the everyday conundrums and sufferings of Berlin's women is the film's mise-en-scène. A sharp focus on the space in *Straßenbekanntschaft* reverses common interpretations of the work as either a *Trümmerfilm* or a street film from the Weimar era, or a mixture of both.[10] The streets in *Straßenbekanntschaft* may be empty, dark, and somewhat desolate, but the film does not actually feature any real or stylized ruins, either observed directly on the streets nor seen through the windows of Marion's or Walter's apartments. Instead, a giant advertisement for the detergent Persil provides the background for one of the conversations between Erika and Walter, suggesting that Berliners' daily agendas have changed from dealing with rubble to restoring a nicer, cleaner, more intact urban environment. Moreover, as Annette Brauerhoch has pointed out, the big-city street in Pewas's film is freed from any threatening connotations, although it is captured in a style that borrows heavily from Weimar's infatuation with the male voyeur's gaze and with the stark contrast between light and shadow.

Whereas in Weimar-era film the street is an alluring yet dubious space onto which the male's anxiety about female modernity and mobility is projected, in this postwar work the street becomes a positively encoded space, especially for the women in the film. Despite what the title suggests, the chance acquaintances that lead to the spread of sexually transmitted diseases do not take place in the street at all. The broad vistas of the street or other open public spaces in the city captured in Bruckbauer's wide-angle shots is transformed instead into the stage for the fortunate, redemptive, and joyful encounters: that is where Erika meets Walter, who eventually rescues her when she faces virtual homelessness; that is where Marion spots her husband returning after the war and causes all city traffic to stop for a moment; it is there, in the open, next to the streetcar terminus station where the intimate conversations between Marion and her friend Olly, the fellow street-car conductor, take place; and, finally, it is there where the happy reunion between Erika and Walter occurs at the end of the film.

In *Straßenbekanntschaft*, the symbolism of the ruins so prevalent in earlier postwar productions gives way to a careful exploration of the domestic arrangements and living conditions within various apartments and women's self-consciousness and self-presentations in those apartments. Critics such as Ulrich Kurowski saw in Peter Pewas's work an "overvaluing of the decorative elements" ("Übeschätzung des Dekorativen") and a filmic mix of "fashion show" and "advertisement" ("filmische Modenschau und Reklame")—offering perhaps the best insight into an everyday reality that female viewers did not live in, but certainly would very much like to be transported to.[11] In order to explore women's everyday realities, the film ventures almost exclusively into interiors, and these cinematographic explorations seem to reflect the various characters' deep desire to settle into a pleasant home. The first dramatic sequence involving Erika takes place in her parents' home, which she openly detests. Her outburst mentions all of the unbearable features of that place while the camera documents, in frame after frame, the darkness and bareness of the place: the discolored quadrangles on the wall where the pictures used to hang, the empty plate, even the windows lacking glass and covered up with cardboard ("Wie soll ich mich wohlfühlen in diesem Loch mit den verpappten Fenstern?" asks Erika). After she runs away, the young woman faces the real possibility of homelessness as she finds out quickly in a conversation with a landlady that "no rooms are rented to women," only "to men." She also does not seem to possess the "currency" needed to barter for a shelter in postwar Germany, namely food or fine linen ("etwas Nahrhaftes," "feine Bettwäsche") As chance would have it, Erika soon meets her savior, Walter, who invites her to stay in his apartment. While he outlines the advantages of his current dwelling situation, with a particular emphasis on the material comforts that it offers ("seidene Tapeten," "grüner Leuchter," "fliessendes Wasser") and as Erika repeats the list approvingly, the camera zooms in on these attractive features in quick succession. She accepts Walter's offer and moves in with the understanding that this is a purely platonic relationship—she does not have to pay him with sex for being offered the luxury of a real home.

The longing for a proper place to live is prominent in the second plot line as well. As Herbert returns to Berlin from the prisoner-of-war camp, he is surprised that his wife has never received his letters during the last couple of years—this is because he has sent them to the old address. In the meantime, Marion explains proudly and cheerfully, she has moved to new apartment in Prenzlauer Berg and it is supposedly a bigger and better one, but cozy as well, as they still have the old furniture. That Herbert subsequently takes care of this place also seems an unusual, subtle, and benevolent cinematic commentary on the comfort that postwar Germans, both men and women, took in possessing a safe and pleasant domestic setting.

After donning one of his wife's aprons, he mops the floor, shakes the rug, and cleans up around the house during the day while Marion is at work.

More than anything else, however, it is women's appearances and rituals of self-presentation, self-staging, and grooming that convey this film's sympathetic endorsement of material indulgencies and of women's newly gained postwar self-confidence as real or potential consumers. Such scenes seem to be in direct conflict with the narrative points and the original didactic charge of the film, but since they are exquisitely staged and photographed, their aesthetics is much more effective and moving than their moral messages. Although women's untamed materialistic desires are supposed to be condemned by this "educational film" ("Aufklärungs-film") as consumerist impulses that lead into real physical danger, the two relatively long scenes in which Erika and her friend Else (played by Ursula Friese) put on the coveted transparent silk stockings are filmed with gentle empathy for the characters rather than with condemnation. Instead of constructing caricatures of materialism, the camera offers us a benevolent peek into two instances of young women's narcissism.

Unlike *Die Mörder*, we don't have here a parade of different costumes presented by a single protagonist; rather, we have the whole spectrum of fashion options distributed among the cast. The choice of costume depends on the specific social situation of the respective woman, and that outfit provides a powerful visual commentary on the personal drama of that female character. For most of the film, Erika appears—in a relatively plain and modest outfit, a white shirt and a darker skirt, but what attracts immediate attention is the glossy sheen of its fabric, possibly satin, which gives her, in a subtle way, an unusually stylish appearance. Her dressing style of unostentatious elegance did not go unnoticed by the critics, who praised the "optic perfection" and the "realistic documentary value" of the film.[12] She was identified as the "one that is nicely and neatly dressed" ("schön und sauber Gekleidete") and it is her clothes that mark the progress she has made in postwar Germany already: from the "tattered clothes" and "torn shoes" ("die zerfetzten Kleider," "die kaputten Schuhe") that were Erika's only option during the war (and that she complains about bitterly in her short monologue before running away from home) to this neat outfit that is suitable for both work and the dancing party she is going to.[13] Erika's sober stylishness is reminiscent of Susanne Wallner's and at the same time stands in stark contrast to the dresses of the women dancing with abandon at the "black-marketeer orgy." Ultimately, Erika's looks are juxtaposed directly to Annemie's, the hostess (played by Alice Treff), whose glamorous outfits, as the Berlin newspapers reported at the time with indignation, had to be rented from a West Berlin designer salon for the then-astronomical sum of 3,000 deutschmarks.[14]

The most interesting fashion display in the film, and perhaps most appealing to the audience because is strikes a middle ground between

Fig. 20. Still from *Straßenbekanntschaft* (1948) showing
Marion (Ursula Voß) in her new dress.

extreme austerity and extreme glamour, is associated with Marion, who
puts on quite a show for the audience when she arrives home from work
after a visit at the hair dresser's. Unaware that her husband is actually
not in the apartment, she starts telling him about her new and "amazing
hairdo," coquettishly touching the sides of her head. She walks around
the apartment, setting down her shopping bag on a table and quickly
checking her appearance in the mirror. The camera follows her, showing
in full length and from all sides the extraordinary, elegant dress she has
on, a dress that is a stark contrast to the more or less utilitarian outfits
she wears at work. As if coming straight out of the pages of a fashion
magazine, the dress is made out of two materials, white tulle combined
with strips and patches of colorful embroidered fabric that accentuates
the waist and sleeves and lengthens the hem. Overall, her relative affluence on display at this moment and her enjoyment of bourgeois comforts are coded positively and endorsed visually on the screen, if not by
the script.

Running counter to the ideological and educational message of the film, Marion's amazing sartorial and overall material progress is retrospectively contextualized and condoned by her moving monologue later, at daybreak in the kitchen. In it she recounts her life during the war and immediate postwar years. In this monologue she seems to speak for all women, for Marion says "we women" ("wir Frauen"): "Hardly anyone of you knows how we women lived at home. Every morning—off to the factory, coming back late at night, hungry, to a cold room. Then there is the air raid siren, fear and hopelessness. Isn't it understandable then that we want to console ourselves? And how much do we want: some warmth, food, a colorful dress, a head scarf, some joy in order to learn to laugh, finally."[15] This statement expressed a common sentiment among women in the postwar period. By staging such implicit mini-fashion shows, postwar films acknowledged a very personal aspect of the quest for normality and rebuilding that was quite relevant to women in Germany after the war: the quest to look good and be comfortable.

Martina (1949)

The West German film *Martina* (1949) can be considered a curious thematic and stylistic counterpart to DEFA's *Straßenbekanntschaft*, although it had quite a different production history. Whereas the DEFA film was a result of an official government assignment to create an "educational product," *Martina* was released after an elaborate publicity campaign aimed at piquing audiences' curiosity and ensuring, ultimately, a huge commercial success for the film. At the beginning of October 1948, many newspapers appearing in the Western zones carried the following announcement: "Mädchen Martina als Hauptdarstellerin in einem kommenden Berlin-Film gesucht. Alter 18 Jahre, Hauptbedingung: Gefallener Engel." (Wanted: A girl, Martina, to play the main character in an upcoming Berlin film. Age: 18. Main requirement: Fallen angel.)[16] According to one newspaper article, "Who Will Become Martina?," there were hundreds of responses not only from actresses but also from young women with various backgrounds—"Sekretärinnen, Verkäuferinnen, Studentinnen, Kellnerinnen, Friseusen und Modistinnen" (secretaries, saleswomen, students, waitresses, hairdressers, and models)—who imagined that it would not be too difficult to play a Berlin girl who has slipped off the right path, but ultimately finds her way back into decent life.[17]

Hoping to "become the next Hildegard Knef," many of the young candidates filled out a questionnaire, attached a recent photograph, and sent their application to the Comedia-Gesellschaft in Berlin. They were promised that about two dozen of these pictures would be published in *Illustrierter Telegraf* and these lucky girls would at least have fifteen minutes of fame.[18] At the end, the title role was assigned to seventeen-year old Jeanette Schultze, a graduate of DEFA's fully state-funded Schauspielstudio für Bühne und Film, who had started her career in *Die Brücke* (The Bridge, 1948, directed by Artur Pohl) and in another film directed by Rabenalt, *Anonyme Briefe* (Anonymous Letters, 1949).[19] Cornell Borchers, who also began her film career in *Anonyme Briefe*, took the role of Martina's sister, the physician. These became the two very young and recently discovered actresses whose photogenic and perfectly made-up faces appear in close-ups throughout the film, facing the audience directly or obliquely, from a reflection in a mirror.

The process of filming also drew the public's attention. Although the majority of the work was completed in the Tempelhof Studios in Berlin, a few scenes at the beginning were shot in front of the Schöneberg City Hall, and the director, Rabenalt, made a media event out of this. A week ahead of the filming he published an announcement in the Berlin daily newspapers encouraging Berlin housewives to come to the set if they wished to appear as unpaid extras in the film *Martina*.[20]

The film recounts the struggles of a young *Berlinerin*, Martina, who has lost her family during the war. She engages in black-market deals and prostitution to survive, as a result of which she is tried as a minor and sent to a reform school. She escapes, tries to reconnect with her older sister, and looks for new beginning. In the course of the narrative, her past traumas are revealed and healed, her true identity is gradually recovered, and the path toward a career and a successful life in postwar Germany is cleared of obstacles.

Despite the unusual publicity surrounding the film, its reception after its premiere on August 10, 1949, was mixed. Similar to *Straßenbekanntschaft*, *Martina* encountered rejection as well as enthusiastic acceptance, and the reactions to both films were driven by comparable motivations. Many audience members were annoyed by yet another *Trümmerfilm*, another film on the topic of postwar trauma and recovery, based on a poorly written and overtly didactic script and with a fairytale ending. For East German critics, the opening of the film caused an additional displeasure. A black screen appears showing an image of a bear tearing its chains surrounded by a text "Filmed in blockaded Berlin" (the bear is a traditional symbol of Berlin). With this image the filmmakers referred defiantly to the difficult material conditions—rationed electricity and goods during the Blockade—under which the work was made.[21]

Yet numerous critics saw the film as an "authentic document of the times" ("echtes Zeitdokument") that paid tribute through its title character to the uneasy fate of many young women in the postwar years, with sympathy and without prejudice.[22] Critics saw the film as an attempt to finally liberate women from the stigma associated with terms such as *Fräulein*, *Amiflittchen*, and *Veronika*. These designations were commonly used to refer to young German women who struck up relationships with US soldiers. Additionally, the cultural stereotype of the *Fräulein* implied youthfulness, promiscuity, and a strong orientation towards consumerism.[23] In the context of the time and with its strong negative connotations, *Fräulein* was in stark contrast to *Trümmerfrau*.

However, the protagonist Martina only seems to be a *Fräulein*. Her story is somewhat different: she is presented as the victim of tragic circumstances and sensationalist media reports that she fights against, until she manages to find her way back into postwar German society.

Martina Riess is introduced as a girl who lost her parents during an air raid at the age of sixteen. Amidst the chaos of the last war months she has also lost contact with her sister Irene and become a *Flakhelferin* (anti-aircraft auxiliary). For a long time she believes that she had killed a man who tried to rape her and is tortured by feelings of guilt. After the end of the war, she tries to forget about her traumatic experiences and chooses a new identity, calling herself Ernestine Kusczinski, Tinny for short, and presents herself as the girlfriend of an American GI, Johnny. In reality, however, she is involved in the criminal scene of postwar Berlin and works for black-marketeers and pimps. Her actual boyfriend is Donny, not Johnny, and he is no American, but a German crook who uses her recklessly for his criminal schemes.

After multiple arrests, she is sent to a reform school for girls, where she manages to escape and reconnect with Irene, now an established neurologist, trained in psychoanalysis. In her sister's nicely furnished apartment she meets the Swedish reporter Volker, whom she manages to convince in the course of time that she is not a "Chesterfield-Girl" or a "Schoko-Lady" or any type of "Fräulein" that he is constantly photographing for the illustrated magazines abroad, because the female audience "can't get enough of these images." At the end of the film, Martina is also healed from the trauma, regains her original identity, and enters into a happy relationship with Volker.

The central figure of Martina is a suitable point of departure for any analysis that attempts to recover the status of this film both as foreshadowing the 1950s and in intensive dialog with earlier rubble films, such as Mizzi in . . . *und über uns der Himmel* and especially with the female protagonists in the DEFA productions *Die Mörder sind unter uns* and *Straßenbekanntschaft*. Like Erika, Martina is presented as a self-absorbed, independent, and rebellious young woman, on the run and on the brink of getting into serious trouble with the authorities. Both young women seem to reject vehemently the ethos of their parents' generation, whom they hold responsible for the war and the ensuing chaos, and seek a complete break with the past. That break with the past horrors of war is defined not only by the radical gesture of assuming a new identity (Ernestine instead of Martina) but also in terms of unabashedly embracing the offerings of the present, and more specifically, American-flavored consumption: smoking American cigarettes, listening to jazz, reading *Life* magazine, eating good meals, and wearing fine clothes. Both women's rapacious hunger for life's pleasures is simultaneously an expression of a deep yearning for normality and stability in everyday life. Upon entering her sister's apartment, Martina, very much like Erika during her visit to Walter's home, can't help but walk around and admire all signs of peacetime material comfort: the nice furniture, the intact wallpaper, and the beautiful paintings on the wall. Ultimately, both Erika and Martina will find a suitable solution to their postwar homelessness that will offer a loving male partner as well as a cozy living space.

Notably, the character of Martina harks back also to the first postwar film production with a Soviet license, *Die Mörder sind unter uns*. It combines features of both the female protagonist, Susanne Wallner, and the male protagonist, Hans Mertens. Like Hans Mertens, the *Heimkehrer*, Martina suffers from the psychological effects of a wartime trauma. Troubled by their memories, both the former Wehrmacht officer and the *Flakhelferin* seek refuge in the shady milieu of black-market dealers and dance bars. Only when they lose consciousness—on the operating table (Martina) or in the hospital (Mertens)—are they able to confront their past traumas. Unlike Mertens, however, Martina is completely healed at the end of the film, in the clinical sense of the word, for her sister applies psychoanalytical methods of treatment while Martina is in a state of hypnosis. For Mertens, many questions about the future linger.

The comparison to Susanne Wallner also reveals striking similarity. Like Wallner, Martina connects to "normality" as she takes up a creative activity, drawing. Martina's sketches, portraits, and caricatures draw the attention of her new friend, the Swedish reporter Volker. With his help she manages to sell them to a newspaper and get her first respectable job. Martina resembles and even surpasses Susanne Wallner most of all in terms of her elegant appearance. She, too, dazzles with the rich palette of outfits that are appropriate for the various occasions, which the camera reveals every time in long close-ups: a light-colored raincoat with a shiny strip at the edge of the collar, neat blouse-and-skirt ensembles, and smartly cut dresses. This emphasis on elegant costume in the film is reinforced by the appearance of Irene, Martina's sister, who, being several years older than Martina, presents a slightly different style of dresses, but equally elegant and, more important, in abundance so that she can easily lend some of her clothes to her sister. Such a double visual spotlight on the variety of elegant outfits must have been noticed by the audience—it certainly irritated some male critics. Wolfdietrich Schnurre sarcastically remarked that the film's female characters wore "excellently cut clothes that could fill up whole fashion magazines" ("ausgezeichnet geschneiderte Garderoben, die ganze Modejournale aufwiegen")[24]

One sequence in the film draws particular attention not only to current fashion, but also to the concrete practices associated with its creation. The scene takes place in Irene's apartment just as she is preparing to host a Christmas party. Martina arrives unannounced—she had just run away from the reform school—and soon asks her sister to lend her some nice clothes for the evening. During the next two minutes we witness her skillful preparations for the party, as her image is quadrupled on the screen: we see her in profile as well as her triple reflection in the three-part mirror, while she gives postwar women audiences a lesson in beauty care and grooming. Displaying a quite revealing piece of sexy lingerie, Martina proceeds to shave her armpits and then, visibly dissatisfied with the trendiness of the dress lent by her sister, goes on to alter it with the help of some scissors. While she is cutting up the old-fashioned dress (or more likely, judging by the results, cutting out parts of the dress to remove the sleeves and widen the décolleté), she is glancing at a page of a magazine propped on the table. The image depicted in the fashion magazine seems to be providing the inspiration and the exact directions for her work with the scissors. Once she has finished transforming the dress, Martina makes a dazzling entry into the dining room, where all the guests, including her sister, look at her with amazement. To Irene's incredulous remark about what has happened to her dress, Martina replies nonchalantly, "Chic, was?"

This scene of Martina's transformation was particularly relevant to the female viewers among the audience in that specific historic moment. First of all, it gives a visual lesson in grooming for the modern woman. The short but detailed filmic representation of the process of cutting and sewing combines references to two common fashion discourses of the postwar years. First, it demonstrates the application of the familiar principle "From old make new" ("Aus alt macht neu") that has been in place in the fashion media actually since the war years. Second, and more important, it depicts Christian Dior's New Look, with its pronounced feminine silhouette, thin waist, tightly fitting bodice, a longer and fuller skirt, and narrow, slouching shoulders, which had been taking hold in Europe since early 1947, including in Germany, though not without controversy. In any case, by early 1948 the phrase "New Look" had entered the vocabulary of the mass media and the associated visuals had conquered women's imagination in war-ravaged Germany.

As much as this sequence in *Martina* is staged as a spectacle for the voyeuristic male gaze, it is also a narcissistic exhibition of women's pleasures associated with fashion and perhaps even as an anticipation of the material insouciance, abundance, and indulgent consumerism of the 1950s. It demonstrates what women have learned from reading the postwar women's and fashion magazines. Such a perspective is very much in tune with the discussions and presentations in the magazines of the late

Figs. 21a and 21b. Martina (Jeanette Schultze) transforms an
old dress into a New Look outfit in *Martina* (1949).

1940s, whence both Erika and, to a greater extent, Martina were taking
their cues and passing on the fashion advice to their female audiences.
Gertrud Recke, the costume adviser and designer for the two films, was
translating the magazine pages into film costumes. She was well aware of
the mass-mediated fashion trends and their importance for women's postwar experiences, since she herself happened to be a regular contributor to
the magazines.

Costume Designers and the New Look

Little is known about Gertrud Recke. She is credited for the costume
design of almost a dozen films between 1942 und 1955, the best known
among them being *Die Mörder sind unter uns* (1946) and *Ehe im Schatten*
(1947, DEFA, directed by Kurt Maetzig). After the Munich-based couturier Bessie Becker, Recke seems to have been one of the most influential
and sought-after costume designers of the 1940s, making a smooth transition from her work in wartime productions of the Third Reich to the
postwar years. Both Recke and Becker, along with a few other women,
started working in the film industry at a time when many of the male
designers on staff were recruited into military service, which opened
unprecedented professional opportunities for young and unknown female
fashion designers. Their careers in film lasted till the mid- to late 1950s,
but the works of the immediate postwar years form a definite highlight
in their professional accomplishments. The short illustrated article published in April 1949 in the magazine *Film Illustrierte* especially targeted
the attention of "the female film fans" ("die weiblichen Filmfreunde") by
introducing a less-known and less-prolific costume designer for film, Irmgard Hartmann, but its statement is very relevant to Recke's work: "Fashion plays a big role in contemporary film. The dresses worn by the actors
save us a trip to a fashion show. The influence of film in this sphere cannot

be overestimated. Films must show 'real' costumes. It takes knowledge, skill, and taste to design New Look costumes. Fräulein Hartmann, known from her contributions to contemporary fashion magazines, must be well familiar with the script in order to grasp the atmosphere and the milieu. . . . She designs most of the costumes, but frequently outfits must be obtained on loan from fashion salons."[25]

Parallel to her work for the movies, Recke published illustrations and short texts on fashion in the Berlin-based monthly *Mosaik: Das Weltbild der Frau*, which was founded in 1947 under a license from the British occupation authorities by the professional master seamstress (*Schneidermeisterin*) and Social Democratic activist Annedore Leber.[26] Like other publications aimed at an exclusively female audience, *Mosaik* had an extensive section dedicated to fashion and supplied patterns as well. In the inaugural issue, October 1947, the publisher included a statement that summarized the mission of the numerous such magazines that cropped up in the wake of the war: "This monthly magazine will display the harsh, sober, and not particularly attractive colors of our present time that form the background of our daily life. Yet we expect that the bright spots of those sides of life that are cheerful, lovely, and full of human warmth will illuminate the dark canvas of our postwar existence. In combination with the glow of the big world out there, it will point to the goal that we have to pursue."[27] One of these "highlights" that originated in the "big and faraway world" was undoubtedly Christian Dior's Ligne Corolle collection, which had been launched in Paris earlier that year and had spontaneously been described as a "new look" by Carmel Snow, the editor in chief of *Harper's Bazaar*.

After its premiere in February 1947, Dior's collection enjoyed unqualified success in Paris, New York, everywhere in Europe, and worldwide. Many experts agree that it remains the most influential single event in fashion history.[28] Emblematic for the New Look was an exaggeratedly feminine silhouette, marked by a tiny, often corseted waist, ample hips, narrow shoulders, and a long, voluminous skirt. In the course of the subsequent decade, until Dior's untimely death in 1957, the hemlines moved up and down, and skirts went from full to narrow and back again, but the New Look preserved a recognizable stylistic continuity.

The immediate transnational appeal of Dior's controversial fashion style was based, as Ilya Parkins has demonstrated, on a complex temporal logic.[29] Its "revolutionary" quality was derived, paradoxically, from the gesture of reclaiming what we may consider an older, more conservative, if not precisely historically definable, ideal of feminine beauty. To the dismay of many, Dior reversed the effects of a previous fashion revolution that had been instigated by another French designer, Paul Poiret: around 1900. Poiret eliminated the "three-dimensional dress" with its tight corset and various upholstering and let the garments flow naturally around the body. Many claimed that after the New Look, the New Woman associated with modern femininity of the 1920s and to a certain extent in the 1930s was gone.

Clearly, however, Dior was reacting to wartime iterations of the feminine in Paris and elsewhere in Europe, which included utilitarian clothing based on austere designs that corresponded to the reality of rations and extreme fabric scarcity. The designer thought that women were quite tired of reconfiguring old men's suits, uniforms, drapery, and table clothes and fragments of old clothing into new garments, and were ready at least to dream of something new, even if they couldn't own it. In additional, some historians have claimed that the New Look presented an important symbolic point of departure from or even helped repress the shameful memories of fashion under the Vichy regime and Nazi occupation, during which collaborationist couturiers introduced "vogue for folk styles" and proposed a return to medievalist, rustic ideals of femininity.[30] In any case, the New Look launched by Dior in 1947 set the tone for the important cultural process of breaking away from a painful war and postwar past to embrace a new sense of normality, based on an image of exaggerated femininity, enhanced consumption, and freedom from material want.

In December 1949 Dior arrived in Germany with his models for sold-out shows in Hamburg and Heidelberg upon the invitation of the leading fashion biweekly magazine *Constanze* (founded in April 1948 in Hamburg).[31] Although *Constanze* has always given itself credit for bringing the New Look to West Germany, the public in the West and the East was already familiar with Dior's name and styles.[32] The coverage in women's and fashion magazines started in mid- to late 1947. First to report about the new trend hailing from Paris was the Berlin-based fashion paper *Chic*, founded under a French license, and the biweekly illustrated *Heute*, published by the American military authorities.[33] Both venues unequivocally endorsed this "revolution of fashion" as the material expression of a new femininity that bade the postwar ruins farewell and was to become the ideal of the coming years: "Two men from Paris's haute couture, Jacques Fath and Christian Dior, created the new peacetime woman: gentle, feminine, and most likely seductive, if she knows how to play along ("die Frau des Friedens: zart, weiblich und höchst wahrscheinlich sehr verführerisch, wenn sie zu spielen versteht").[34] Starting in June 1947, in every issue *Chic* featured designs by Christian Dior and New Look–inspired models with long skirts, hour-glass waists, and soft, sloping shoulders. The articles called Dior "the creator of new feminism" ("der Schöpfer des neuen Feminismus") and expressed complete and unquestioning embrace of the New Look in both text and sumptuously illustrated features.[35]

Other women's magazines, such as *Mosaik*, were also quick to publish accounts of Dior's ascendance in Europe, but they were much more ambivalent about this revolution. In an article "Are Legs out of

Fashion?," the publication's fashion editor outlined the complete imprac-
ticality (not to mention utter unaffordability) of Dior's new style for the
regular German woman and speculated that many would certainly not be
happy at all: "The whole cut, the whole silhouette, all the frills complete
with corset, feathered hat, and veil point to the capricious and ladylike
style that can be seen in the French fashion magazines and that seems
borrowed from a different century. These changes signal the beginning
of a complete transformation of fashion. And they will be met everywhere with worry."[36] Yet on the same page, next to this critical article,
the magazine published at least a dozen illustrations of designs reflecting
Christian Dior's New Look. This duality of rejection and acceptance, of
reservation and enthusiasm, of condemnation and embrace, was to typify
for Dior's mass-mediated reception in Germany: the editorial text would
be cautious, reticent, or outright critical of the New Look's implications
for women's everyday fashion practice, while the elaborate visuals—photographs and drawings—would exhibit details about the House of Dior
and document the ways in which leading German designers were already
bowing to its decrees.

Curiously, the leading fashion magazine, *Berlins Modenblatt*, delayed
its coverage of Dior's new line by almost a year after its first appearance
in the Paris salon, most likely out of concern that German women would
find it both extravagant and unaffordable to take to Dior's fashion dic-
tate.[37] Then, in January 1948, it published an extensive article under the
title "Über kurz oder lang . . ." (About short or long . . .; a pun because
kurz oder lang also means "sooner or later" and "the long and the short
of it"), in which the magazine's fashion editor, Anna Paula Wedekind-
Pariselle, took stock of recent developments and the current situation:

> A Paris fashion designer, not of the old guard . . ., but one of the
> young, audacious ones, has the, let us be honest, absurd idea of
> reviving the most unflattering fashion that was ever invented. And
> he is successful with it worldwide! . . . He is revolutionizing fashion,
> rejecting everything that has hitherto been viewed as beautiful; he is
> even trying to reintroduce the corset and is managing to do so! He
> . . . hides the legs. In an age that is trying everywhere to fight for the
> equality of women, he turns women into helpless delicate creatures,
> whose wasp waists rise up as they once did, slender and fine out of
> a mass of fabric. . . . Paris has received the new line with enthusi-
> asm; from England we hear that the long (however, usually tight)
> skirt has prevailed, and from America there are reports of vociferous
> diverging opinions. . . . "Long or short" is also the subject of heated
> debate here at home but tending to mere rhetoric.[38]

Despite its pointed critique of the purported fashion revolution, the
magazine did not fail to publish in the same issue illustrations of six New

Fig. 22. Dior's models arrive in Hamburg, *Constanze*, no. 1, 1950.
Staatliche Museen zu Berlin, Kunstbibliothek.

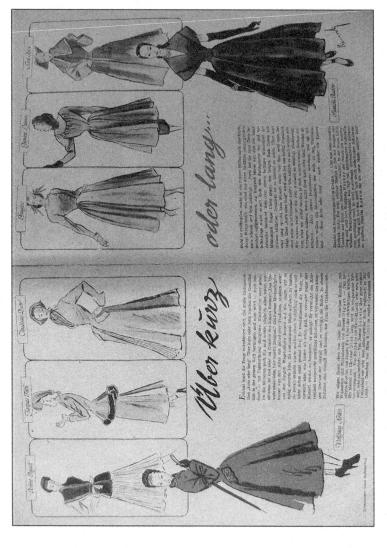

Fig. 23. Discussion of the New Look in *Berlins Modenblatt*, January 1948.
Staatliche Museen zu Berlin, Kunstbibliothek.

Look designs by Christian Dior, Jacques Fath, Jeanne Lanvin, and Nina Ricci, among others, as well as two Dior-inspired outfits by the German designers Wolfgang Nöcker and Sinaida Rudow. Thus, the rhetoric of "wait and see and don't rush to accept any of these crazy ideas" was immediately undermined by the tempting images. It seemed that the new Paris style was there to stay, and soon, all fashion publications in Germany found themselves giving advice to their readers on how to adapt to the new guidelines, especially to the decree of a longer skirt that required so much more fabric than it was feasible to find under the conditions of rations and general shortage. The desire to be in sync with European trends and international style, however, was prevailing; this was the yearning to move away from the shameful past, from postwar practices of thrift, inventiveness, and patchwork, on to a new era of seemingly boundless opulence and abundance. By April 1948, when the new summer models were premiered, fashions in Berlin as represented on the pages of the magazines were indistinguishable from those in Paris. Virtually all Berlin couturiers—from Heinz Oestergaard and Gehringer & Glupp to Charlotte Glückstein, Melitta Gründt, and Sinaida Rudow—had adopted the New Look.[39] *Straßenbekanntschaft* was reviewed in the same April issue that presented the German versions of the New Look and celebrated their irreversible triumph.

It is noteworthy that fashion magazines distributed in East Berlin and the Soviet Occupation Zone kept pace with the trend and kept their reader abreast of developments in Paris, despite the editors' consistent ideological reservations vis-à-vis any fashion decrees coming from the capitalist West. *Die Frau von heute*, a socialist women's magazine published by the antifascist women's committees, repeatedly acknowledged that, East and West, "Our young women wish strongly to live and be allowed to enjoy their youth . . . They take pleasure in dancing, even if they are surrounded by ruins. . . They like going to the movies and the theater and are interested in fashion."[40] Therefore, the magazine offered regular advice on how to adjust or simplify the New Look to the prevailing conditions without compromising the general silhouette.[41] Two Berlin-based designers Ursula Schewe and Hanni Christ were often featured on the pages of the magazine, and when their work became daringly close to Dior's models, the editor needed to provide a qualifying, almost apologetic explanation:[42]

> In the same way that is it possible to adapt our hair styles to those of the Parisian or American woman, we can borrow from a fashion that we principally reject some points of inspiration that can serve us well. The designers Hanni Christ and Ursula Schewe have found good solutions: their designs follow the style of the new fashion without imposing on the wearer the dictatorship of the New Look. The leave

it to the customer to adopt those elements that appeal to her. Most of the models are made for export, but "export" often means sales within Berlin. This is the reason why these salons follow the new trend more closely that we consider right.[43]

Here, as it was common in other magazines, the strong reservations voiced in the text were routinely dwarfed by a two-page spread filled with the sumptuous illustrations of at least a dozen Dior-inspired models. The New Look was to be seen at the March 1948 Leipzig Trade Fair, where fashion designers from all four occupation zones were putting their export production on display. "The New Look is here—not in its Parisian, English, or American form, but in its German one. The many orders placed are proof that it can be also pleasing," announced the journalist for *Die Frau von heute* who visited the fair.[44]

The availability of fabrics and other materials remained the biggest concern for German women who were trying to follow the new fashion, especially if they wanted a dress that called for a longer and fuller skirt. For women who lived the American occupation zone, part of the solution was the CARE (Cooperative for American Remittances to Europe) packages donated to German citizens by US individuals and relief organizations. Initially the CARE packages contained predominantly food, but in February 1947, 35,000 packages of a new type arrived in Berlin: the "CARE Blanket Package." In addition to food the packets contained two woollen Army surplus blankets and a "complete set of sewing supplies."[45] Leading designers at the New York Dress Institute—Claire McCardell, Madame Eta, and Emily Wilkens—had developed patterns that were meant to help Berlin women fashion for themselves "practical and good-looking garments out of utilitarian blankets." Lilly Daché also designed a hat to be made out of the scraps that were left over when the coats are made.[46] The German illustrated press publicized the patterns that had been developed especially for the CARE packages so that "impatient women" could sew their own garments, and according to various reports, fashion designers around Germany were ready to work out a whole new line of winter coats.[47] The shipments of fabrics to Berliners increased in volume during the Berlin Blockade, and even though many in both the illustrated press and fashion industry were forced to shrink their operations or leave the city and move to West Germany, the regular fashion cycle in Berlin with its spring and autumn shows, the launching of new lines, and even the delivery of exported items abroad was sustained.[48]

Schultze, Borchers, and Trowe as "New Look Girls"

With all the media saturation, very likely by 1948 the female audience expected to see the New Look on the silver screen as well, especially when it came to the representations of contemporary women. When the light-hearted DEFA comedy *Träum nicht, Annette!* (Don't Dream, Annette!, 1949, directed by Eberhard Klagemann), with the viewers' darling Jenny Jugo in the title role, was released in early February 1949, the inconsistency of costume was immediately picked up in the press: "Women audience members have noticed that during the day Annette (Jenny Jugo) runs around in New Look outfits, while she goes out at night in a skirt that hardly reaches her knees." This mixture of extravagant New Look and anachronistic old look was seen by some critics as a sign that the DEFA-film was "neither contemporary, nor anti-capitalistic" ("weder zeitnah, noch antikapitalistisch").[49] The explanation for this stylistic inconsistency, which partially exonerated the film's costume designer, Hans Kieselbach, was that the filming of *Träum nicht, Annette!* had begun before the war and was completed under new, somewhat chaotic production conditions in 1948.[50]

The contestants for the role of Martina, on the other hand, did not want to leave anything to chance. When they responded to Comedia's call for actresses in late 1948, they made sure that their photographs portrayed them in outfits of the latest fashion. Reporting on the sensational contest and its "650 contenders from all four occupation zones, despite the Blockade," *Berliner Filmblätter* featured the photographs of eight "new-look-Mädchen" who had been called for auditions.[51] In the years following the premieres of both *Straßenbekanntschaft* and *Martina*, in a similar fashion as *Die Mörder sind unter uns* and . . . *und über uns der Himmel*, the young, attractive, and previously unknown actresses were catapulted into a brief stardom. Of course that depended on a strong media presence in the mass-circulation women's and fashion magazines and the publication of numerous illustrated stories that blended filmic and extrafilmic appearance of these actresses, their public and private lives. In Jeanette Schultze's case, the cultivation of star allure started even before the premiere of the film, with numerous articles revealing her charisma and beauty as an actress.[52] Photographs of Gisela Trowe and Jeanette Schultze, along with Hildegard Knef and Heidi Scharf, were featured in an article that discussed new hairstyles for 1949.[53] As much as they served as guidelines for the new styles, the actresses' images and the corresponding commentary on Trowe's "unruly flying hair" ("ungebändigt flatternde Haare") and on Schultze's "preference for uncoiffed hair" ("Vorliebe zum Unfrisierten") also contained clear references to their recent film roles in *Straßenbekanntschaft* and *Martina* as rebellious young women.[54] Cornell Borchers's star persona, on the other hand, was shaped very much after Hildegard Knef's model for stardom: the publicity around her emphasized the balance of youth and intelligence, reserve and beauty, and, most important, her potential to have a career in Hollywood and become an international star.[55]

The infatuation with the young film stars was surprisingly strong in East German fan magazines as well: glamorous photographs of Trowe and Scharf appeared on the covers of different issues of the DEFA journal, *Neue Film-Welt*, and the two young film actresses worked in both West and East German film productions.[56] The same was true for other filmmakers: the directors A. M. Rabenalt, Wolfgang Staudte, and Peter Pewas, the cameraman Georg Bruckbauer, the composer Werner Eisbrenner, and the costume designer Gertrud Recke were among those working alternately or simultaneously in DEFA and Western projects.[57] Surprisingly, against the background of the Berlin Blockade and intensifying political tensions between the East and the West, at the movies people were not as divided as one might have expected: they were dreaming the same dreams of the unlimited pleasures of consumption.

Fashion discourses from late 1947 to 1949, the years preceding the advance of the economic wonder (*Wirtschaftswunder*), testify in an unmistakable way how German women in both the East and West considered affluence and material prosperity a legitimate and acceptable realm of fantasies, even if not yet a reality. The embrace of the New Look meant an eager anticipation of a future possibility, not necessarily immediate application in everyday practices. Through the proliferation of the new fashion in both print media and the silver screen, German women's tastes and desires were cultivated in the spirit of the New Look, in the spirit of a new internationalism, and their gaze was directed further away from the rubble and more toward a future world of increased consumption.

5. Consuming Fashion on the Screens of the Early 1950s: *Modell Bianka* (1951), *Frauenschicksale* (1952), and *Ingrid: Die Geschichte eines Fotomodells* (1955)

THIS LAST CHAPTER revisits three films from the early 1950s—two DEFA productions and one West German work—that all took exception to the general trends in filmmaking in their respective industries and engaged in critical ways with the realities that it was their intention to address. More specifically, however, they engaged with the realities of the rise and establishment of postwar consumer culture in Germany on both sides of the Cold War divide.

In 1991, the unification of East and West Germany led to the dissolution of the DEFA studio in East Berlin, forty-five years after its founding. On the eve of this event, the East Berlin cinema Babylon organized a retrospective called "The Early Years, back then in Berlin" ("Frühe Jahre—damals in Berlin"). In a press release from April 15, 1991, the organizers emphasized their preference for stories of everyday life in the city that defied the strict ideological divide between East and West. Thus, they stressed, the 1951 *Modell Bianka*, "a unique DEFA film about the early development of the fashion industry in the German Democratic Republic," was a perfect match for the series (it was screened on April 23, 1991).[1] Yet this was not the first time that the film had been included in a commemorative retrospective. In 1979, *Modell Bianka* was re-released as part of the series "30 Stories for the 30th Anniversary" ("30 Geschichten zum 30. Jahrestag") of the founding of the German Democratic Republic.[2] It was shown along with Slatan Dudow's *Frauenschicksale* (Destinies of Women, 1952), a film that was made just a year later and was considered to be one of the "aesthetically most important films" of the time, according to the same 1979 re-release protocol. Both works were included in the anniversary retrospective in 1979: set in the fashion industry, both works reflected "women's yearnings in the first postwar years" and were considered worthy of a second look as valuable cultural documents.[3]

In the context of West German filmmaking of the early 1950s, a comparable film is *Ingrid: Die Geschichte eines Fotomodells* (Ingrid: The

Story of a Fashion Model, 1955, directed by Géza von Radvanyi), also set for the most part in the fashion industry. The film's main character, a single female character with a trajectory of tumultuous personal growth, melodramatic love troubles, and an ultimate professional realization, is shown against the background of social and economic developments of the early postwar years in West Germany. *Ingrid* offers a realistic insight into the workings of the capitalist model of fashion production and dissemination with its emphasis on the star designer and the hierarchical, highly competitive star system in general, as well as on excessive glamour and the drive for international recognition.

Seen next to each other, these three works display striking generic differences. *Modell Bianka* is a light-weight comedy about amorous relations that end happily; the *Frauenschicksale* is an ambitious study of five intertwined female characters and their connection to the gradually strengthening socialist order; *Ingrid* directs a rather melodramatic limelight on the life story of a young woman in the West who overcomes various obstacles on her way to personal and professional happiness in the Federal Republic.

Despite belonging to different genres, the three films share some similarities and complement each other in an auspicious manner, especially in the ways they transform fashion from an element of the mise-en-scène into the primary multilayered and complex theme of their plots that is inseparable from the development of the female protagonists. Revealing cultural documents of their time and as part of the wider East and West German media landscapes, these films testify to the importance of fashion production, fashion accessibility, and fashion-related entertainment to women as citizens in the two emerging German states, whose desire to participate in the cycle of consumption is undeniable and requires further exploration. *Frauenschicksale* and *Ingrid* also offer critical insight into the variety of ways that average consumers negotiated the commodity world constructed by their respective political regimes.

A broader common ground for understanding these three films is the economic and political conditions that shaped the East and West German societies of the early 1950s. The currency reform of June 1948, preceding the dramatic Berlin Blockade by a few days and the founding of the two states by a year and several months, was seen as a definitive caesura, a watershed moment in German postwar history.[4] The deutsche mark was introduced by the Western Allies in their occupation zones and West Berlin to enable the rapid implementation of the Marshall Plan, eliminate the black market, and create a more favorable ratio between available goods and the amount of money in circulation. These measures, deemed by historians as by and large successful, quickly cleared the way for a free-market system in the West, while the East was firmly set on a course toward planned socialist economy.

The immediate consequences in the summer of 1948 in the West were, indeed, visible and impressive: the stores filled up immediately with of all sorts of consumer goods that had been unobtainable for years, and the long lines in front of them disappeared, thus ending the rationing system. For many West Germans, Michael Wildt writes, the currency reform and the transformed shop windows "symbolized the end of the war years and times of deprivation."[5] It marked the long-expected return to "normality" and a move toward attaining prosperity. The following years, known as the *Wirtschaftswunder* (economic miracle), led to a consumption boom that included the tendency of West Germans to acquire massive quantities of new clothing, known as the *Kleidungswelle* (clothing wave).[6] In the short run, the downside of the currency reform was a rapid increase in prices and a significant widening of the social gap between rich and poor that in some places led to strikes and protests.[7] Moreover, the pace of achieving prosperity was not as swift as often assumed—the majority of working-class West Germans continued to live frugally well into the 1950s.[8]

While the Federal Republic of Germany (FDR) was rebuilding its consumer industries quickly with capital from the Marshall Plan, in the German Democratic Republic (GDR), large-scale démontage, nationalization of production facilities, and the introduction of state-planned economy was slowing down the already devastated economy. A *Wirtschaftswunder* simply did not happen in the GDR. The East German leadership and its press organs attacked the "shop-window politics of the West" that came in the aftermath of the currency reform and the adopted Marshall Plan, but struggled to find ways to satisfy the needs of their own constituency. By the late 1940s, the desires and fantasies of a well-developed consumer culture were reemerging in the GDR, despite the dire material conditions. Even in the midst of numerous clothing problems (*Bekleidungsprobleme*), consumers were abandoning the practices of making new from old and voicing their demands to be able to buy a wider variety of new manufactured apparel in stores.[9] In 1948, the year the currency reform, Soviet authorities undertook measures to combat the burning issues of consumer goods shortages and persisting black markets in their occupation zone, including East Berlin, by having their own currency reform and introducing the business organization (*Handelsorganisation*). The HO presented a centralized system of stores to sell consumer goods produced in the newly nationalized factories. These new establishments were supposed to rival the West and display "high-quality," "outstanding," even "luxury items" at affordable prices. Both the service and atmosphere in these stores were supposed to be distinctive and pleasing. Ideological campaigns were launched to boost workers' productivity by virtue of an improved work ethic and the challenge of socialist competition (*Wettbewerb*) as opposed to the cruel capitalist system of *Konkurrenz*, competition between companies. Even a public discourse of customer complaints was tolerated to a certain extent in order to improve on the quality of the offerings.[10]

However, while the West German reforms had returned goods to the stores for legal, ration-free purchases and had sucked up large portions of excess cash circulating on the black market, the East German reforms failed to produce the same effects due primarily to a continuous lack of goods available for legal purchase. Consequently, chronic shortages and rationing of consumer products persisted well into the 1950s. Even with all the propaganda surrounding the new HO-stores, they embodied a contradiction within the socialist system: the stores were meant to rival the West's abundance, but they themselves turned out in reality to be—if they could be stocked properly—full of expensive and unattainable goods that engendered social critique und resentment within the GDR. Paradoxically, the historian Katherine Pence has concluded, rather than quenching East Germans' thirst for more appealing and inexpensive goods, the HOs and the propaganda that accompanied their establishment promoted consumer desires, tastes, and interests that could rarely be satisfied in the East and could be fulfilled more effectively in the sparkling capitalist West.

The three films discussed here reflect on many aspects of the emerging East and West consumer worlds and seem to capture a shared middle ground between the two German societies, one beyond the diametrically opposed practices associated with capitalist and socialist systems. All three films reveal women's widespread involvement in fashion from early on after the war, mainly as seamstresses in the industry, sometimes as designers and models. The two DEFA productions openly acknowledge the consumer needs of postwar women in the GDR and their desire for new and beautiful clothes. *Modell Bianka* does this in a light, comedic format, adhering more to the principles of UFA entertainment than those of socialist realism. The film completely ignores the existence of the rival West German state and turns selected deficiencies of the socialist system of fashion production into occasions for humorous and amusing situations. *Frauenschicksale*, however, chooses to juxtapose the exploitative and cruel capitalist conditions in the West, to the more humane and fair socialist system of production in the East. *Ingrid* indulges in a sumptuous portrayal of West Germany as a consumer paradise, but does not shy away from revealing, partly with irony and partly with melodramatic pathos, the dark sides of capitalist success and material abundance. It takes a strong individual with willpower, good looks, and plenty of luck, like the title character Ingrid, to survive and succeed in male- and consumption-dominated Western society.

Modell Bianka

In the early 1950s, entertaining films on contemporary topics were largely missing from the film programs in East Germany, and DEFA was searching for material that would make people laugh as it simultaneously addressed contemporary concerns.[11] The issue was discussed at length at party meetings and DEFA conventions, and on the pages of the leading film journal in the East, *Neue Film-Welt*. But it turned out to be a difficult task to make films that would effectively entertain and espouse the correct ideological message at the same time. Recent comedies such as *Kein Platz für Liebe* (No Place for Love, 1947, directed by Hans Deppe) and *Träum nicht, Annette!* (Don't Dream, Annette!, 1948, directed by Eberhard Klagemann) turned out to be too lightweight, devoid of serious content, and somewhat disconnected from reality—in other words, mediocre films.

The director Richard Groschopp seemed to be aware of that conundrum as well. Echoing DEFA's concern about the entertainment value of its productions ever since the founding of the studio, Groschopp, who had not yet directed a full-length feature film, wrote in early 1951, "The people's call for funny films has not stopped. . . . But to create funny films for our new people is a serious, difficult, and responsible task. The search for new ways in the light film genres is at its most necessary and most complex."[12] Groschopp also complained that his fellow filmmakers treated the audience's desire for "cheerful" ("heitere") films with disdain, and when they did embark on such a project, they planned it as a "small-scale" production to be completed within the shortest time frame and on a minimal budget.[13] Groschopp decided he wanted to direct a film that would combine the audience's desire for film entertainment with another popular demand, namely "the desire for fashionable and tasteful clothing" ("der Wunsch nach modischer und geschmackvoller Kleidung").[14] As he recalled in a 1987 interview with Ralf Schenk: "Only a short time after the end of the war, the people wanted to have fashionable stuff. But there was a complete lack of materials" ("Die Bevölkerung verlangte schon kurze Zeit nach dem Krieg durchaus nach modischen Dingen; aber es mangelte vorn und hinten an Material").[15]

With the help of the DEFA dramaturg Wolfgang Krüger, Groschopp developed a script that both overturned the trend of neglecting the entertaining genre and addressed a central concern in the GDR, the desire for fashionable clothing. Thus, *Modell Bianka* was conceived as "a joyful film with a complicated plotline full of misunderstandings and confusions." An enormous amount of effort and resources were invested in filming on location to create extensive complicated scenes on the steep ski slopes in Saxony, and in creating in a studio an exact replica of the setup of the fashion show from the autumn Leipzig Trade Fair in 1950.[16] Set entirely in the fashion industry, the film's spectacle conveyed to its audience optimism and pleasure and at the same time offered an understanding of the concept of socialist competition. In a lengthy preview two months before the premiere, the *Berliner Zeitung* was pleased to recommend to the audiences this "cheerful contemporary fiction film" that "the women in our audience with a sharp eye for fashion" should not miss.[17]

The film tells the story of two fictional state-owned companies in the clothing industry, the Berlin-based Berolina and the Leipzig-based Saxonia, that see each other as competitors, especially when it comes to presenting their designs at the Leipzig Trade Fair. Both companies are state-owned companies called *volkseigene Betriebe*, or VEBs, for clothing. VEB Saxonia's young and enthusiastic fashion designer, Jochen Rauhut (played by Siegfried Dornbusch), has sketched two fabulous designs, one labeled "Bianka" and the other "Gitta." But Jochen is frustrated because his creative ideas are rejected by his coworkers as too lavish and inappropriate to adopt for mass production. He protests loudly and passionately, "But people today want to have better things!" And his commitment to his fellow citizens' consumer desires clashes with the chief cutter's stern reminder, "eight percent less fabric must be used!" ("acht Prozent Stoff muss gespart werden!").

When Saxonia's director, Johannes Müller (played by Joseph Peter Dornseif), offers the young designer to come along on a business trip to Berlin as compensation for his frustration, Jochen agrees. Once they arrive in Berlin, however, Jochen's anger is not mollified, as the boss continues to refuse to accept his designs. Impulsively Jochen gives his designs away to a stranger in a bar who happens to be working for Berolina. The fashion sketches reach Berolina's chief designer, Ursel Altmann (played by Gerda Falk), and her friend, the chief dressmaker, Hilde Meißner (played by Margit Schaumäker). The two skillful women immediately sew beautiful new outfits based on Jochen's designs and start wearing them. In fact, they decide to wear them on the train to a ski resort in the Erzgebirge, where both Berolina and Saxonia employees were being sent on vacation by their trade unions as a reward for excelling achievements in the workplace. While learning to ski on their winter vacation the teams from the two competing garment companies happen to meet. As expected, some romantic entanglements ensue, including last-minute fallouts involving the two Berolina girls, Ursel and Margit, and the two Saxonia employees, Jochen and his friend Gerd Neumann, a chief salesman, played by Fritz Wagner.

All conflicts, personal and professional, are ultimately resolved during the Leipzig Trade Fair. Realizing that neither one of the companies will succeed at the fair on its own, the rivals Saxonia and Berolina reconcile and join forces. A culminating seven-minute sequence at the end of the film features a magnificent fashion show, and the two companies emerge as collaborators on the design of the "Bianka" design, a "transformation" dress. Berolina's chief designer, Ursel, models the various transformations of the outfit, while Saxonia's sales director, Gerd, serves as a master of ceremonies. The film's message is that by joining forces rather than fiercely competing, ultimately the two companies win together all the awards.

This summary of the film's content already hints at the rather thin and awkwardly constructed plot and dialogues, which were immediately criticized in GDR newspapers. Phrases such as "too light," an "unsuccessful model," a "damaged item" were used as headlines by the press in its attacks on the film.[18] Yet what the film lacked on the plot level it seemed to compensate for fully on the level of spectacle, especially in its thorough engagement with the theme of fashion, a subject of great interest to women in East Germany. Despite the grumblings of some critics, audiences made the film a hit.[19] Tapping into the old UFA tradition of escapist entertainment and reusing elements of successful, familiar genres of the 1920s and 1930s such as the fashion farce (*Konfektionskomödie*) with its setting in the ready-to-wear clothing industry, and the mountain film (*Bergfilm*), especially in the long scenes of skiing in the mountains, this unpretentious DEFA production satisfied some immediate needs for homegrown amusement. Some other marketing devices borrowed from the Weimar period also helped boost its popularity, such as the premiere of the film in the DEFA-Theater Kastanienallee and subsequent screenings accompanied by fashion shows organized by the HO.[20]

Modell Bianka was quickly seen by more than 4 million viewers, even though it premiered in June 1951 in the midst of a brutally hot summer, before there were any open-air theaters, as director Groschopp recollected.[21] Half a year after the premiere, popular demand kept the film running in theaters, prompting the West German magazine *Der Spiegel* to note: "The demand for such lighthearted productions in the grey and exhausted by work East is very high. This can be seen in the example of the little unpretentious movie *Modell Bianka*, which shows nice clothes, scenes in the snow and a romance. Contrary to DEFA's expectations, this film provided a very quick return on its high-cost investment"[22]

With its central focus on the design of nice-looking clothes, *Modell Bianka* was bound to be a crowd pleaser. Its mixture of appropriate degrees of authenticity and fantasy not only resonated with some of its audiences' real experiences in the GDR, but perhaps also enticed them with an enjoyable visual indulgence of otherwise inaccessible fashion items. As Hans Ulrich Eylau wrote in his review for the *Berliner Zeitung*, "This movie is a pleasant encounter of good-looking and well-dressed young people, which is a rare occurrence in our films" ("Dieser Film ist eine angenehme Begegnung mit gut aussehenden, gut angezogenen jungen Menschen—und die sind in unseren Filmen sonst ziemlich rar geworden").[23] In an article in another party-controlled newspaper, "Which Films Women Want to See," *Modell Bianka* was singled out also as the type of film that would be especially attractive to young female workers in the GDR.[24]

The film announces its preoccupation with the topic of fashion early, during the opening credits, as they run against the background of a sumptuously unfolding fabric with a shepherd's plaid design. Transitioning from the credits to the establishing shots, the camera enters the large manufacturing hall of VEB Saxonia, signaling that the film will deal specifically with the production side of fashion. By featuring sweeping views of the large factory floors with scores of female workers bent over sewing machines, the film also echoes the official party line that the only way to ensure an adequate supply of clothes for everyone was to establish large-scale, state-owned production companies for the mass production of apparel, rather than to support a multitude of smaller private companies that relied on home workers, *Heimarbeiterinnen*, as was common in the prewar and immediate postwar period.[25] The sense of authenticity is reinforced by the fact that Groschopp filmed both sequences on location in VEB Fortschritt, a well-known clothing factory in Berlin, with the actual women workers as extras.

Already in this first sequence another real issue within this branch of East Germany's state-owned planned economy is raised right away: the film viewer eavesdrops on the conversations among the women workers on the floor who complain about malfunctioning and old sewing machines that make the completion of their jobs so difficult. At the same time, both workers and supervisors agree that they should maintain the high quality of the products, despite the deficient material conditions, and do their best in preparation for the competition at the Leipzig Fair.

It may be surprising to hear such grumblings right at the opening of this DEFA film, but problems with the availability and quality of women's clothes were among the issues that were actually permitted as subjects of criticism and public discussions in the GDR in the early 1950s. Complaining about issues related to clothing in letters to the press and to the party leadership became a unique aspect of East German consumer citizenship, especially among women.[26] Public campaigns to raise the quality of textile production were also common, as attested by the activist Luise Ermisch's combative slogan initiated in 1949, which persisted for years: "Kollegen, produziert Qualitätskleidung!"[27] In an article published in *Neues Deutschland* under the same title in 1951, Ermisch, a former seamstress, appealed passionately to the party leadership for the need to support fashion shows, organized at factories and at the Leipzig Fair, and argued that the goal was to promote processes that would result ultimately in higher-quality clothes: "A fashion show is not only an entertaining event. More than anything else, especially when it takes place in our people-owned companies, it could stimulate the competition between the different companies and be enriched significantly by the workers' critical input."[28]

To its predominantly female and urban audiences, *Modell Bianka* also demonstrated convincing familiarity with the workings of the traditional Berlin-based industry, its sites and history, and conveyed with unabashed candidness the pleasures as well as the problems related to owning beautiful new clothes. To the extent to which the workings of the two companies were presented realistically in the film, they both were modeled after the Berlin-based VEB Fortschritt, a premiere production site for East German fashion, founded in 1949 and covered extensively in the GDR press, in daily newspapers and women's magazines alike.[29] Furthermore, VEB Fortschritt's production was well known to the female audience, as it was most frequently featured both in the pages of *Die Frau von heute* and in regular reports about fashion shows in the Soviet-controlled part of Berlin.[30]

In an outdoor sequence at the beginning of the film Johannes Müller, VEB Saxonia's director, and Jochen Rauhut arrive in Berlin to procure fabrics from a central supply facility. As the two men emerge from a subway station, the frame freezes briefly on the sign for the Hausvogteiplatz subway station, which serves as a nostalgic reminder to the audience that this area was the traditional center of Berlin's *Konfektion*.[31] The brief cinematic focus on the sign also suggests the GDR's claim to inheriting, resurrecting, and continuing this venerable tradition. The impression is confirmed as the camera then quickly steers away from Hausvogteiplatz, careful not to show any of the surrounding ruins, and closely follows the two men as they reach their nearby destination—a large and impressive early-twentieth-century six-story building whose sign reads "Deutsche Handels-Zentrale Textil."[32] For the Berliners in the audience, this will have been a filmic confirmation of what they had read in numerous celebratory newspaper articles announcing that "the threads of *Konfektion* come together again at Hausvogteiplatz" ("Denn wieder laufen die Fäden der Konfektion am Hausvogteiplatz zusammen").[33] According to these reports, the newly renovated building there that housed the Center for State-Owned Wholesale Trade (*Zentralstelle des volkseigenen Großhandels*) also functioned as central storage for all the textiles that were distributed to the companies. As the protagonists enter the building, the film continues to tread a fine line between reality and fantasy, manipulation and wishful thinking.

The very first peek into the storage room reveals a glimpse of socialist materialist abundance. Contrary to the typical real-life experience of empty shelves and insufficient consumer goods for sale, these storage spaces are filled from floor to ceiling with rolls and rolls of fabric. This carefully constructed cinematic sight of plenty resembles in many ways what one could find on the fashion pages of popular women's magazines in the East, such as *Neue Berliner Illustrierte* and *Die Frau von heute*: there, too, the emphasis is on the display of a wealth of resources—often unimaginable in real life—as if to encourage their audiences' vicarious consumption.[34] Back in the film, the two company men and Frau Schulze, the director of the rival, VEB Berolina (she wears an elegant black fur coat), are all free to browse around as they choose whatever they like from a variety of nice-looking fabrics. They stop here and there to run their fingers approvingly over the high-quality fabrics. Given the abundance of resources viewable in this scene, it is hard to understand why mandated cuts of 8 percent were announced in the previous sequence. And why has Saxonia rejected Jochen's beautiful designs if the availability of nice fabrics is not a problem, as one can see from the visual abundance of this sequence? The film does not offer any logical answers to these questions, other than that such a contradiction is needed in order to propel further development of the comedic plot.

The cinematic images of beautiful clothing are associated primarily with the appearances of the two female protagonists, Ursel and Hilde. They are shown at their workplaces designing various stylish dresses and often trying them on themselves during the production process, thus putting on intermittent fashion shows for the film audience. They are also wearing the new outfits "Bianka" and "Gitta" on the train ride to the ski resort, walking to the restaurant and back to their compartment so that everyone on the train can admire their looks. In the mountains, there is an opportunity to showcase some winter fashion, although it is not as spectacular as the dresses we have seen up to this point. In fact, Groschopp's ambition to display as many beautiful outfits on screen as possible, especially the ones relating to winter sports, turned out to be a challenge for DEFA's costume department and particularly for the film's fairly inexperienced *Kostümberater*, the costume consultant Gerhard Kaddatz. So Groschopp's wife "kindly lent [the production] many of her own dresses and sweaters" for the star actress Gerda Falk (playing Ursel) to wear in the film.[35]

Finally, Ursel and Hilde convince the audience that not only can they design and sew beautiful clothes, they can also model them: they present Berolina's and Saxonia's production during the fictional Leipzig Fair. This reinforced a point frequently made in the East German fashion press, that under socialist conditions there are no professional models (*Mannequins*) of the old, prewar type; rather, the regular working women of different ages, designers, as well as potential consumers, are entitled to model at the fashion shows and even serve on juries.[36]

Modell Bianka incorporated some features of a documentary film. Many of the contemporary reviewers noted that the most spectacular of all fashion displays in the film takes place in a long sequence re-creating the Leipzig Trade Fair.[37] Richard Groschopp had started his professional life with the production of advertisement and education films during the 1930s and continued as a cameraman for the East German *Augenzeuge* newsreels. He considered the short documentary *Leipziger Messe 1946* (The Leipzig Trade Fair 1946, directed by Kurt Maetzig), which he had shot and edited, a highlight in his career up to that point.[38] Building on his extensive expertise in commercial filmmaking, Groschopp wanted to recreate the spectacle of the runway and the atmosphere at the Leipzig Fair as authentically as possible. The architect Arthur Naumann built a replica of the Leipzig Fair runway in the Babelsberg studio, and various original stage decorations used during the fashion show were borrowed from Leipzig for a hefty fee.[39] VEB Fortschritt supplied the garments modeled during the fictional onscreen show and at several points of the Leipzig Fair sequence, and Groschopp also spliced in some archival film footage.[40]

As the camera crosscuts between the action on the runway and the drama in the wings, it creates a sequence in which all themes of the plot come together and all previous tensions are resolved. The Leipzig Trade Fair closes the narrative frame, for it has been announced at the beginning of the film as the ultimate goal toward which both companies were working. The Leipzig Trade Fair, which reemerged in August 1945 with a small display and on a much larger scale in February 1947, became an early symbol of projected normalization and of promised prosperity. In the wake of the currency reform and the onset of the Cold War, it became the showcase for the GDR's industrial production, including items of clothing and textile. These displays were meant to convince the world of the socialist consumer economy's superiority over the West's capitalist one.[41] The Leipzig Trade Fair also embodied the idea of a friendly competition among production units, within the GDR and among the Socialist Bloc countries (Czechoslovakia, Hungary, Poland, Bulgaria, Romania, and the Soviet Union), a concept that, as we see in the film, was the specific response of the political leadership to the deficient supply of consumer goods in the Soviet zone.[42] By encouraging "friendly competition" among different state-owned production companies, the GDR leadership hoped to increase efficiency at the workplace and enhance the overall quality of the output. Or, as the director of the fictional Saxonia company declares in the film, "Competition should serve as an incentive for bigger and better production" ("Wettbewerb muss Ansporn sein für bessere und größere Leistung"). The idea of competition, especially in the field of fashion, was extended to include some West German and West Berlin salons that also participated in the fair. Starting in the spring of 1947, fashion shows (*Modellmodenschauen*) and fashion competitions (*Modewettbewerbe*) became a regular feature of the fair. They took place twice a day at the theater Leipziger Schauspiel or in the Ringmessehaus;

the morning show was for domestic and foreign guests, and the afternoon show was for the specialists in the industry.[43]

At the beginning of the Leipzig Fair sequence in the film, Jochen, who is still upset that Berolina has "stolen" his "Bianka" design, comes up with the idea for the two companies to present jointly under the motto "Designed by Saxonia, produced by Berolina." With some trickery he manages to win everyone on both sides over to his idea. As a result, both Gerd, from Saxonia, and Ursel, from Berolina, appear together onstage, he in the role of an announcer, and she as a model who demonstrates quite professionally the *Verwandlungskleid* "Bianka" in all four of its variations: from a travel suit into a sporty dress, then into an elegant afternoon dress, and finally into a fancy ball gown.[44] It is certain now that this design will win the big prize at the fair. At the same time this culminating scene in Leipzig serves as an occasion for romantic reconciliation, as the two couples (Gerd-Ursel and Jochen-Hilde) get together again. Gerd presents on the stage not only the "Bianka" design but also his future bride, Ursel, who is wearing it. Thus, the formulaic happy ending merges both the achievement of the prescribed political goal, winning the socialist competition, and the realization of the romantic dream—the marriage of the sweethearts.

Not until this final sequence of the film does the audience actually get to admire the eponymous dress in all of its transformations. If one is to believe the journalistic coverage, *Verwandlungskleider* were all the rage at fashion shows in East in the early 1950s.[45] In a story on a fashion show organized by the DDR-publishing house Für die Frau (publisher of the magazines *Die Frau von heute*, and *Für Dich*), the party organ *Neues Deutschland* reported that "the transformation dresses were by far the biggest sensation. With the help of a few extra scraps of material, a dress can be transformed into four or five different outfits."[46] Such dresses could often be seen at the Leipzig Fair as well. In fact, "one almost got dizzy from many transformation dresses" that after going through several changes were transformed from business suits into sleeveless summer dresses. "The audience exploded in wild applause," wrote the reporter for the *Berliner Zeitung*.[47] In this context it is understandable why Groschopp was determined to make the *Verwandlungskleid* "Bianka" stand out from the rest of the costumes in the film and assigned its design expressly to the "most highly valued DEFA-designer" ("der geschätzteste Kostümbildner") Walter Schulze-Mittendorff.[48]

The *Verwandlungskleid* "Bianka" in the film also became a focal point of critical attention: very much like its counterparts on the catwalks in Leipzig and Berlin during that time, it was received with a mixture of admiration and rejection. While such types of dresses gained applause, won prizes, and generally pleased audiences at fashion shows in the GDR, the press was often critical of their extravagance and unsuitability for

Fig. 24. Poster for *Modell Bianka* (1951), presenting the "Bianka" design at the Leipzig Fair. Deutsches Filminstitut. Frankfurt am Main.

ordinary working-class women. *Neues Deutschland* called the *Verwandlungskleid* "an unfortunate model" and voiced direct ideological objections against it: "A visit to any store would reveal that our state-owned industry, despite some material deficits, can create much more tasteful and imaginative outfits than that frumpy 'designs' that no woman would ever want to wear."[49]

Read against the background of real-life economic and political developments in divided Germany, this film is also intriguing for its obvious intentional omissions. In the style of the good old traditional UFA entertainment films of the early 1940s, *Modell Bianka* avoids any overt political propaganda and references to sensitive political or social issues of the day. Missing from the screen, for example, is any awareness of the current political division, of the existence of West Berlin or the Federal Republic, or of any competition with the more affluent West. Although the film's plot touches upon the theme of material scarcity and touts the idea of *Wettbewerb* (without the adjective "socialist" that usually preceded it in the press) as a way of overcoming problems, this competition remains internal, within the GDR, and has the main function of creating a source of dramatic conflict at the very beginning of the film. This notion is reinforced by the absence of any international participants in the Leipzig Fair sequence, whereas in reality fashion competitions (*Modekonkurrenzen* or *Bekleidungswettbewerbe*) among the countries in the Socialist Bloc were a common practice, and the women's magazines featured numerous colorful reports on their pages.[50] These international competitions, initiated by the GDR and Czechoslovakia in 1950 and gradually expanded to include other socialist countries, were a major source of prestige, pride, and legitimation for the East German state in public discourses about fashion.

It is noteworthy that *Modell Bianka* does not mention another major event for consumers of fashion in the East, namely the ration card for clothing (*Punktkarte*), which was introduced in the Soviet occupation zone and East Berlin on January 1, 1949, after the currency reform, and was in use until the end of 1951.[51] The new "points card" was a crucial aspect of GDR's early consumer experience, as it extended practices familiar from the wartime and early postwar years well into the 1950s. *Neues Deutschland* published several articles in the course of 1949 containing details about the logistics of the card and expressing the firm conviction that "now there will be considerable improvement in the planned supply of the shoppers in the East sector with textiles, whereas the West Berliner continues to live in uncertainty."[52] The introduction of the new ration card was praised, paradoxically, as a "resurrection of his Majesty, the Customer" and was credited for "the happiness of men and women alike who can now acquire new clothing items with the card."[53] The women's illustrated press dedicated numerous issues to explaining exactly how the card works—it came in five different categories, A through E—and featured numerous designs that could be purchased with the card, but the film made no mention of these practical matters.[54]

Also significant is the avoidance of the word *Mode* in the film's narrative in favor of the repeated use of *Konfektion*, *Konfektionär*, and *Konfektionsfirma*. These rhetorical gestures signal the rejection of the Western notion of capitalism-driven fashion cycle and its exclusive "haute couture," favoring instead reconnection to the venerable prewar institution of *Konfektion*, serially produced ready-to-wear clothing, with its roots in East Berlin, at Hausvogteiplatz. This was paired with the style of the fashion show very much in the prewar tradition of parading the clothes on a catwalk with a jury and a live audience that applauded the show.

Also absent are any scenes of retail spaces or of ordinary German women actually shopping for, purchasing, trying on, and wearing any of the clothes designed in the state-owned companies. The struggles and frustrations of the regular consumers in Berlin, Leipzig, or any other East German city are also ignored. With the exception of the brief sequence filmed on Hausvogteiplatz and the long scenes of skiing in Erzgebirge, the film remains hermetically encapsulated within the closed-off sites of production, VEB Berolina and VEB Saxonia, and within the world of display of the Leipzig Trade Fair, which was equally isolated in its exclusivity.

This fictional cinematic construct seems to mirror the state of affairs of the East German clothing industry in the early 1950s, which was often the object of criticism: it was good at creating exquisite sartorial *Modelle* suitable for showcasing at national and international competitions, but failed to satisfy the needs of regular consumers by producing sufficient quantities of nice-looking, comfortable, and practical clothes for everyday use.[55] Ultimately, the reproach often leveled at the Leipzig Trade Fair applies to the film as well, namely that for average East German consumers the fair and the film both presented a utopian fantasy rather than a reality; they both put on a show of consumer goods—nice dresses—that were exceptional rather than typical, accessible to a privileged few but not to the working-class masses.[56]

Frauenschicksale

Slatan Dudow's *Frauenschicksale* premiered only a year after *Modell Bianka*, in June 1952, but the difference between the two DEFA productions was marked. *Modell Bianka* was the debut feature of a rather inexperienced team and despite its success with audiences was considered by officials at the time to be a light fare and an unfortunate return to the commercial cinematic tradition that DEFA was supposed to transcend. *Frauenschicksale*, on the other hand, was the work of a seasoned director with proven credentials in socialist filmmaking that went all the way back to the Weimar Republic.[57] Dudow's ambitious new film was DEFA's second production in color and was a response to the state-controlled company's desperate search for stories for socialist audiences that are serious and engaging as well as entertaining.[58] It is perhaps no surprise, then, that fashion was a focal point in this cinematic event, too, in the shape of a particular blue dress strongly desired by one of the characters in the film and later designed for mass production by another character. As was often the case with *Modell Bianka*, the authorities thought it particularly fitting to pair the public film screenings throughout the country with fashion shows and to organize local premieres of the film in clothing factories.[59]

As the title suggests, the film presents the intertwined life stories of several contemporary German women—Anni Neumann, Barbara Berg, Renate Ludwig, Ursula Krenz, and Hertha Scholz—from 1948 until the World Youth Festival (*Weltjugendfestspiele*) held in Berlin in 1951.[60] Directly or indirectly, their fates have been shaped by the war: Hertha, the now-widowed oldest of the five, was a resistance fighter during the Nazi period and has become both a party functionary and an activist for women's and children's rights. She also serves as a mentor and friend to Barbara, a law student, who then becomes one of the first female judges of the GDR. Anni, Renate, and Ursula, the youngest characters, are all around sixteen years old in 1948 and have grown up amidst the deprivations and traumas of war. Having lost both parents in the war, rebellious Ursula has been raised by her grandparents and also in a state-run orphanage. Her life turns around as she starts working at VEB Fortschritt, and with the support of her colleagues she becomes a student at the university. Anni's working-class family in West Berlin, plagued by poverty and unemployment, is trying to hold her back as she dares to pursue a better life for herself in East Berlin. Renate has grown up during the war without a father, although her mother has struggled to survive and dotes on Renate's much younger half brother.

Three of the younger women—Barbara, Anni, and Renate—find themselves enchanted by the charms of a womanizer, the West Berliner Conny Lohmüller. In a quick succession, he seduces them, has a brief relationship with each woman, and then abandons them, occasionally leaving behind devastating consequences. Barbara is so distressed that she almost gets hit by a truck as she walks dazed through the streets of Berlin; Anni gets pregnant and is fired from her job as a sales assistant in a fashion salon; and Renate ends up in jail after inadvertently killing her bother, a jolting act committed while stealing her mother's money with the intention of using it to buy a fancy dress in the hopes of pleasing Conny.

A few other women with typical postwar life stories are introduced episodically and briefly as well. Frau Becker has lost her livelihood and family during the bombing of Dresden in 1944 and is reunited with her child, Christel, four years later. We also catch brief glimpses of the comfortable domestic lives of two affluent West-Berlin women, Betty Vogt and the Baroness Isa von Trautwald, who have exquisite designer dresses delivered to them and custom-fitted at their own elegant homes.

At the end of the film, all of the women whose lives have been followed closely by the narrative achieve significant personal and professional success. Barbara becomes is a well-respected judge who tackles difficult cases and marries her colleague, Dr. Gebhardt. Anni, a single mother, is recognized as one of the best workers at VEB Fortschritt, and her child is happily raised in the nearby child-care center run by the state-owned company; lastly, Renate is released from prison after a reduced two-and-a-half-year sentence and is in a happy relationship with her co-worker, Helmut.

In terms of both narrative and visual representation of femininity, *Frauenschicksale* is the only DEFA film that is preoccupied with the Cold War's evolving politics of consumption, which, as recent research has shown, was critical for the development of both the East German and West German national identity in the postwar years. Yet Dudow's treatment of the subject is much more nuanced, serious, and sensitive than *Modell Bianka*. The film uses fashion to trace the process of gradual formation of the new female consumer in the GDR within the context of conventional gender politics, material deficiency and hardship, and intensive competition with the West.

The starting point of this development seems quite conventional: fashion exists in order to please the male's exacting gaze. Each of the women that Conny is dating is shown posing in front of a mirror and checking out her dress, lipstick, and make-up to ensure that her dandyish West Berlin boyfriend will be happy with what he sees. Conny himself either showers his lovers with compliments on their outfits after examining them with a knowing eye—"You look lovely," "What a pretty dress you're having on!"—or actually tries to shape the young women's appearance by making very specific recommendations. Each encounter between Conny and one of his lady friends revolves around fashion, and it is clear that the women become extremely self-conscious about their appearance when in his presence. Betty's first line in the film is, "Do you like this dress?" and upon hearing Conny's repeated positive response, the couple starts dancing a waltz across the frame and into the bedroom. When this very same dress is delivered to Betty's home from a fashion salon by "the little dressmaker" ("die kleine Modistin") Anni, Conny uses the occasion to start flirting with the young girl. During their subsequent date, Anni, a working-class girl, is slightly embarrassed and apologetic: "My dress is not as nice as your lady's," to which Conny responds with a recommendation: "A spring green dress would suit you well." For his next lover, Renate, he has different advice: "A pale-blue dress will suit you nicely." All the women go along quite willingly and often foolishly with this game of attraction and seduction as they model in front of the mirror, with narcissistic pleasure as well as in anxious anticipation of Conny's judgment.

As a result, the film viewers become witnesses to an amazing fashion display, especially during the first half of the film, while the actresses are inspecting their clothes privately in mirrors or presenting them proudly in public. We experience a wide range of sartorial possibilities, from Barbara Berg's elegant purple dress to her smart professional outfit to Renate Ludwig's and Anni's simple colorful day dresses to the outrageously extravagant outfits worn by decadent West German women. Vera Mügge, the woman responsible for *Frauenschicksale*'s wardrobe, was one of the best-known and most sought-after costume designers in both the East and the West throughout the 1950s. Unlike many of her colleagues at DEFA and in West German studios, she was no stranger to color film, having met the significant challenges posed by UFA's very first use of Agfacolor film in the 1941 production *Frauen sind doch bessere Diplomaten* (Women Are Better Diplomats, 1939–41, directed by Georg Jacoby). Now Mügge transformed this DEFA production into an opulent visual spectacle.[61] In her work for *Frauenschicksale* she takes full advantage of the use of the updated Agfacolor film with a carefully selected pallet of hues that not only correspond to the fashion trends of the early 1950 but also work well even when there are changes in natural light conditions when filming in daylight and by night. The film's costumes drew some criticism by DEFA officials for contributing significantly to the cost of production. In his meticulous efforts to get all details right, for example, Dudow insisted on having Conny's coat and other pieces of attire custom-made in one of the designer salons on the Kurfürstendamm.[62] But the film's costumes were undoubtedly admired and appreciated by the audience.

The piece of clothing that receives the most cinematographic and narrative attention in the film is an elegant pale-blue designer dress that Renate spots in a display window in West Berlin. She decides to obtain it at any cost in the hope that wearing it, she can lure back her lover, Conny. When the shop assistants in the elegant store refuse to let her even try the dress on, suspecting that the East Berliner cannot afford it, Renate becomes all the more determined to find the money to buy it. She acts impulsively and recklessly to get the money, and she does purchase the blue dress, but her actions cause the inadvertent death of her brother. She is arrested soon thereafter, is sent to stand trial, and is given a two-and-a-half-year prison sentence.

Meanwhile, Anni, who has been heartlessly fired by the owner of the West Berlin fashion salon, crosses the sector border to East Berlin and finds work at in a branch of VEB Fortschritt on Greifswalder Straße. There she not only finds meaningful employment but also, within only two years and with much encouragement from her colleagues, is able to realize her dream of becoming a dress designer.[63] After seeing a gorgeous, high-quality pale-blue fabric, she proposes to design a fashionable dress for mass production. When it is finished, Anni's dress looks identical in cut and design to the one purchased by Renate in West Berlin, hinting that German women in East and West actually share the same taste, the same understanding of what is fashionable, and, ultimately, the same consumer desires. The two systems differ only in modes of production and distribution. Under capitalism, the dress shop and the couturier design bear the mark of exclusivity: expensive fashion is produced under harsh, competitive conditions by selected salons for a select few. Under socialism, even the poor but talented seamstress can rise to become a dress designer and, together with communally minded clothing factory workers, can produce attractive, modestly priced clothing that is easily available to the average GDR woman in the HO-store.

Indeed, in the final sequence of *Frauenschicksale*, after Renate's release from prison and a triumphant drive through the city, festively decorated on the occasion of the World Youth Festival, she and her new boyfriend, Helmut, join the frantically shopping crowds in the HO-Kaufhaus on Alexanderplatz (seen in documentary footage incorporated into the film). Encouraged by the shop assistant and by Helmut, who praises the high quality of the material, Renate tries on a beautiful sky-blue dress—the one designed by Anni—that looks exactly like the one sold in West Berlin that got her into trouble in the first place. Despite her initial hesitation, Renate accepts the dress as a present from Helmut, and the two walk in a happy embrace out of the store. Thus, the satisfaction of Renate's consumer desire coincides with the image of the two happy lovers at the end of the film.

The film's excessive attention to the desirability and importance of clothes for the women, exemplified with particular dramatics by the pale-blue dress coveted by Renate, prompted a strong reaction by various party authorities and regular viewers in the East German press: "And isn't it outrageous, from a psychological standpoint, that at the beginning of her new life, [Renate] would be wearing the very same dress that caused her all that trouble in the first place? Most of the viewers expected a different reaction when the blue dress was offered to her. Why did it have to be almost the same dress as the one from West Berlin?" wrote A. Künnemann in *Neues Deutschland* in an angry review of the film.[64] Other critics, without directly addressing the topic of clothes, took issue with the representation of the women's desires—for love, social recognition, and material stability. The most vehement critique came from the Demokratischer Frauenbund Deutschlands (DFD) and the party organ *Neues Deutschland*, which accused Dudow of undermining the concept of socialist realism by portraying the women in the film as gullible and easily seduced by the material bounty of the West. Dudow responded with a lengthy article in *Neues Deutschland*. He defended his position, arguing that a film focusing on all aspects of the plight of German women after two world wars was long overdue. Furthermore, he stressed that if a story is set in Berlin, the director had an obligation to show "how the two worlds meet" and what capitalism's "decadent influence" is.[65]

The ideological friction caused in certain circles by *Frauenschicksale* proves that engagement with the question of consumer desire in the GDR was indeed justified. Its narrative, as well as Dudow's response in the press, did validate the needs of socialist women as consumers in the most direct, unapologetic, and sympathetic way. This is made evident in the courtroom scene, when Renate is put on trial for causing the death of her brother. The entire discussion revolves around the right to wear nice clothing. Instead of offering an explanation for her actions in her statement, Renate poses the questions: "But what's wrong with wanting to possess a pretty dress? Don't I have the right to have a little happiness?" ("Was soll denn schlecht daran sein, dass ich ein schönes Kleid haben wollte? Habe ich nicht auch das Recht auf ein bißchen Glück?"). The judges on the panel do not challenge this right—in fact, they agree with her, and go even further, asserting it as a right that should apply to "the millions of other women" and that "one should work hard to achieve." According to the judge, Renate's predicament was not entirely her fault, and many women, he states, succumb to the "false glitter of a doomed social system." He implies that the solutions to legitimate desires have to be found for East German society as whole. Thus, the film openly acknowledges the legitimacy of consumer desire under the conditions of deficits and unfair competition with the affluent West, deeming the satisfaction of this desire as a crucial task for the state.

At the same time, the film also offers a path of action, one that is completely in line with some party-endorsed initiatives. The film's proposed solution does not involve the simple cinematic disregard or elimination of desire, but the adequate production and distribution of desirable, affordable, and high-quality consumer items for the mass of consumers that can be obtained in an HO store. When Anni comes across the nice, blue, high-quality fabric and decides to create a new collection of fashionable dresses for the working women, who most deserve it, some of her colleagues comment, "Are you planning to design again for the ladies from Ku'damm?" Anni quickly dismisses their objections. Some scholars have recognized in this scene similarities to Luise Ermisch, a seamstress in the VEB Halle clothing factories who started the "movement toward higher quality" ("Qualitätsbewegung") in 1949, appealed for raising standards in the production of women's garments, and developed a work flow that would lead to improved standards.[66] Following the commercial success of the lighthearted *Modell Bianka*, *Frauenschiksale* doubled down on the adamant assertion that East German women were no less interested in looking nice and sophisticated as consumers of fashion than their Western sisters. Their wishes and needs should neither be regarded as betrayal of socialist ideals nor discounted as frivolous.

Ingrid: Die Geschichte eines Fotomodells

In its relationship to the theme of fashion, *Ingrid: Die Geschichte eines Fotomodells* (1955, directed by Géza von Radvanyi), differed significantly from the two DEFA productions. It features lavish costumes presented at even more lavish fashion shows that are intended to be understood as the products of an exclusive West German haute couture that is on par with the international standards set in Paris. The film shows us mostly spectacular evening attire created by inspired star designers of international renown. Its emphasis is on the mystery and serendipity of the creative process and the power of popular success—not on the details of mass production for the average consumer. The fashion spectacle shown in *Ingrid* was a true celebration of the newly acquired prosperity that resulted from the *Wirtschaftswunder* in the Federal Republic.

Yet this film diverges from the aesthetic standards espoused by the majority of shallow entertainment fashion movies that West Germany produced in the course of the early 1950s. *Ingrid* presents a more complicated and nuanced picture of the capitalist fashion world from the point of view of a female protagonist whose career is both spectacular and unusual. It is markedly different from the light-fare fashion-oriented products in the old-school UFA style such as *Fürst von Pappenheim* (The Prince of Pappenheim, 1952, directed by Hans Deppe) and *Unschuld in tausend Nöten* (Innocent in a Thousand Notes, 1951, directed by Carl Boese, released in Austria under the title *Das Mädel aus der Konfektion*).[67]

Because of their unoriginal plots and clumsy dialogue, some critics characterized the latter films, both set in the milieu of designer salons, as unimaginative and derivative remakes of popular fashion farces from the 1920s and 1930s, likening them somewhat derisively to serially produced pieces of clothing: *Konfektion* put together on the principle of "Aus alt mach neu."[68] However, the films tried to compensate for plot shortcomings by staging the most spectacular displays of the production of fashion, choreographed by contemporary fashion designers. Both *Fürst von Pappenheim* and *Unschuld in tausend Nöten* introduce a type of successful West German entrepreneur and his romantic escapades with his beautiful models working in his designer salon.[69] Both farces feature the former UFA starlet Hannelore Schroth, "1938's youthful film ideal" ("das Film-Ideal der Jugend von 1938") in the role of a star model whose main function within the thin plots of the films was to parade the collections of the prominent Berlin-based designers Sinaida Rudow-Brosda and Ursula Schewe.[70] These movies predictably received extensive coverage in the illustrated press such as the magazine *Film- und Mode-Revue*, primarily for the filmed fashion shows and the explicit advertisement of Berlin couture.[71] Initially, *Unschuld in tausend Nöten* was even greeted with sympathy and enthusiasm because this work, produced by the legendary

Fig. 25. Poster for *Ingrid: Die Geschichte eines Fotomodells* (1955).
Deutsches Filminstitut. Frankfurt am Main.

Artur Brauner at his new studio in Berlin-Spandau, Central Cinema Company-Film GmbH (CCC), signaled the long-awaited return of filmmaking to West Berlin.[72] Ultimately, however, the two fashion farces were mercilessly panned in serious film reviews for recycling old forms of unpretentious entertainment.[73]

This was not the case with *Ingrid*. This film impressed the critics with its ambition to combine entertainment with realism, cinematic sophistication with socially and politically relevant content. Along with shedding light on a variety of practices in the revived fashion industry against the background of triumphant economic reconstruction and advancing prosperity in the West, this production impressed mainly with its aim to revisit the developments of the last ten years through the live story of Käte Bienert (played by Johanna Matz), who adopts the artistic name Ingrid after the dress whose creation she inspired and which she presents at shows with huge success. The film draws an epic arc and recapitulates a familiar array of themes from the distinct point of view of the young woman who came of age right around 1945 and who, several crisis-laden years later, has settled into a successful professional life and found personal happiness. The themes include the chaos, displacement, and confusion among the ruins of the war; the emerging Cold War divisions; the ugliness and dangers of the booming black market; the quick revival of the fashion and related entertainment industries along with the opportunities they offer to young women; and the triumphant economic reconstruction and advancing prosperity in the West.

The film opens around 1949 or 1950 with a lavish fashion show of glittering wedding gowns presented to an elegant audience sitting at dinner tables along the elevated catwalk. Against the background of slow dance music, crystal chandeliers, and exotic decor of palm leaves, the models, holding the numbers of the designs, parade in a circle. The camera, steadily fixed on the parading models, alternates between low and high angles, revealing either the audience's point of view at the spectacle or a more omniscient perspective of the public and atmosphere of the event. It turns out that this is not simply a fashion show but a pageant to choose the best model, "Miss Mannequin." Soon the winner is announced: "Number Ten," and the young woman with that number reenters the stage triumphantly to the wild applause of the public. This film clearly puts a premium on exclusivity and high style, unlike the fashion displays in DEFA films, such as the one at the Leipzig Fair in *Modell Bianka*, where the practicality and usability of clothing in everyday context is emphasized. In *Ingrid*, the venue is also important—a luxurious hotel with a well-dressed, refined audience, reflecting the newly acquired prosperity and consumer affluence in West Germany.

The show's choreography and presentation style are strongly reminiscent of the Miss Germany pageants that were popular in the 1920s

and 1930s until the Nazis banned them in 1933 as expressions of cosmopolitan decadence.[74] By 1948, however, beauty and fashion competitions
(*Schönheits- und Modekonkurrenzen*), frequently merged into a single
event, had been resurrected with remarkable speediness in the Western
occupied zones and received wide media coverage as signs of rapid normalization of life.[75] They quickly became the subjects of mindlessly escapist, but also extremely popular revue comedies such as *Johannes und die
13 Schönheitsköniginnen* (Johannes and the 13 Beauty Queens, 1951,
directed by Alfred Stöger) and *Der bunte Traum* (The Colorful Dream,
1952, directed by Géza von Cziffra), which were filmed in color, featured sumptuous costumes, and "enticed the viewers into a careless stroll
through the land of dreams and charms."[76]

In its quasi-documentary style, the opening sequence of *Ingrid* is
almost indistinguishable from the reports in the West German newsreels
about the first reestablished beauty pageants taking place throughout
West Germany. The merger of beauty, fashion, and postwar trauma in
this competition, won by the fictional film protagonist, must have also
reminded the audience of the first highly-publicized actual postwar contests: Miss Berlin, Miss Mannequin, and Miss Germany. In those contests
fashion models who had recently survived family tragedies, displacement,
and misery were elected the most beautiful German women. According
to the journalist Katja von Glinski, these stories found "an amazing reso-
nance" ("einen erstaunlichen Widerhall") with the public and drew attention to the lives of young women in particular.[77]

The best known of these contestants was Susanne Erichsen, for whom
the international media invented the term "a German Fräuleinwunder"
and whose life story during and after the war was remarkably similar to
Ingrid's in the film. After years of displacement and incarceration as a
refugee during and after the war and some tedious months as a cutter in
the Bavaria film studios in Geiselgasteig, she was discovered by the Salon
Flacker in Munich and the fashion industry in September 1948, when she
began modeling. She was chosen Miss Mannequin of Munich in 1949 and
Miss Germany in 1950.[78] In the 1950s, Erichsen was West Germany's
star fashion and photo model with numerous international engagements,
but remained loyal to the Berlin-based designer salon of Gehringer &
Glupp, where she had a steady contract throughout the years.[79]

The name of the new Miss Mannequin, the main protagonist in our
film, becomes known the next day when she is interviewed by a journalist, Robert (played by Paul Hubschmid) for a cover story in an illustrated
magazine, at the insistence of a photographer, Walter (played by Paul
Edwin Roth) who has fallen in love with her at first sight. We learn that
she is Käthe Bienert, a Viennese who has been displaced by the war. The
interview serves as occasion for a long flashback in which Käthe recounts
her life at the end of the war: losing her parents in the turmoil, moving

from Silesia to live with relatives in Thuringia and, from there, making her way to the West, near Hamburg, where she is at first placed in an internment camp. This seems to be a typical, traumatic postwar experience of many young women: it is the story of difficult survival, of hunger, of encounters with the black market, disorientation, detention, and rape. Many contemporary critics pointed out that in *Ingrid* this story is retold cinematically with sober realism, "free of sugary clichés," "free of erotic antics," and without melodramatic pathos that were common on the West German screen of the 1950s.[80]

Käthe's career in the fashion industry starts as an auspicious escape, made possible by her sister, from the shady criminal world that she has been involved in. A benevolent roommate who is a chief dressmaker (played by Alice Treff) offers her a job as a seamstress (*Nähmädchen*) at the designer salon where she works as *Directrice*. Here Käthe will have to learn to sew and to do "real work" ("wirkliche Arbeit"), which means that she will work hard for very little money ("wenig Geld und sehr viel zu tun"). As in the DEFA films, the profession of the seamstress is presented here as a "natural" but labor-intensive career path for uneducated young women in postwar Germany. In the West, however, the conditions are less egalitarian than in the East and the dreary job of the ordinary seamstress is juxtaposed to the glamour of a select few highly successful star models within the same company. The overall conditions of the industry are also signified by the availability of money and the trend toward luxury. In a stark contrast to the crowded, oppressive domestic conditions under which Käthe and her roommates live, the sequence introducing the fashion salon opens on large presentational space resembling a theater stage with a rotating platform in the middle. On it, accompanied by live music, a female model is revolving slowly, as motionless as a statue. Mimicking an artist desperate to find inspiration, the chief designer, D'Arrigio (played with charming irony, almost without words by Louis de Funés), looks at the decked-out model with narrowed eyes and grimaces in dissatisfaction. As the camera moves back and the frame widens, we see how he is surrounded by piles of flowing fabric and a small army of assistants who helpfully hand him different materials. At the end of the scene, the fashion king retreats to his throne-like armchair and motions the model to step down from the rotating platform. From her annoyed reaction back in the dressing room, it becomes clear that the couturier did not find the model inspiring enough to help him create a new design for a dress, "Ingrid," that he has dreamed up but not quite realized.

When the *Directrice* picks the newcomer seamstress Käthe to step on the stage, scantily clad in a revealing bodice, the designer D'Arrigio is instantly attracted by her beauty. On the spot he creates the design "Ingrid" on her slowly rotating body in a realistic reenactment of the process typically followed by star designers of the time, from Christian Dior and Pierre Balmain in Paris to Heinz Oestergaard and Hans Gehringer in Berlin.[81] The breakthrough with this dress becomes the miraculous starting point of Käthe Bienert's ascending path as a fashion model with the artistic name "Ingrid." ("All of us have been renamed," she explains later, "I am now called Fräulein Ingrid.")

Visually, this transition from an anonymous seamstress to the dazzling career of a prominent model is presented by a long pan of the camera in a dark production floor filled with lifeless clothes stands that fade into a close-up on an elegant and brightly lit catwalk. A quick succession of shots shows Käthe perform with professional poise and charm at the most glamorous fashion shows in Germany as well as abroad. The final scene in the sequence takes place at the Hamburg airport, where a live radio broadcast reports how an airplane has just arrived from Paris and angel-like models in beautiful white gowns were descending on the tarmac—Käthe, of course, is one of them. A group of cameramen are filming the models stepping down the stairs for the newsreels in movements choreographed very much like a premiere fashion show. The culmination of Ingrid's success is her subsequent selection as "Miss Mannequin," which brings the flashback to an end.

Curiously, after telling the story of the victimized refugee girl who gained a new identity and name, the camera does not return to Käthe Bienert's face, where the subjective narrative of the flashback began, but lands instead in the middle of a discussion between the two journalists, Walter and Robert. They question themselves and their motives: Should they publish their story or not, and, if so, how are they going to narrate it? The two men finally decide to construct a photo-essay entitled "Ingrid—die Geschichte eines Fotomodells" as a kind of Cinderella story of success and transformation by juxtaposing "before" and "after" pictures of her ("Lagerinsassin–Königin, Aschenbrödel–Fotomodell, Elend–Glanz," as Robert formulates the layout's principle).

In this somewhat sensationalist mass-media account as well as in Käthe's own retrospective view of her early life, the magic is equated to a fairy-tale-like breakthrough in the fashion industry, which requires a lot of luck: having the right physical appearance, being in the right place at the right time, and being discovered by the right men. Needless to say, this fashion and media world is ruled by powerful men, D'Arrigio and the journalists Walter and Robert, who govern by whim, have enormous influence on mass taste, and determine, often single-handedly, the fate of the women in the industry. The subsequent segment, in which Käthe poses for fashion photographs, underscores the position of passivity that she is reduced to, despite—or perhaps because of—her newly gained fame. As a professional model, she is constantly an object of scrutiny and observation and is continuously reminded to smile in a particular way. It seems that in acquiring popularity, renown, and new artistic identity, Käthe Bienert has lost her own voice and control over her story.

Throughout the remainder of the film, the title female character maintains an interesting balance between dependency and autonomy in both her personal and professional life. She has a complicated relationship with the two men, Robert and Walter. As her affair with the arrogant and often unreliable Robert results in a pregnancy that he wants terminated, Käthe decides to leave him. A modernist montage of shots of city traffic, close-ups on grotesquely staring eyes, and images from a fashion parade changing and repeating in quick succession alludes to Käthe's nervous breakdown right before she makes up her mind to leave the fashion world, give birth, and keep her child without Robert's knowledge. Walter is supportive and understanding of all her decisions, but his affections, albeit appreciated, are not returned. After a short break following childbirth, Käthe returns to her modeling career. Her work for a female-owned fashion firm in Hamburg has a dramatically different meaning now: the single mother Käthe has acquired the autonomy and confidence of a fashion professional who is earning money to support herself and her child, while maintaining complete control over her life.

The happy ending of the film conforms to a pattern established in earlier postwar productions, typical of both East and West Germany such as *Straßenbekanntschaft* and *Martina*: after all obstacles and misunderstandings the couple reunites to live as a family, and the promise of obtaining a nice, modern, and, in this case, brand-new living space is embraced. Perhaps responding to the generational aspirations of East and West Germans who rebuilt their cities in the early 1950s and found adequate housing, the final sequence portrays Robert and Käthe visiting the construction site of the high-rise where they will have an apartment. Detailing the amenities of their future domestic spaces with nearby playgrounds and linking them firmly to the future happiness of the couple, this scene presents a West German cinematic parallel to the East German reconstruction program as exemplified in DEFA's *Roman einer jungen Ehe* (1952, directed by Kurt Maetzig). Here, an extensive element of the narrative celebrates the opening of Berlin's Stalinallee (now Karl-Marx-Allee) and of its buildings with spacious, light-filled apartments for working- class families; this theme is intertwined with the prospects of the young couple's happy life together.

Despite its realistic, nuanced, and multidimensional treatment of the life and career of a young woman in postwar Germany within the context of the fashion industry, *Ingrid* failed to spark strong audience interest. Although it offered an opportunity to review the recent experience of a whole generation in a story that was marked by both loss and economic gain, hard work and material prosperity, habitual dependency and emancipation, the West German public more or less rejected that form of cinematic entertainment.[82] The display of fashion—thoughtfully connected to Käthe Bienert's various professional experiences in life, experiences that not only oppress and exploit, but also bring opportunity and material stability—was not enough to attract a large audience.

As previously discussed, the consumer culture and widespread interest in fashion that reemerged directly following the war continued to develop in the subsequent years and was shared by women in both the Soviet and the Western occupation zones. The evolving politics of consumption after the founding of the two German states was critical for the development of both the East and West German national identity in the postwar years. Contrary to what we imagine, the East German media were attuned to the needs and desires of women as Cold War divisions sharpened with the advance of the *Wirtschaftswunder* in the Federal Republic and the lack thereof in the GDR. The DEFA films *Modell Bianka* and *Frauenschicksale* reaffirm with different stylistic means and within different genres that women in the East, too, insisted on adequate, sufficient in quantities, and high-quality clothing for their basic everyday needs, despite the inability of the state to provide for these needs. And whether explicitly acknowledged or not, Western haute couture and its forms of public presentation, continued to serve as models and standards that the East followed, imitated, and appropriated in its own fashion industry and in the spectacles offered on its silver screens.

Epilogue

B Y REVISITING A selected body of East and West German films, this book has traced the cinematic developments that paralleled the recovering and the renewed flourishing of the fashion industry during a string of postwar crisis periods in Germany: from the end of Second World War to the early postwar years, through the Berlin Blockade, the founding of the two German states, and to the early phase of the Cold War. Reexamination of these films, along with the relevant fashion media reports, offers critical and often alternative reflection on this relatively short time span, in which democratization, recovery, and rebuilding after the war took place. The immediate postwar period, a span of only about ten years, was marked by such a rapid process of normalization in everyday life and in real and vicarious consumption and entertainment that by the mid-1950s the events of the previous decade seemed like distant history. Retrospective, self-congratulatory narratives of the quick progress made in the course of that period abounded on film and in the printed media, in the East and the West. In this process the media often chose fashion-related themes and the spectacular display of the women's changing styles to express visually the dramatic advances taking place, especially in women's lives.

In 1953, a small movie company in Wiesbaden, Trans-Rhein-Film, released a series of five short documentaries (*Kurz-Dokumentarfilme*), each one twelve to fifteen minutes long, that were distributed by United Artists Co. GmbH and shown in theaters before the main feature.[1] The five films were all titled "A Short Trip through Time" ("Kleine Reise durch die Zeit") and had different topics and main protagonists exemplifying a typical development of the recent years. Each documentary featured a humorously rhymed voice-over narration, musical accompaniment by the popular cabaret performer Peter Igelhoff, a fictional main character played by a nonprofessional, and a visual narrative based on a mix of documentary footage and scenes filmed on a set. Of the five short documentaries, the one most interested in incorporating a variety of historical footage and in shedding light of the life of women after the war is *Kleine Reise durch die Zeit mit Ursula* (A Short Trip through Time with Ursula, 1953, directed by Wolfgang Kiepenheuer).

Ursula—Ulla for short—is introduced as a "fashion student" ("Modeschülerin"), and the film announces that it will recreate this young woman's experience in search of self-realization in the course of the years since the end of the war. The starting point is the panorama of a city reduced to ruins—it looks like Hamburg—with figures rummaging among the debris and frenzied scenes at the black market. The lonely figure of Ursula is shown wandering aimlessly in the city and observing silently and from a safe distance the sites of struggle and chaos. She asks, "Where was there any meaning in this new beginning?" ("Wo war in diesem Neubeginn der Sinn?"). The documentary narrative then zooms in on the postwar situation involving clothing: fragments of garments are used as currency in black-market deals or traded at special barter "rag trading" (*Lumpenaustausch*) centers. "One had nothing but rags and scraps" ("Man hatte nichts als Lumpen und Fetzen"), the voice-over narrator explains, while the camera focuses on the old uniforms with swastikas that are being shredded, the strips of cloth forming a huge pile.

A dramatic cut leads the viewer into the orderly space of a dressmaker studio were women work on sewing machines. Ulla, wanting to acquire some practical skills, gets herself s job as a seamstress and learns to sew dresses out of old military bed linen. Soon, the first postwar fashion shows follow suit. Although celebrated as hopeful signs of recovery, these fashion shows are characterized by the film as "a pale imitation of glamour, a weird butterfly dance in gray" ("ein schwacher Glanz, seltsamer Schmetterlingtanz in grau"). Ulla finds these clothes "remarkably ugly." Her personal response to the unsatisfactory postwar conditions in the quest for a meaningful new beginning is to enroll in art school to study drawing and eventually become a fashion designer herself.

In the course of her studies, Ulla witnesses all aspects of postwar recovery—the rebuilding of the cities and the factories with the help of the Marshall Plan, and the rebirth of commerce. She learns to capture the spirit of the budding economic boom in her own sketches and drawings. Her first original fashion design is a dress, which she names "Transatlantic," made of a printed fabric with images of various sea vessels, an implicit gesture of gratitude for the bales of cotton that arrive from the United States on Hamburg's docks and fuel the rebirth of the textile industry. Ulla's extensive fashion education includes browsing in old illustrated magazines and becoming familiar with fashion history. This is strongly implied by the extensive documentary footage incorporated into the *Kurz-Dokumentarfilm* of fashion shows shot for the very first Pathé, Messter, and Tobis newsreels, from the 1910s through the late 1940s.

Ulla's training wouldn't be complete without a visit to the undisputed capital of global fashion, Paris, and to the beating heart of that world, Christian Dior's salon, where the young German designer gains plenty of inspiration to create her own New Look dress. The dress proves to be a huge success on the Kurfürstendamm as well as in stores around the world. Ulla seems to have accomplished her goal and to be firmly on a path to further professional triumphs.

The DEFA feature film *Besondere Kennzeichen: keine* (Distinguishing Features: None, 1956) could be considered an East German counterpart to the West German Kurz-Dokumentar. It was Hans Kunert's directorial debut and was based on a radio-play written by Berta Waterstradt. It has a longer fictional format, but with its stark realism and almost documentary atmosphere, this work, too, presents a retrospective overview of the enormous progress made by East German society in overcoming the effects of the war.[2] As Klaus Wischnewski, DEFA's premiere film critic, wrote in a long analysis of the film, "it resembles a documentary, because it does not tell a story, but reports on a development" ("[Der Film] hat etwas von einem Dokumentalfilm, der keine Geschichte erzählt, sondern über eine Entwicklung berichtet").[3] Like *Kleine Reise durch die Zeit mit Ursula*, *Besondere Kennzeichen* places a young woman "without any distinguishing features," Gerda Krause (played by Erika Müller-Fürstenau), at the center of the action in order to recreate the typical female experience of the postwar period. Although she is a widow with two small children at the end of the war, Gerda's fate very much resembles Ursula's: in order to survive, she takes on a job as a seamstress in one of the large state-owned clothing companies in Berlin, presumably the VEB Fortschritt.

Dressmaking sustains Gerda's young family throughout the rough and hungry rubble years after 1945. But this first job turns out to be only a stepping-stone on the way to achieving the bigger dream of her life, becoming a teacher. As a teacher, Gerda returns with her students on a school trip to the clothing company, proudly shows them around, and takes them to a fashion parade that showcases the beautiful models produced by the state-owned clothing industry. Mixing in ample documentary material from the DEFA archives, the extensive sequence of the fashion show at the end of the film marks a high point in the narrative: in this sequence Gerda's personal and professional triumphs blend with the impressive accomplishments of the GDR textile industry, which by the mid-1950s is seen to have overcome the significant difficulties and shortages of the immediate postwar years and is able to satisfy East German women's insuppressible desire for elegant outfits for everyday wear.

Both films, the low-key fictional *Besondere Kennzeichen: keine* and the much more tendentious *Kleine Reise durch die Zeit mit Ursula*, convey the confidence of their filmmakers and audiences that enough historical distance has been gained by the mid-1950s to appreciate the upward postwar path of the postwar fashion industry in both West and East Germany. In that sense both films are retrospective, evoking many of themes touched on in this book. They remind us of the paradoxical juxtaposition between ruined, rubble-filled cities and resurrected prewar rituals. They tie the postwar efforts for economic recovery to the struggles, initiatives, and ambitions not of *Trümmerfrauen* but of women engaged in the various creative and productive aspects of the fashion industry. Without explicitly commenting on the political divisions between the German Democratic Republic and the Federal Republic of Germany or making overt comparisons, each film promotes its own specific view of recent history. *Kleine Reise durch die Zeit mit Ursula* emphasizes the crucial impact, in the West, of the Marshall Plan on the speed and scope of the industry's revival, and particularly the economic assistance delivered by the United States. *Besondere Kennzeichen: keine* acknowledges the role of the new socialist institutions, the state-owned factories and schools, and their supportive communities in helping individuals find their footing in life and realize their professional dreams. In addition to providing oblique political comment, both films hint at the undeniably major driving force that was common in varying degrees to both halves of postwar Germany, namely "consumption" and the desire to normalize it.

These two retrospective films are also symptomatic of the regrettable shortcomings of such celebratory narratives, which are visible also in the fashion spreads in the print media during that period. More often than not, mass-media visualizations of women's fashion in magazines and on the silver screen reflected pipe dreams, retold fantasy scenarios, and encouraged vicarious consumption instead of reflecting on what was actually available or affordable to the East or West German female consumer. Yet such trends had a considerable social and political function in wartime and in the postwar years. For example, postwar couture disseminated as a normative image a vision of the autonomous, professionally accomplished woman, and many middle-class women did indeed carve out an independent existence as white-collar workers within the fashion-related professions.

More important, however, the zeal to mark the positive developments of the preceding decade often eclipses any critical consideration of the fate of the once-prominent German fashion industry during the years of Nazi reign. The resurrection of the fashion out of the ashes caused by Allied bombing was acknowledged in these films. The resurrection out of the ashes of an industry sector on the bones of people whose businesses had been expropriated and "Aryanized" under the Nazi regime was not. Neither West nor East German media made any serious effort to engage with the this painful history and come to terms with it. Hence, I have made a point of shining a light on one forgotten story: the Jewish designer Charlotte Glückstein, who returned to Berlin after being incarcerated in a KZ, reestablished a successful career, and dedicated her efforts to catering to the specific tastes and needs of the women of Berlin, a city in the process of reconstruction.

This cultural history of the long decade of the 1940s is intended to be selective, focusing in on facets of the era that have been ignored in other accounts of both film and fashion history. My aim was to revisit fiction films and fashion media accounts for forgotten memories preserved in them. As the Weimar film expert Anton Kaes has observed, the "complex fictional constructs" that we call films "unlock the viewer's hidden wishes and fears, liberate fantasies, give material shape to shared moods and dispositions."[4] When we reread these films and the fashion discourse interwoven into them as interventions into cultural and political life, we seek to reconstruct an alternative, more nuanced history of women's experiences in that period, a history that reveals the continuity between the wartime and postwar periods and the surprising commonality between the East and the West, the socialist and capitalist systems, in the early Cold War years. In the course of my research I have unearthed abundant archival material that has helped me develop and advance my hypotheses. However, much remains to be done to add more detail to this fascinating picture. My hope is that this volume will spark curiosity in other scholars to pursue further research in municipal and national collections and in business records and statistical offices, to widen the geographical scope of this history beyond Berlin.

Appendix 1. Principal Costume and Fashion Designers: Biographical Notes

Bessie Becker (1919–71), listed in credits also as Irmgard Becker-Schulte or Irmgard Becker, spent her formative years in Berlin. From 1937 to 1940 she studied at the Fashion and Textile School on the Warsaw Bridge (Textil- und Modeschule an der Warschauer Brücke), initially fashion drawing (*Modegraphik*) and subsequently costume design. In the 1940s Becker worked as a costume designer for Berlin theaters as well as for UFA, where she provided the costumes for five wartime productions, including *Großstadtmelodie* (1943) and *Meine Freundin Josefine* (1942), two films with extensive scenes set in a fashion salon and around fashion shows. At the end of the war, in 1945, Becker moved to Munich, where she resumed work for both theater (Münchner Kammerspiele) and film. She is listed as the costume designer in the credits for thirteen West German film productions between 1947 and 1959. Among her most prominent works are: *. . . und über uns der Himmel* (1947), *Zwischen gestern und morgen* (1947), *Film ohne Titel* (1948), *Das doppelte Lottchen* (1950), and *Nachts auf den Straßen* (1952).[1]

Irmgard Bibernell (1910–99) was born in Berlin and trained at the Lette-Verein. After working as an apprentice and star model at the famous Gerson Salon, Bibernell started her own independent career as a designer. In 1934 she cofounded with Heinz Schulze the fashion salon Schulze & Bibernell; after 1941 it became a member of Berliner Modelle GmbH and a well-known supplier of costumes for the stage and film. Bibernell was known as the personal couturier of movie celebrities such as Zarah Leander, Marika Rökk, and Inge Meysel. After 1945 she relocated to Hamburg and rebuilt her business with the help of her friend the publicist Axel Springer. She designed the costumes for the postwar productions *Film ohne Titel* (1948; working with Bessie Becker) and *In jenen Tagen* (1947).[2]

Alfred Bücken (1910–?) designed the costumes for twelve UFA period dramas between 1939 and 1945 (*Der Tanz mit dem Kaiser, Diesel, Träumerei*) and for twenty West German productions between 1950 and 1959. Bücken's extensive personal archive, including many sketches, is available in the Filmmuseum Frankfurt.[3]

Ilse Fehling (1896–1982) studied costume design at the Reimann School for Applied Arts in Berlin from 1918 to 1920 and subsequently also sculpture at the Bauhaus in Weimar with Georg Muche and Johannes Itten. Between 1933 and 1940, Fehling designed the costumes for twenty films, among them some acclaimed productions such as *Das Mädchen Irene* (1936, a film with a fashion salon at the center of its plot), *Eskapade* (1936), *Die Kreutzersonate* (1937), and *Casanova heiratet* (1940). From 1936 to 1940 she also worked as chief costume designer (*Chefausstatter*) for Tobis-Europa and was responsible for developing a concept for reusing and reappropriating available costumes and props. Fehling resumed her work as a costume designer for the movies in the 1950s and contributed to half a dozen West German films.[4]

Manon Hahn (1908–93), a native of Breslau (now Wrocław), completed training as a photographer in Munich at the age of eighteen, before moving to Austria to study fashion design at the famous Vienna Art School for Women (Wiener Frauenakademie), from 1928 to 1932. At the age of twenty-five, Hahn started working for UFA, designing costumes for thirty-eight films before the end of the Second World War. Her big break came with the assignment to design the costumes for Reinhold Schünzel's *Amphitryon* (1935). After that Hahn became a sought-after costume designer working for big-budget historical films such as *Boccaccio* (1936), *Capriccio* (1938), *Prinzessin Sissy* (1938), and *Münchhausen* (1943). After 1945 Hahn spent several years writing and drawing for the Berlin-based fashion press, contributing to the fashion sections of *Telegraf, Spandauer Volksblatt, Der Nacht-Express, sie,* and other publications, signing her pieces as "Manon." She resumed work as a costume designer for West German film in 1953, thereafter adding another eighteen productions to her record.[5]

Margot Hielscher (1919–2017) was born in Berlin and trained as a fashion designer in the 1930s, before joining UFA as a costume consultant in 1939. She designed the costumes for five films: *Hurra! Ich bin Papa!* (1939), *Lauter Liebe* (1940), *Kora Terry* (1940), *Auf Wiedersehn, Franziska!* (1941), and *Der Gasmann* (1941). During the same period, her musical and acting talents were discovered and she started performing in films. After 1945, Hielscher became known exclusively as an actress and singer.[6]

Eva Lemke (1893–?) studied art and design in Paris from 1924 to 1932. Upon her return to Berlin she started teaching part-time at the School for Textile and Fashion in Berlin and directed the workshop associated with the school, which produced costumes for theater and film. In 1942, after lengthy considerations by the administration, Lemke was appointed the director of the school, despite the fact that she had not joined the Nazi Party. She is credited with the costumes for the propaganda film *Jakko* (1941). After the war she turned to fashion journalism and published in the Berlin fashion magazines *Chic* and *Berlins Modenblatt*, using the bylines "E.W." and "Ewa Lemke." In 1949, Lemke also became a professor of fashion drawing at the Institute for Fine Arts in West Berlin (Hochschule für Bildende Künste in West-Berlin), known since 1975 as Hochschule der Künste (Institute of Arts). No further biographical information is available.[7]

Gerda Leopold designed the costumes for ten films between 1939 and 1943, among them *Frau nach Maß* (1940), *Mädchen im Vorzimmer* (1941), . . . *reitet für Deutschland* (1941), and *Die goldene Spinne* (1943). After her marriage to the cameraman Walter Pindtner she was listed in credits also as Gerda Leopold-Pindtner.[8]

Vera Mügge (1911–84) is credited for the costumes in fifty-one films from 1939 to 1974, the majority of them in the 1940s and '50s. She was trained at the Berlin School for the Applied Arts (Berliner Gewerbeschule) in Charlottenburg and started her career at UFA in 1939. Mügge was primarily responsible for the costumes in the first AGFA-color German film, *Frauen sind doch bessere Diplomaten* (1941), the notoriously anti-Semitic *Die Rothschilds* (1940), and thirteen other films until 1944. In the first long postwar decade, she worked mostly for DEFA (*Rat der Götter*, 1950; *Corinna Schmidt*, 1951; *Das verurteilte Dorf*, 1952) and for some West German productions such as *Beate* (1948) and *Am Tag als der Regen kam* (1959), as well as for DEFA coproductions with Sweden such as *Fräulein von Scuderri* (1955) and *Die Spielbank-Affäre* (1957). After 1958, Mügge moved to the West and was associated for many years with Arthur Brauner's studio CCC-Film.[9]

Ilse Naumann (1905–83), a Berlin native, studied costume design at the Reimann School for Applied Arts in Berlin-Schöneberg. Naumann worked for theater and film. She designed the costumes for eight film productions between 1937 and 1942, including the costumes for the stars Grete Weiser, Heinz Rühmann, Olga Tschechowa, Marianne Hoppe, and others.[10]

Hildegard Ordnung (1910–?) studied fashion design and illustration at the Lette-Verein, a prominent Berlin school for applied arts, from 1926 to 1929. After working for the publisher of *Der Bazar* in 1930 and the well-known department store Nathan Israel from 1930 to 1934, Ordnung became a freelancer and joined the Reichskammer für Bildende Künste in 1936. With special permissions from the Reichsfilmkammer, she was hired to design the costumes for five Tobis-Film and UFA productions between 1942 and 1945: *Der große Preis* (1944), *Kollege kommt gleich* (1943), *Leb' wohl, Christina* (1945), *Die Jahre vergehen* (1944), *Die Hochstaplerin* (1944). Immediately after the war she started working as an illustrator for the fashion press, most prominently for *Berlins Modenblatt*, where her regular contributions continued into the late 1950s. No further biographical information is available.[11]

Maria Pommer-Pehl, also known as Maria Pommer-Uhlig, is listed as the costume designer in the credits for over thirty film productions between 1938 and 1944, among them *Es leuchten die Sterne* (1938), the successful comedy *Ein Mann auf Abwegen* (1940), and *Robert und Bertram* (1939). No biographical information is available.[12]

Gertrud Recke, listed in some credits as Gertraud Recke or Gertraude Recke, worked as a costume designer in Berlin for both theater and film. She outfitted four pre-1945 films (*Meine Frau Teresa*, 1942; *Die Degenhardts*, 1944; and *Weiße Wäsche*, 1942) and ten postwar film productions, among them some iconic German films: *Die Mörder sind unter uns* (1946), *Ehe im Schatten* (1947), *Straßenbekanntschaft* (1948), *Berliner Ballade* (1948), and *Martina* (1949). No biographical information is available.

Sinaida Rudow (birth name Besrutschenko; listed in credits also as Sinaida Rudow-Brosda or Sinaida Rudnow), was daughter of Russian émigrés. She established her salon, Esté, in Berlin in the early 1930s and became a member of Berliner Modelle GmbH in the 1940s. The costume designer Günther Brosda (1918–80) joined the salon in 1939 as an intern, after his graduation from the School for Fashion and Textile in Berlin. After the war Rudow and Brosda became business partners in the newly established Rudow & Brosda Salon, which emerged as one of the most prominent and luxurious establishments in postwar Berlin. Sinaida Rudow was known as the couturier to many celebrities (Olga Tschechowa, Hilde Seipp, and Brigitte Horney) and alone or with Brosda designed the costumes for ten West German films between 1951 and 1958. Rudow & Brosda was dissolved in 1961, and Sinaida Rudow relocated to Munich.[13]

Ursula Schewe (1918–?), a Berlin native, received her master's certification in fashion design and tailoring from the respected Meisterschule für Mode in Munich. In 1941, then twenty-three, Schewe returned to Berlin and opened her own salon, Modewerkstätte (Fashion Workshop) at Wielandstrasse 30, in Charlottenburg. Her boyfriend, Arno Tanski, helped her financially and logistically. The establishment flourished despite wartime shortages and restrictions. Miraculously, Schewe's salon survived the air raids intact and continued production after the war. In the immediate postwar months, she took orders from the Soviet occupation forces and the wives of Soviet officers. She showed her first postwar collection at the Leipzig Fair in 1946, and it was featured in various Berlin fashion magazines. In the 1950s Schewe cemented her reputation as a couturier to prominent celebrities, Miss Germany contenders, and actresses in West Berlin and abroad (such as Giulietta Massina). Her salon had more than fifty employees. In 1951 she was commissioned to design the costumes for *Unschuld in tausend Tönen* (also titled *Das Mädel aus der Konfektion*), which premiered at the newly founded Berlin International Film Festival. Ursula Schewe married a millionaire, Walter Hadamovsky, moved with him to Caracas, Venezuela, and closed her fashion salon in 1959.[14]

Walter Schulze-Mittendorff (1893–1976) studied sculpture at the Academy of Arts in Berlin. In 1920 he was introduced to Fritz Lang and became involved the production of *Der müde Tod* (1921). In the course of his long career in film he collaborated on many Fritz Lang classics, including *Metropolis, Nibelungen,* and *Das Testament des Dr. Mabuse.* After 1933 Schulze-Mittendorff got more and more involved in costume design. In 1935 his name was listed as both a sculptor and a member of the costume design team in the film credits of the film adaptation of Kleist's *Amphitryon.* During the late 1930s he also worked for Erich Engel (*Der Maulkorb*) and Veit Harlan (*Der Herrscher*). Helmut Käutner's *Kleider machen Leute* (1940), an elaborate costume film set in the nineteenth century, was a turning point in Schulze-Mittendorff's career. It was his first film as a costume designer, under contract with the production company Terra-Filmkunst. Because this company was under the control of the Nazi Ministry for Propaganda, he was excused from military service and had an easier time protecting his half-Jewish wife from persecution. After the war Schulze-Mittendorff worked for the DEFA film studios, where he was the costume designer for almost forty feature and children's films, including *Wozzeck, Der Untertan,* and *Die Geschichte vom kleinen Muck.* At the same time he also worked for the Berliner Komödie and Volksbühne theaters. After the building of the Wall in 1961, Schulze-Mittendorff, who lived in West Berlin, decided not to renew his contract with the DEFA studio. Between 1962 and 1968, he worked on eighteen West German television and movie productions, collaborating once more with Falk Harnack and Wolfgang Staudte, who had also left DEFA and East Germany.[15]

Gertrud Steckler, a chief costume consultant and designer for UFA since 1939, oversaw the production of the costumes for twenty-three films between 1936 and 1951, among them *Immensee* (1943), *Wunschkonzert* (1940), *Die Frau meiner Träume* (1944), and *Augen der Liebe*

(1943/1951). She specialized in costumes for revue films. The dress that Steckler designed for Marika Rökk in *Die Frau meiner Träume* was widely discussed in the film and fashion press at the time. No further biographical information is available.[16]

Reingard Voigt, a Bauhaus-trained artist who studied with Paul Klee from 1929 to 1930, designed the costumes for fifteen films produced by the Terra, Tobis, and UFA companies in the period from 1938 to 1944, including the last wartime color film, *Ein toller Tag* (1944; it premiered in 1954), and *Achtung! Der Feind hört mit!* (1940). No further biographical information is available.[17]

Appendix 2. Films and Newsreels Discussed

Feature Films

Achtung! Der Feind hört mit! (Attention! The Enemy Is Listening!). Directed by Arthur Maria Rabenalt. 1940. DVD, Avondale, AZ: rarefilmsandmore.com, n.d.

Besondere Kennzeichen: keine (Distinguishing Features: None). Directed by Hans-Joachim Kunert. 1956. DVD provided by Progress-Filmverleih.

Das himmelblaue Abendkleid (The Sky-Blue Evening Gown). Directed by Erich Engels. 1941. DVD. Avondale, AZ: rarefilmsandmore.com, n.d.

Der bunte Traum (The Colorful Dream). Directed by Géza von Cziffra. 1952. Viewed in at the Deutsche Kinemathek, Berlin.

Die Mörder sind unter uns (The Murderers Are among Us). Directed by Wolfgang Staudte. 1946. *The Murderers Are among Us.* DVD. Berlin: DEFA Stiftung, 2016.

Die Sünderin (The Sinner). Directed by Willi Forst. 1954. DVD. Berlin: Studiocanal, 2000.

Film ohne Titel (Film without a Title). Directed by Rudolf Jugert. 1948. VHS. Indianapolis, IN: German Language Video Center, n.d.

Frau nach Maß (Custom-Made Woman). Directed by Helmut Käutner. 1940. DVD. Avondale, AZ: rarefilmsandmore.com, n.d.

Frauenschicksale (Destinies of Women). Directed by Slatan Dudow. 1952. DVD, *Destinies of Women.* Amherst, MA: DEFA Film Library, 2007.

Frischer Wind aus Kanada (A Fresh Wind out of Canada). Directed by Heinz Kenter. 1935. DVD. Avondale, AZ: rarefilmsandmore.com, n.d.

Fürst von Pappenheim (Prince von Pappenheim). Directed by Hans Deppe. 1952. Viewed at the Deutsche Kinemathek, Berlin.

Großstadtmelodie (Melody of a Great City). Directed by Wolfgang Liebeneiner. 1943. DVD. San Francisco: Reichskino, n.d.

Illusion in Moll (Illusion in a Minor Key). Directed by Rudolf Jugert. 1952. Viewed at the Deutsche Kinemathek, Berlin.

Ingrid: Die Geschichte eines Fotomodells (Ingrid: The Story of a Fashion Model). Directed by Géza von Radvanyi. 1955. DVD. Avondale, AZ: rarefilmsandmore.com, n.d.

Johannes und die 13 Schönheitsköniginnen (Johannes and the 13 Beauty Queens). Directed by Alfred Stöger. 1951. Viewed at the Deutsche Kinemathek, Berlin.

Kein Platz für Liebe (No Place for Love). Directed by Hans Deppe. 1947. Viewed at Progress Film-Verleih, Berlin.

Kleine Reise durch die Zeit mit Ursula (A Short Trip through Time with Ursula).
Directed by Wolfgang Kiepenheuer. 1953. Viewed at the Bundesarchiv/Filmarchiv, Berlin.

Kollege kommt gleich (The Colleague Will Come Immediately). Directed by Karl
Anton. 1943. DVD. Avondale, AZ: rarefilmsandmore.com, n.d.

Leipziger Messe 1946 (The Leipzig Trade Fair, 1946). Directed by Kurt Maetzig.
1946. Viewed at the Bundesarchiv/Filmarchiv, Berlin.

Mädchen im Vorzimmer (The Girl in the Lobby). Directed by Gerhard Lamprecht. 1940. DVD. Avondale, AZ: rarefilmsandmore.com, n.d.

Martina (Martina). Directed by Arthur Maria Rabenalt. 1949. DVD. Berlin:
Magic Picture, 2011.

Meine Frau Teresa (My Wife Teresa). Directed by Arthur Maria Rabenalt. 1942.
DVD. Avondale, AZ: rarefilmsandmore.com, n.d.

Meine Freundin Josefine (My Friend Josefine). Directed by Hans H. Zerlett.
1942. DVD. Avondale, AZ: rarefilmsandmore.com, n.d.

Modell Bianka (The "Bianka" Design). Directed by Richard Groschopp. 1951.
DVD. Berlin: Icestorm Entertainment, 2006.

Nachts auf den Straßen (Nights in the Streets). Directed by Rudolf Jugert. 1952.
DVD. Avondale, AZ: rarefilmsandmore.com, n.d.

Roman einer jungen Ehe (Novel of a Marriage). Directed by Kurt Maetzig. 1952.
DVD, *Story of a Young Couple*. Amherst, MA: DEFA Film Library, 2006.

Straßenbekanntschaft (Street Acquaintance). Directed by Peter Pewas. 1948.
DVD, series name Peter Pewas Filme 1932–67. Fridolfing, Germany: absolut
Medien, 2004.

The Man Between. Directed by Carol Reed. 1953. DVD. Berlin: Studiocanal,
2015.

Träum nicht, Annette! (Don't Dream, Annette!). Directed by Eberhard Klagemann. 1948. Viewed at Progress Film-Verleih, Berlin.

Unschuld in tausend Nöten (Innocence in a Thousand Notes). Directed by Carl
Boese. 1951. Viewed at the Deutsche Kinemathek, Berlin.

Vor uns liegt das Leben (Life Lies before Us). Directed by Günther Rittau. 1948.
Viewed at the Deutsche Kinemathek, Berlin.

Wege im Zwielicht (Paths in the Twilight). Directed by Gustav Fröhlich. 1948.
DVD. Berlin: Magic Picture, 2010.

Zwischen gestern und morgen (Between Yesterday and Tomorrow). Directed by
Harald Braun. 1947. DVD. Munich: Edition Filmmuseum 45, 2010.

Newsreels Viewed in the German Bundesarchiv/Filmarchiv Berlin,

Blick in die Welt
Der Augenzeuge
Die deutsche Wochenschau
Die neue deutsche Wochenschau
Welt im Film

Notes

Introduction

[1] The film was produced by Stella-Film GmbH in Berlin and was one of the so-called exchange films (*Austauschfilme*) between the West and the East. It premiered at the end of 1948 in Cologne, and was shown in both West, in July, and East Berlin, in September, with screenings in West and East Germany throughout 1950. See Bauer, *Spielfilm Almanach, Band 2: 1945–1955*.

[2] See Münchner Stadtmuseum, *Aus 2 mach 1*. On the continuities between war and postwar practices of dealing with clothing shortages as reflected in selected feature films, see Hampicke, "Flotter Mangel, fesche Reste."

[3] Riederer, *Wie Mode Mode wird*, 60. (Translation by the author; all translations are by the author unless otherwise noted.) Marietta Riederer (1906–86) worked in Paris alongside Helen Hessel and published in the *Frankfurter Zeitung*'s supplement *Für die Frau* until 1938. During the war years she worked in Germany and contributed fashion drawings, alongside the texts by Susa Ackermann, to the weekly periodical *Das Reich*. After the war, Riederer settled in Munich, but from the mid-1950s until the late 1970s she also traveled widely across Europe, contributing fashion reports to *Die Zeit*, *Die Süddeutsche Zeitung*, *Annabelle*, the German edition of *Vogue*, and occasionally to *Der Spiegel*. See Ganeva, "Die Modeschriftstellerin Helen Hessel," 341.

[4] Riederer, *Wie Mode Mode wird*, 61.

[5] The practice is recounted in multiple sources. See, for example, von Kardoff, "Vier Frauenbildnisse von heute."

[6] A survey performed in 1948 posed the question "What would you do if all of a sudden you come in the possession of 1000 D-Marks?" Fifty percent of the participants answered that they would buy clothing (*Bekleidung*), and the percentage among refugees was even higher, 60 percent. See Bundeszentrale für politische Bildung, *Neubeginn und Wiederaufbau*, 29.

[7] "Phantasie gegen leere Kleiderschränke," *Die Neue Zeitung*, October 28, 1945: "Da wären etwa die alten Decken aus dem Luftschutzkeller. Jetzt brauchen sie das Tageslicht nicht zu scheuen—und Einfallsreichtum kann aus ihnen einen schicken Mantel, eine Jacke oder lange Hose, eine Wickelrock oder dergleichen zaubern. . . . Also: Einfärben, zerschneiden, . . . nähen, steppen—und fertig ist das gute Stück. Manches vom modischen Standpunkt aus gesehen 'hoffnungslose' Kleid wird durch Einstricken von Rollkragen, Ärmeln oder Miederteilen aus farbigen Wollresten nicht nur bedeutend hübscher, sondern gleichzeitig wärmer."

[8] The most comprehensive account of the Aryanization of the Berlin-based fashion industry is Westphal, *Berliner Konfektion und Mode 1836–1939*. See also Guenther, *Nazi Chic*, and Kremer, *Broken Threads*.

[9] Hanne Voelcker, "Die Wiedererstandenen," *ITEX: illustrierte Fachzeitschrift für die gesamte Textil- und Bekleidungswirtschaft* (henceforth cited as *ITEX*), December 5, 1947.

[10] See Kessemeier, "Die Mode erobert den Kurfürstendamm," and Metzger, "Kurze wirtschaftliche Blüte," 211–14.

[11] See Schmitt, "Die strahlenden Jahre." See also "Die Heimatarbeiterinnen," *Telegraf*, June 25, 1946.

[12] Roessler, "Der Wiederaufbau der Berliner Industrie 1945–1947," 505, 520–21; Janke, "Bekleidungs- und Mode-Metropole Berlin," 61–62.

[13] ann-mary, "Der letzte Schrei." ann-mary was the pen name of the journalist Ann Mary Sigrist.

[14] "Darf man jetzt von Mode sprechen?," *Die Zeit*, April 11, 1946.

[15] See Sywottek, *"Darf man jetzt von Mode sprechen?"*

[16] Liselott, "Mode ohne Kleider," *Berlin am Mittag*, February 8, 1947.

[17] The history of the Leipzig Trade Fair goes back to the Middle Ages. After the war Leipzig fell within the Eastern zone, but it retained its traditional role as a meeting place for Germany's manufacturers and designers.

[18] Hanisch, *"Um 6 Uhr abends nach Kriegsende,"* 13.

[19] Hauptamt für Statistik von Groß-Berlin, *Berlin in Zahlen 1946–1947.*

[20] On the continuity of moviegoing as an escapist endeavor throughout the war and postwar years and for detailed numbers, see Prommer, *Kinobesuch im Lebenslauf,* 89–93, 131–40; Prommer, "Das Kinopublikum im Wandel."

[21] Brandlmeier, "Von Hitler zu Adenauer," 34.

[22] Albrecht, "Kino am Abgrund." See also Szepansky, *"Blitzmädel," "Heldenmutter," "Kriegerwitwe,"* 31.

[23] See Wortig, *Ihre Hoheit Lieschen Müller,* 15–16.

[24] See Baer, *Dismantling the Dream Factory,* 2–3. In 1945, women made up 63.2 percent of the population of Greater Berlin; this portion declined slightly in subsequent years to 59.5 and then to 57.5 percent. See Borneman, *Belonging in the Two Berlins,* 58–59.

[25] Hanisch, *"Um 6 Uhr abends nach Kriegsende,"* 4, 18.

[26] Pleyer, *Deutscher Nachkriegsfilm 1946–1948,* 49, 153–54.

[27] Helmut Käutner, "Demontage der Traumfabrik," *Film-Echo,* no. 5, June 1947.

[28] Note on film titles: The first time a German film title is mentioned in a chapter it is followed in parentheses by an English translation, the year of release, and the name of the director. The German title is used for subsequent mentions. Some longer titles are referred to in a shortened form, for example, *Die Mörder.* See also "Appendix 2: Films and Newsreels Discussed," for a complete list of films discussed in this book.

[29] Helmut Weiß, "Stabilität des Unterhaltungsfilms: Plädoyer für die Traum-Fabrik," *Der neue Film,* no. 1, 1948.

[30] Erika Müller, "Sag die Wahrheit," *Die Zeit*, May 1, 1947; "Stellvertreter bei der Hochzeit," *Der Spiegel*, September 20, 1947.

[31] See Bergfelder, *International Adventures*; Rentschler, "The Place of Rubble"; Shandley, *Rubble Films*. I provide a more detailed discussion of these sources and the topic in chapter 3.

[32] Meyer, "Trümmerkino," 261. For the audience numbers, see also Pleyer, *Deutsche Nachkriegsfilm*, 155.

[33] See Groß, *Die Filme sind unter uns*, 15–16.

[34] Saryusz-Wolska and Labentz, *Bilder der Normalisierung*, 16.

[35] Andrews, "Film and History," 179.

[36] Ibid., 178. This central premise in echoed in Koch, "Nachstellungen: Film und historischer Moment," 229.

[37] Shandley, "Truth Value of Cinema," 95.

[38] Street, *Costume and Cinema*, 9. For more recent examples of the increased interest of film scholars and historians in the connections between fashion and film and the variety of perspectives on the topic, see Munich, *Fashion in Film*.

[39] See Saryusz-Wolska, "Watching Films in the Ruins," 762–82. Dozens of film programs are preserved in the archive of printed materials (*Schriftgutarchiv*) of the Deutsche Kinemathek in Berlin (www.deutsche-kinemathek.de/en/archives/film-archive/general-information). I am grateful to Magdalena Saryusz-Wolska for this helpful reference.

[40] Gertrud Recke worked on four pre-1945 and ten post-1945 films; Vera Mügge was the chief costume designer for fifteen wartime and thirty-five postwar films, eight of them between 1946 and 1953; Manon Hahn is credited for the costumes for thirty-five pre-1945 UFA productions and nearly twenty postwar films, most of them in the 1950s; Bessie Becker (also listed in film credits as Irmgard Becker-Schulte or Irmgard Becker) worked on six prewar, fourteen postwar films (nine between 1946 and 1953); Hildegard Ordnung designed costumes for four prewar films and one postwar production and after the war worked primarily as fashion journalist for different periodicals. See Berger, Reichmann, and Worschech, *Zwischen gestern und morgen*, and also appendix 1; for further information see also filmportal.de.

[41] For example, in Glaser, *Rubble Years*, film is only marginally mentioned; in Hermand, *Kultur im Wiederaufbau*, developments in film and fashion are scattered throughout separate chapters, but the emphasis is primarily on the 1950s in West Germany; Schivelbusch, *In a Cold Crater*, offers a fascinating account of the brisk revival of cultural life among the ruins, but also leaves out completely the fashion media and fashion-related activities; finally, in a more recent exploration, Steege, *Black Market, Cold War*, demonstrates how the Cold War in Berlin in general and the politics of the black market in particular were crafted "from below," by ordinary Berliners, often in spite of or in opposition to the policies of the occupation powers. His account, too, leaves Berliners' fashion and clothing practices out of the picture.

[42] See Pleyer, *Deutscher Nachkriegsfilm*; Shandley, *Rubble Films*; Fay, *Theaters of Occupation*; Greffrath, *Gesellschaftsbilder der Nachkriegszeit*.

[43] Arendt, "Aftermath of the Nazi Rule: Report from Germany," 249.

[44] Arendt, *Essays in Understanding*, 254.

[45] Confino, *Germany as a Culture of Remembrance*. 214.

[46] See Grossmann, *Jews, Germans, and Allies*, 3–5.

[47] Gemünden, *A Foreign Affair*, 72.

[48] There are a number of studies that emphasize markedly regional practices and locally renowned designers of postwar fashion. See Volz, "Trümmermode und New Look"; Prinz, *Trümmerzeit in München*, 303–11; Schütz, "Vom Zuckersack zum Traummodell"; Selheim, "Kleidung und Mode in Bayerisch-Schwaben zwischen 1945 und 1960."

[49] See Heineman, "Hour of the Woman."

[50] For an incisive and extended discussion of the "Fräulein" phenomenon, see Brauerhoch, *Fräuleins und GIs*.

[51] See Heineman, "Hour of the Woman."

[52] Carter, *How German Is She?*, 7. For more on the emergence of the "consumer-citizen" in West Germany as a result of the Marshall Plan, see De Grazia, *Irresistible Empire*, 336–75.

[53] Lennox, "Constructing Femininity in the Early Cold War Era," 67.

[54] Carter, *How German Is She?*, 213.

[55] Baer, "*Film und Frau* and the Female Spectator in 1950s West German Cinema," 152.

Chapter One

Epigraph: H. G. von Studnitz, "Frau Mode filmt. Modisches Zwischenspiel aus dem neuen Ufa-Film 'Frischer Wind aus Kanada,'" *Der Silberspiegel*, February 1935, 48–50: "In der Mode ist der Film Diktator und Gefangener zugleich."

[1] It was a relatively expensive film, costing 2,645,000 reichsmarks (reichsmarks continued to be in use until 1948) to produce, but it brought in 3,156,000 reichsmarks after its run until May 1944 and was thus considered a box-office hit. It was also rated "artistically valuable" ("künstlerisch wertvoll"). See Klaus, *Deutsche Tonfilme*, 158–59.

[2] Freiß, *Die Strickjacke*, 171–72, singles out Renate's knitted jacket (*Strickjacke*) as a symbol of belonging to the rural *Heimat* and to a traditional community.

[3] The popularity of the film and especially of its heroine is recounted in numerous contemporaries' eyewitness accounts. Will Tremper, in *Meine wilden Jahre*, remembers how as a result of *Großstadtmelodie*'s enormous success a record number of young women applied to be licensed as photo-reporters in April 1944: "I saw that because of the film *Großstadtmelodie* a kind of plague had broken out" ("Ich erfuhr, es sei durch den Film *Großstadtmelodie* eine Art Seuche ausgebrochen" (26–27). See also Sachsse, "Im Schatten der Männer," 12–25.

4 Irmgard Becker-Schulte (1919–71), later known as Bessie Becker, provided the costumes for seventeen films, including for some of the first well-known postwar productions such as *Zwischen gestern und morgen* (1947), *Film ohne Titel* (1948), *Das doppelte Lottchen* (1950), and *Nachts auf den Straßen* (1952). After contributing to five UFA films between 1941 and 1943, Becker moved to Munich in 1945, where she worked for both the theater and film and founded her own fashion salon in 1952. For more on Becker, see chapter 4 and appendix 1.

5 On the recognizability of Hilde Weissner and her suitability for the role of a fashion designer (*Modeschöpferin*), see Ernst Jerosch, "Großstadtmelodie," *Film-Kurier*, October 7, 1943.

6 "Die erste Frühjahrsmodenschau von Berlins Modenblatt in der Femina," *Berlins Modenblatt*, no. 5, May 1946.

7 See Veillon, *Fashion under the Occupation*, 39–40.

8 See, "Deutsche Mode in Brüssel," *Der Silberspiegel*, February 1942.

9 According to some counts, there were fewer than twenty war films. See O'Brien, *Nazi Cinema as Enchantment*, 119.

10 Rentschler, *Ministry of Illusion*, 16–18.

11 Ibid., 19.

12 See Bruns, *Nazi Cinema's New Women*, 45–46.

13 O'Brien, *Nazi Cinema as Enchantment*, 9.

14 Arthur Maria Rabenalt, "Meine Frau Teresa," *Film-Kurier*, January 2, 1943, 10. Quoted in Lange, *Das Kino als moralische Anstalt*, 166.

15 See Lant, *Blackout*, 75–76.

16 See Hake, *Popular Cinema of the Third Reich*, 191. Among the very few explorations of the function of costume in individual German wartime entertainment films is Warth, "The Reconceptualization of Women's Roles in Wartime National Socialism," 219–30.

17 Davidson, "Working for the Man, Whoever That May Be," 244–45.

18 Arthur Maria Rabenalt, Wolfgang Liebeneiner, Josef von Báky, and Rudolf Jugert are among the many film directors who began their careers during the Nazi period and continued equally successfully in the immediate postwar years. A number of young female designers, too, started around the 1940s and contributed to the quick rebirth of both the fashion print media and costume design right after the war. Among them were Hildegard Ordnung, Gertrud Recke, Bessie Becker, and Vera Mügge.

19 See Aly, *Hitler's Beneficiaries*.

20 Ibid., 97. Aly quotes extensively from Heinrich Böll's wartime correspondence with his future wife, Annemarie, where such items of clothing are extensively enumerated and commented upon.

21 Swett, *Selling under the Swastika*, 187.

22 For most detailed accounts, see the chapter "War Years" in Guenther, *Nazi Chic*, and Sultano, *Wie geistiges Kokain*, 30–31.

23 Sultano, *Wie geistiges Kokain*, 30–31.

[24] Guenther, *Nazi Chic*, 216, provides a note on the different dates to be found in various sources. According to Charman, *The German Home Front 1939–45*, 49, the date of the release of the first *Reichskleiderkarte* was November 16, 1939.

[25] For example, a pair of pajamas was forty-five points; a shirt, twenty points; a towel, a pair of socks, or pair of gloves, five points each. Bigger items such as jackets and suits required sixty points. See Werner, *"Bleib übrig!"* 52.

[26] Quoted in Guenther, *Nazi Chic*, 217.

[27] Walford, *Forties Fashion*, 173–75.

[28] For the reports of the military propaganda that summarized the mood in German cities, especially Berlin, see Wette, Bremer, and Vogel, *Das letzte halbe Jahr*, 142–43.

[29] See "Spendenparade der Wintersachensammlung" and "Frontfürsorge auf höchsten Touren," *Berliner Lokal-Anzeiger*, January 3, 1942; "Das große Fest des Sammelns. Bist Du auch dabei?" *Berliner Lokal-Anzeiger*, January 4, 1942; "Spenden-Wetteifer," *Berliner Lokal-Anzeiger*, January 8, 1942.

[30] See "Alle Hände halfen mit: Die Schauspielerin Käthe Haack in der Nähstube einer Berliner Sammelstelle," *Der Silberspiegel*, February 1942.

[31] "Empfindliche Strafen für Tauschgeschäfte: Neue Anweisungen des Reichsjustizministers, *Berliner Lokal-Anzeige*, January 21, 1942.

[32] For an analysis of the variety of black-market activities in the 1940s, see Zierenberg, "The Trading City," 145–58.

[33] They still advertised the few items excluded from rationing, such as silk stockings and cosmetics products.

[34] Ehrlich, "Die PuC Werkstätten." For more on wartime branding strategies and advertising for clothes as well as other consumer items, see Swett, *Selling under the Swastika*, 185–227.

[35] J.v.M. [Mörner], "Das Verwandlungskleid," *Das Reich*, September 8, 1940. See also "Wollkleider—vielfach verwendbar," *Der Silberspiegel*, September 1942, and "Ein Kleid 7 X gewandelt," *Der Silberspiegel*, January 1943.

[36] See, for example, "Viele Falten, aber mit wenig Stoff," *Der Silberspiegel*, February 1941; "Die Mode spart und bleibt erfinderisch," *Der Silberspiegel*, March 1943; "Zeitbedingte Vorschläge," *Der Silberspiegel*, March 1943.

[37] See the segment "Kleiderschau 'Aus Alt mach Neu' in einem Rüstungswerk," in *Die Deutsche Wochenschau*, no. 714/21, 1944, screened at Bundesarchiv/Filmarchiv Berlin in June 2014. Unfortunately, the audio on the tape was partially missing and the voice-over commentary was not always inaudible.

[38] Maria May, "Der Mode-Stil der Zukunft," *Das Reich*, June 30, 1940: "Durch die Einführung der Kleiderkarte ist eine Erziehung zur Qualität erfolgt, ein Besinnen auf Zweckmäßigkeit, verbunden mit einer kritischen Einstellung in Fragen des persönlichen Geschmacks."

[39] For the private reactions of German couturiers and designers, see Guenther, *Nazi Chic*, 208–9.

[40] "Mode ohne Diktat," *Die Mode*, January 1941.

[41] Ernst Herbert Lehmann, "Mode und die deutsche Sprache," *Die Mode*, October 1941.

[42] May, "Mode-Stil der Zukunft": "Den Versuchungen einer billigen, lediglich dem Sensationsbedürfnis dienenden Nouveaute-Industrie unterliegt man nicht mehr. . . . Die Mode der Vergangenheit war Paris—die Mode der Zukunft liegt bei Großdeutschland." For more on anti-French propaganda and the actual developments of the French fashion industry under occupation, see Guenther, *Nazi Chic*, 210–13; Veillon, *Fashion under the Occupation*. The desired shift of the center of the fashion industry from Paris to Berlin was loudly announced in all propaganda outlets, including the youth magazine *Signal*, which was distributed also in English: "Until Now Paris has been the focus of the world in the realms of fashion, but the creators of the Seine have been clouded in their judgments of what is really beautiful, good and appropriate. . . . Parisian fashion must pass by way of Berlin before a woman of taste can wear it." See *Signal*, no. 9, March 1941.

[43] "Berliner Modell," *Das Reich*, July 28, 1940.

[44] May, "Mode-Stil der Zukunft." For more on Berliner Modelle GmbH, see Guenther, *Nazi Chic*, 191–92; Wagner, "Das Deutsche Mode-Institut 1933–1941."

[45] Companies that exhibited wartime fashion included Corves & Seger (formerly the Jewish-owned firm Löwenberg); Gehringer & Glupp (formerly Auerbach & Steinitz); Kuhnen (taken over by Werner Brüggemann); Horn (formerly Gerson); Suden & Lauer; C. G. Strohbach (Aryanized by three former employees); Frekato, Hansen Bang (taken over by Herrmann Schwichtenberg); Sauer (taken over by Helmuth Witt).

[46] "Hinter den Kulissen," *Die Mode*, February 1941: "Die Berliner Modellvorführungen im Herbst und Frühling sind zwei feststehende Punkte im kulturellen Jahresprogramm der Reichshauptstadt geworden."

[47] "Berlin zeigt," *Die Mode*, August—September 1941: "Die Arbeit der 'Berliner Modelle' findet in der Materialbelieferung Unterstützung bei den amtlichen Stellen." On the plundering of French fabrics, see Veillon, *Fashion under the Occupation*, 39–40; Schmidt, "Raub an allen Fronten," 44–46.

[48] See Sultano, *Wie geistiges Kokain*, 29. Even though the shortage of labor due to mobilization remained a continuous problem for the industry, it created unprecedented professional openings for young female designers and artists.

[49] E. v. Sichard, "Politik und Mode," *Das Reich*, November 17, 1940.

[50] "Berlin zeigt," *Die Mode*, August–September 1941.

[51] Sultano, *Wie geistiges Kokain*, 29.

[52] "Hinter den Kulissen," *Die Mode*, February 1941.

[53] "Germans over Paris," *Vogue*, January 15, 1941.

[54] See "Die Manufaktur der deutschen Mode-Instituts" and "Richtungsschau Berlin," *Die Mode*, February 1941.

[55] "Aus den Kollektionen," *Die Mode*, January–February 1942.

[56] See Veillon, *Fashion under the Occupation*, 94.

57 For more on the media campaigns in Britain geared toward women on the home front, see Kirkham, "Keeping Up Home Morale." See also Kirkham, "Fashion, Femininity and 'Frivolous' Consumption in World-War-Two Britain." as well as Howell, *Wartime Fashion.*

58 M.W., "Mode auch im Kriege," *Die Mode,* March 1941.

59 Audrey Withers, "British *Vogue* Weathers the Storm," *Vogue,* December 1, 1940.

60 See Ernst Herbert Lehmann, "Die 'Vogue' bettelt um Mitleid in Amerika," *Der Silberspiegel,* February 1941.

61 Ernst Herbert Lehmann, "Politisierende Mode in USA," *Die Mode,* November 1941.

62 Lehmann, "Die 'Vogue' bettelt."

63 See "Sex Appeal in Uniform," *Die Koralle,* August 24, 1941.

64 Ernst Herbert Lehmann, "Gemeinschaftskleid," *Die Mode,* February 1941.

65 Maria May, "Die neuen Farben," *Die Mode,* April 1941.

66 Lehmann, "Gemeinschaftskleid": "Denn es wäre falsch zu glauben, dass der Frau durch das Tragen einer Uniform die Freude am schönen Kleid verloren ginge. Im Gegenteil: wenn sich eine solche Frau in ihrem Privatleben befindet, wird sie besondere Freude an schönen Kleidern haben."

67 Ernst Herbert Lehmann, "'Einheitskleid' oder 'Modellkleid,'" *Die Mode,* April 1942.

68 Ibid.

69 "Schöpferisches Spiel mit Samt und Seide," *Der Silberspiegel,* June 1941.

70 "Aus den Kollektionen," *Die Mode,* January–February 1942.

71 Felix Buttlersack, "Das Interview des Silberspiegels mit Benno von Arent," *Der Silberspiegel,* February 1942.

72 Hans Traub, "Mode und Film," *Die Mode,* March 1943: "Wir sahen einen Film, einen von vielen, an irgendeinem Abend. Es war nichts Besonderes an ihm hervorzuheben. Er war keine Spitze. . . . Er war nur Unterhaltungsfilm, oft allzu leicht als Durchschnitt angesprochen, wo doch auch an ihm Leistung und so unendlich viel Kleinarbeit und Mühe stecken. Es blieb nichts von ihm haften, weder für das gespannte Auge, noch für das leidenschaftliche Herz. Und doch machten einige flüchtig hingeworfene Sätze zweier Besucherinnen den Abend wertvoll. Die eine sagte: 'Was war das für eine reizvolle Mode!' Die andere antwortete: 'Ja, fabelhafte Kostüme hatten die an, und diese Aufmachung!'" See also "Mode und Kostüm im Film," *Die Mode,* April 1943; Eva Lemke, "Aus einer Werkstatt für Film-Mode," *Die Mode,* April 1943.

73 Schulze has already been involved in designing the costumes for some of the UFA's productions and was known as the personal couturier of many UFA stars, including Zarah Leander. He did not last long in his job because of his refusal to become a party member and was soon sent to military training. After 1953 he called himself Schulze-Varell. See Auer, *Der Couturier Heinz Schulze-Varell (1907–1985),* 40. See also "Modische Verwandlungen. Zarah Leander in *Die große Liebe,*" *Der Silberspiegel,* January 1942.

[74] See Hans Traub, "Mode und Film," *Film-Kurier*, April 8, 1943; Hans Traub, "Mode und Kostüm im Film," *Film-Kurier*, April 12, 1943.

[75] Traub, "Mode und Film."

[76] Günther Schwark, "Mehr Geschmack in der Filmkleidung. In modischer Hinsicht hat der Film erzieherische Aufgaben," *Film-Kurier*, March 11, 1942: "So und so viele Millionen weiblicher Besucher sehen jährlich die Filme. Sie orientieren sich geschmacklich an den darin getragenen Kleidern. Was müssen junge Mädchen und junge Frauen in kleineren Provinzstädten für einen Eindruck von dem Aussehen einer gutgekleideten Großstädterin bekommen? Sie wissen ja nicht, daß die kultivierte Berlinerin oder Wienerin über solche Modeblüten nur lächeln kann. Was aber dann, wenn diese Angeberkleidung Schule macht, gläubig nachgeahmt wird? Wenn das in breiteren Kreisen für fein gehalten wird, was der Film zuweilen unter dieser Marke modisch ausgibt. Auch in dieser Sicht übernimmt der deutsche Film eine große Verantwortung. Ihrer sollte er sich mehr bewußt werden, indem er Träger des guten Geschmacks wird."

[77] Georg Herzberg, "Mode und Film," *Film-Kurier*, October 17, 1942 (the entire passage): "Wenn man offenen Auges durch die Straßen der deutschen Städte geht, wenn man in die Büros und in die Verkaufsstätten, die Theater, Lichtspielhäuser und Restaurants blickt, dann wird man feststellen können, dass die deutsche Frau auch zu Beginn des vierten Kriegsjahres es noch immer versteht, sich gut und geschmackvoll anzuziehen. Sie tut das trozt aller kriegsbedingten Schwierigkeiten, aus dem instinktiven Gefühl heraus, daß es auch in dieser schweren Zeit nicht nur ihr gutes Recht, sondern auch ihre Pflicht ist, ihr Äußeres zu pflegen und auch in ihrer Haltung den Widerstandswillen des deutschen Volkes zu demonstrieren."

[78] Hake, *Popular Cinema of the Third Reich*, 191.

[79] Ibid.

[80] Jürgen Petersen, "Das himmelblaue Abendkleid," *Das Reich*, September 8, 1940.

[81] Reingard Voigt, a Bauhaus-trained artist who studied with Paul Klee in 1929–30, between 1938 and 1944 designed the costumes for fifteen films produced by Tobis, Terra, or UFA. For more, see appendix 1.

[82] "Jagd nach einem himmelblauen Abendkleid," *Filmwelt: das Film- und Foto-Magazin*, February 7, 1941.

[83] Dietrich, "Frau Mode auf Abwegen"; Dietrich, "Ein heiterer Kriminalfall."

[84] See Strate, "Kleider machen Stars."

[85] "Jagd nach einem himmelblauen Abendkleid."

[86] Dietrich, "Frau Mode auf Abwegen."

[87] Ibid.: "Augenblicklich kann man, wenigstens was Deutschland angeht, von einer sehr vernünftigen Mode sprechen, und der Krieg mag hier in mancher Beziehung regulierend gewirkt haben, weil sich niemand bei der Punktbeschränkung große modische Extra-Touren leisten kann und soll. . . . Doch kleine Dosen von Luxus im Film geniessen wir immer noch."

88 Dietrich, "Ein heiterer Kriminalfall": "Dieser amüsante Film kommt zur rechten Zeit in München heraus, denn jeder denkt gern daran, wie das früher einmal war und jeder weiß, daß ein Jahresanfang wieder einmal so unbeschwert und glücklich begangen wird."

89 "Ein neues Thema der Mode," *Die Mode*, July 1942: "Da das Leben der Frau gegenwärtig in einem nie dagewesenen Maße der Arbeit gehört, ergeben sich für die Mode neue Aufgaben von politischer und sozialer Bedeutung."

90 Hanns Maria Braun, "'Kollege kommt gleich': Erstaufführung in Sendlinger-Tor-Lichtspielen," *Münchner neueste Nachrichten*, November 30, 1943.

91 This theme seems particularly topical in the wake of the mass Aryanization of the predominantly Jewish-owned fashion businesses between 1933 and 1935. By 1938 this process was complete; in the 1943 film, references to Jews are entirely missing.

92 Braun, "'Kollege kommt gleich': Erstaufführung in Sendlinger-Tor-Lichtspielen."

93 See Höhn, *"Fange nie an aufzuhören,"* 24.

94 The magazine *Der Silberspiegel* dedicated a long article with multiple illustrations to the fashion display in the 1935 film. See H. G. von Studnitz, "Frau Mode filmt. Modisches Zwischenspiel aus dem neuen Ufa-Film 'Frischer Wind aus Kanada,'" *Der Silberspiegel*, February 1935. See also G.H., "Frischer Wind aus Kanada: Filmkritik," *Film-Kurier*, March 11, 1935.

95 Most likely, Hildegard Ordnung—like Gerda Leopold, Gertrud Recke, and Manon Hahn—was one of several young female designers recruited by the film industry in the wake of mass mobilization of male employees to the front. Ordnung worked as a costume designer on five films produced by the studio Tobis between 1942 and 1945; after the war she became fashion editor and contributor to numerous magazines such as *Berlins Modenblatt*, *sie*, and *Elegante Welt*. For more on Ordnung, see appendix 1.

96 Hans Martin Cremer, "Die Kostümberaterin und ihr Aufgabenfeld," *Film-Kurier*, November 16, 1940. See also Fritz-Heinz Reinhardt, "Das Geheimnis der Zwischentöne: Der Kostümberater beim Film—Schauspieler werden künstlerisch gekleidet," *Film-Kurier*, December 14, 1940; Lisa Peck, "Eine Kostümberaterin erzählt: Frau Pommer-Pehl über ihre Arbeit für den neuen Bavaria-Film 'Komödianten,'" *Film-Kurier*, February 24, 1941. Maria Pommer-Pehl (also known as Maria Pommer-Uhlig) is listed as the costume designer in the credits for over thirty productions between 1938 and 1944. For more, see appendix 1.

97 Margot Hielscher (1919–2017) studied fashion design from 1935 to 1939 and started working for UFA in 1939. She designed the costumes for six wartime films, most notably for *Auf Wiedersehn, Franziska* (Good-bye, Franziska, 1941, directed by Helmut Käutner), in which she also took on a small acting role. After the war she switched tracks and became an actress and a singer. She is best known for playing the lead role in *Hallo, Fräulein!* (1949, directed by Rudolf Jugert). For more on Hielscher, see appendix 1.

98 Veillon, *Fashion under Occupation*, 124.

Chapter Two

Epigraph: "Modebarometer: steigend," *Heute*, June 15, 1947: "Das sieht man im Straßenbild von Berlin—Frauen, die ausgesprochen schick und modisch wirken. Dabei sind die Kleider nicht extravagant, es ist der Gesamteindruck, der entscheidet. Die Berlinerin beweist aufs Neue ihren Sinn für Mode, für das, was 'in der Luft liegt.' Sie greift nicht nach den Sternen, sondern nach dem Realisierbaren. Sie sucht und findet das richtige Kleid, für ihren Typ und—für Berlin heute!"

[1] Alice Bronsch (1910–?) was a well-known fashion illustrator who had worked for Ullstein publications (*Die Dame, UHU*) throughout the 1930s and 1940s. In the 1950s she was recruited to work for *Film und Frau*. The phrase "Fashion for Fräuleins" is borrowed from a headline that appeared in the British *Daily Mail*, December 14, 1945: "Life Returns to the New Germany with New after-the-Defeat Styles and Fashions for Fräuleins." It reappeared in the magazine *sie*, January 13, 1946. *sie* described itself as a *Wochenzeitung für Frauenrecht und Menschenrecht* (Weekly Newspaper for Women's Rights and Human Rights).

[2] Isaac Deutscher, "Berlin—September 1945," *The Economist*, September 29, 1945, 4467.

[3] Frisch, "Notizen aus Berlin und Wien," 183–84: "Fast alle mit einem Bündel, einem Rucksack oder einer Schachtel. Neben Gesichtern, die wie aus Lehm und Asche sind, gibt es andere, durchaus gesunde, aber ebenso verschlossen und fast maskenhaft; erst nach einer Weile bemerkt man die Armut am Kragen und an den Ellbogen. Noch hält sich Berlin in seinen letzten Anzügen. Die Frauen, auch wenn sie Hosen und schwere Schuhe tragen und ein Kopftuch, sind meistens sehr gepflegt, das ist schön. Und wichtig. Für sie sind es die Haare, die Lippen, die Fingernägel; für den Mann ist es die Fahne, woran er seine Selbstbeachtung heftet, und auf eine Weise, die sich kaum nennen läßt, bleibt um die Frauen eine viel größere und echtere Hoffnung."

[4] "Magnet für Modemacher," *Der Spiegel*, Janruary 4, 1993, 132–36. The article provides a good overview of the development of Berlin as a fashion center from the mid-nineteenth century till the 1990s.

[5] Frisch, "Notizen aus Berlin und Wien," 183: "Am Kurfürstendamm gibt es wieder die ersten Schaufenster, klein aber schmuck und sauber und geschmackvoll. Ein Labsal für das Auge. . . . Es ist die begreifliche Lust, wieder einmal etwas Ganzes zu sehen, etwas Sauberes, etwas Schönes."

[6] Wagner, "Die Mode in Berlin nach 1945," 130–31. For more on the transformation of Charlottenburg into the new center of Berlin's fashion industry from 1945 through the 1950s, see Goos and Heyde, *Kleider machen Frauen*. For more on the move of the production site of fashion from Hausvogteiplatz in the East to locations in the West of the city, see "Magnet für Modemacher," 134–35; H.V. [Hanne Voelker], "Hausvogteiplatz," *ITEX*, February 27, 1948, 8.

[7] Quoted in Metzger and Dunker, *Der Kurfürstendamm*, 214. For data on the recovery of West Berlin's garment industry, one of the city's "biggest economic branches," see "Die Bekleidungsindustrie" in Industrie- und Handelskammer zu Berlin, *Die Wirtschaft Westberlins 1945–1955*, 31–32.

8 The other four industries were the electrical industry, machine manufacturing, the chemical industry, and food production. See "Das darf Deutschland produzieren: Der Industrieplan für die deutsche Nachkriegswirtschaft," *Spandauer Volksblatt*, April 4, 1946. See also Industrie- und Handelskammer zu Berlin, *Die Wirtschaft Westberlins 1945–1955*, 7, 31–32.

9 Berlin Municipal Council, *Das erste Jahr*, 82.

10 Ibid., 81–83. Similar articles reporting the establishment of nearly 400 fashion-related businesses appeared in the daily press as well. See "Berliner Industrie auf Touren," *Der Nacht-Express*, March 29, 1946.

11 E.K. [Emmy Klaß], "Wieder Berliner Konfektion," *Der Nacht-Express*, September 3, 1946.

12 See the files from Claussen's postwar business archive, "Claussen Nachlass," in Heimatmuseum Charlottenburg-Wilmersdorf, Archiv, box 3422, reviewed by author in Berlin, July 2009 According to court documents, Hans W. Claussen, born in 1906, in partnership with his wife, Irma Claussen, purchased the garment business of Ursula Steinlein in January 1938. Whether or not this transaction is considered part of the Aryanization taking place during the same time period remains an open question. No other documents have survived to provide a definite answer.

13 Several newspaper ads placed by "Claussen-Kleider" announcing the company's intention to buy up used evening dresses and theater costumes to obtain silk, velvet, brocade, tulle, and lace. See *Der Nacht-Express*, April 15 and 22, 1946.

14 ann-mary [Ann Mary Sigrist], "Einfach und praktisch, das Gebot für den Export: Das Neueste aus der Metropole," *Spandauer Volksblatt*, June 22, 1946; E.Kl. [Emmy Klaß], "Erste Herbstmodensinfonie," *Der Nacht-Express*, October 22, 1946.

15 ann-mary, "Der letzte Schrei."

16 See folder, "Bilder vom ersten Friedens-Modentee." Nardi was a prominent journalist who contributed to a number of Berlin-based newspapers and magazines. Cordula Moritz (1919–95), a fashion journalist for *Der Tagesspiegel* between 1946 and 1980, in *Die Kleider der Berlinerin*, 86–87, recalls getting inspired by images of *Flickenkleider* she had seen and sewing herself a dress made partly of a bedcover, partly of different pieces of fabric. See also Grit Thönnissen, "Ein perfekter Schnitt," *Der Tagesspiegel*, September 28, 2015.

17 See also, "Praktische Hilfe: Das Flickenkleid," *Neue Berliner Illustrierte*, 1945/5.

18 Similar developments were observed in other fashion centers in German-speaking Europe after the end of the war. The first fashion show in Vienna took place on July 20, 1945, and there were ten more before the end of that year. See Feike, *Vom Vorhangkleid zur Dreamline*, 36–47, and Bönsch, "Kleidung nach dem Krieg," 102–6. In Munich the first fashion show was organized in April 1946, quickly followed by other export shows. See Epp, *Kleider machen Münchner*, 12–13. In both Vienna and Munich, the rebirth of the fashion show for an audience that included the military occupying forces was interpreted by the media as

a hopeful sign of optimism and determination to overcome the hardships of the present.

[19] See Heinz Mohr's reminiscences of the revitalization of the industry and its professional association in Ackermann, *Couture in Deutschland*, 24–25. The first show of the Guild of the Garment Trade took place in the Royal-Club on the Kurfürstendamm. See "Modenschau Frühjahr 1946," *Der Nacht-Express*, March 12, 1946. The first show of the Circle of Berlin Fashion Designers took place in the theater Komödie am Kurfürstendamm, in October 1946. See Emmy Klaß, "Sie kurbeln die Mode an," October 25, 1946.

[20] Riess, *Berlin! Berlin!*, 58. See "Stühle werden gesucht," *Berliner Zeitung*, April 28, 1946; "Stühle für Modenschau gesucht," *Neues Deutschland*, April 6, 1947.

[21] Strehl-Firle, *Und danach war alles anders*, 13.

[22] Hartung, "Wer in der Mode lebt," 49. See also Altman, "Spirit of Optimism," 18.

[23] "Modenschau am Funkturm," *Illustrierter Telegraf*, August 4, 1946.

[24] Borgelt, *Das war der Frühling von Berlin*, 220–21.

[25] See "Modenschau 1948 und bei einem Berliner Modeschöpfer," *Illustrierter Telegraf*, October 21, 1948.

[26] For analysis and a detailed history of the AFAs, see Harsch, *Revenge of the Domestic*.

[27] "Wo ein Wille ist, ist ein Weg," *Die Frau von heute*, February no. 1, 1946, 8–9.

[28] A.H., "Es war ein goldener Sonnentag: Das Sommerfest des Frauenausschusses am Funkturm," *Die Frau von heute*, October no. 2, 1946. The article features numerous photographs from both fashion shows and explains that the sewing rooms of the AFA provided 4,000 orphans with a set of underwear, a piece of sleepwear, and a dress or a suit. The fabrics were donated by the International Red Cross.

[29] "Vom Fenstervorhang zum Winterkleid," *Illustrierter Telegraf*, November 10, 1946. The article and several photographs feature students at work at Viktoria Fashion School in Berlin. In October 1946, *Der Nacht-Express* reported that a new fashion school was opening in Frankfurt, directed by Emmy Grasegger. Interest was said to be so high that only half of the 300 candidates from all four occupation zones could be admitted. See "Wieder eine Sorge weniger: Akademie der Mode," *Der Nacht-Express*, October 1, 1946. In the eastern sector, the Textil- and Modeschule der Stadt Berlin resumed its operations in the fall of 1945. See the extensive and richly illustrated articles "Neubeginn des Modeschaffens," *Neue Berliner Illustrierte*, 1945/4, and "Berliner Mode: Wie sie neu began und wie sie heute aussieht," *Neue Berliner Illustrierte*, 1945/7. The professional school located in Friedrichshain near Warschauer Brücke in the eastern sector was an institution with a long and venerable tradition going back to 1874. It functioned throughout the war, until late 1944, then reopened in 1945. The Textil- and Modeschule was renamed the Ingenieurschule für Bekleidungstechnik (Engineering School for Garment Technology). In the 1990s it merged with the Ingenieurhochschule Berlin (Engineering Institute). See also the long illustrated

article by Hanne Voelcker, "Kommende Meister: Von der Arbeit der Fachschule für Textilindustrie und Mode," *ITEX*, December 19, 1947.

[30] See Oberschernitzki, *"Der Frau ihre Arbeit!"* 204–9. For reports on the shows prepared by the class of fashion designers and illustrators in the famous Lette-Verein, see Helene Beer, "Fünf Töchter und kein Mann. Kostümschau der Modenschule zum 80. Jahrestag von Lettehaus," *Die Frau von heute*, April no.1, 1946, 2–3; G.Z., "Modeschülerinnen zeigen ihre Künste. Arbeitsschau der modischen Klassen für Schneiderei und das graphische Gewerbe," *Der Nacht-Express*, October 15, 1946.

[31] On Germany's only professional school for fashion models in Berlin, see "Mädchen, die zweimal gehen lernen müssen: Die Mannequinschule," *Der Nacht-Express*, June 24, 1946. The following year brought more such establishments. See the advertisement for the Yorck Studio modeling school, *sie*, August 24, 1947, 12.

[32] "Auch Mannequinns sind knapp," *Der Spiegel*, May 24, 1947.

[33] "Ilse und das Ruinenkostüm," *Der Augenzeuge*, no. 5, May 1946. For more on *Der Augenzeuge*'s reporting on fashion, women's issues, and consumption, especially in the 1950s, see Schwarz, "Der blockübergreifende Charm dokumentarischer Bilder, 203–34.

[34] "Phantasie gegen leere Kleiderschränke," *Die Neue Zeitung*, October 28, 1945.

[35] For example, the press reported of the arrival of 6,000 family members of the American military forces in Berlin in April 1946. See "Amerikaner in Berlin," *Spandauer Volksblatt*, April 9, 1946. In describing the audience at the first postwar shows and the clients of fashionable clothing, Hartung, "Wer in der Mode lebt," also mentions "ladies of the easy trade" ("Damen des leichten Gewerbes") and girlfriends of the occupation troops who had the necessary disposable income or barter goods in the form of food, cigarettes, or alcohol.

[36] "Auch Mannequinns sind knapp."

[37] "Berlin am Nachmittag," *ITEX*, December 19, 1947, is a report on a fashion show presented by the designer Hans W. Claussen that also emphasizes the importance of the members of the occupation forces as both customers and suppliers of fabrics: "Berlin am Nachmittag—das heißt vorläufig noch nicht, wie es sich präsentiert, sondern was es in den Mode-Ateliers arbeitet, um Aufträge aus den Kreisen des Besaztungsangehörigen bewältigen zu können, von denen oft das Material zur Anfertigung geliefert wird."

[38] "Auch Mannequinns sind knapp."

[39] Ibid.

[40] "Mode kennt keine Grenzen," *Für Dich: Die neue illustrierte Frauenzeitung*, December 15, 1946. Melitta Stegenwalner (1919–2010) started working for Tobis-Film in 1939, tailoring film costumes; it was there that she met Alfred Gründt. The two married after the war and founded their own business in Berlin, Modehaus Gründt. Melitta was the creative driving force behind it, while her husband was the accountant. From the late 1940s until 1961, according to press coverage, Melitta Gründt was one of the most original Berlin couturiers. For more, see Anselm Neft, "Melitta Stegenwalner: Wie in der Konfektion, so im Leben," *Der Tagesspiegel*, June 24, 2010. See also "Frühjahrsmoden: Melitta Gründt,"

Illustrierter Telegraf, March 18, 1948. "Modeschaffen in Berlin," *Die Frau von heute,* January no. 1, 1947.

41 "Deutscher Modeschöpfer Hugo Flacker vor Amerikanerinnen," *ITEX,* March 21, 1948, 12.

42 Located in the Nürnberger Strasse in Schöneberg, the Femina Bar had been a legendary spot on the nightlife scene since the late 1920s. The Soviet authorities ordered it to reopen in June 1945, along with other clubs in the area that offered cabaret and live music every night. After July 1945 it continued its activities in the American sector and was a popular hangout for the military of all four allies, who were looking for entertainment in Berlin. After 1950, it became a popular jazz club. See Chamberlin, *Kultur auf Trümmern,* 172–73.

43 See the publicity "*Berlins Modenblatt* zeigt am 26. und 27. März in der Femina einen Querschnitt durch das Modeschaffen Berlins: Frühjahrsmodenschau," *Berlins Modenblatt,* no. 3, March 1946. See also "Modenschau," *Welt im Film,* April 8, 1946, available in Bundesarchiv/Filmarchiv. That particular segment of the fashion show was filmed by the famous cameraman Fritz Arno Wagner.

44 "Die erste Frühjahrsmodenschau von Berlins Morgenblatt," *Berlins Morgenblatt,* May 1946.

45 See advertisements in *sie,* May 26, 1946, 8.

46 See Lott-Almstadt, *Die Frauenzeitschriften von Hans Huffzky und John Jahr.*

47 Ruth Andreas Friedrich (1901–77) was a journalist who started her career in the 1930s with the magazine *Die junge Dame* and participated in the underground resistance against the Nazis. In the immediate postwar period Friedrich resumed her work as a journalist and contributed to many weekly magazines, including *sie* and *Lilith.*

48 Mary Hamman and Nancy White, "Schaff' Dir Deine Mode!" *Heute,* May 15, 1946, 25–27. See also "Mode in Amerika," *Heute,* August 15, 1946; "ILGWU: Geschichte und organisatorischer Aufbau einer großen amerikanischen Industrieorganisation," *Heute,* January 10, 1946.

49 For circulation numbers and distribution, see Lott-Almstadt, *Die Frauenzeitschriften von Hans Huffzky und John Jahr,* 354–55.

50 Peter Weidenreich, "Zeitungsparadies Berlin," *Die Neue Zeitung,* January 11, 1946.

51 Ibid. For more on the thriving press in Berlin, see Reiche, "Berlin: Zukunft nach dem Ende."

52 See Schwarz, *Wochenschau,* 73, 295–342.

53 See Stitziel, *Fashioning Socialism,* 188. Stitziel quotes the only woman on the Politburo, Elli Schmidt, a trained seamstress who in a speech in 1960 retrospectively mused that in the immediate postwar period, "Our women did not ask how the clothing that they wore looked like. We were all very happy if there was enough to wear, when we got shoes on our feet."

54 Ruth Andreas Friedrich was surprised at how much the postwar audience cared about such a frivolous topic as fashion, sometimes even at the expense of serious political discussions. To that observation her managing editor at *Lilith,* Werner

Eggert, responded, "This is an inevitable compromise if you want to sell a paper these days. Democratic reeducation just cannot happen without any talk about cosmetics, diets, and fashion. Eggert quoted in Friedrich, *Zeitfunken: Biographie einer Familie*, 275: "[Es ist] klar, dass es ohne Konzessionen nicht geht, wenn man ein Blatt auch verkaufen wolle. Also wird die Erziehung zur Demokratie mit Kosmetik-, Diät- und Modethemen entsprechend aufbereitet."

55 "Muß Mode sein?" *Berlins Modenblatt*, no. 8, August 1946, 15–16: "Ich freue mich immer, wenn nett angezogene Fahrgäste in meinem Wagen fahren. Es ist so, als ob sie Sonnenschein mitbringen in die oft dunkle Atmosphäre des mit Blechen verdunkelten Wagens."

56 The two officials were Dr. Otto-Fritz Oehmichen, responsible for the Textile and Garments Department in Berlin's municipal government, and Erich Hoffmann, administrator in the finance division.

57 *sie*, editorial, December 19, 1945, 4.

58 See Hannelore Holtz, "Zwei Stunden im Märchenland: Modenschau am Nachmittag," *Der Nacht-Express*, October 31, 1946.

59 A.L. [Annedore Leber], "Mode—?" *Die Frau von heute*, February no. 1, 1946, 21: "Endlich frei von der Uniform und dem Zwang sucht [die moderne deutsche Frau] nach Wegen und Möglichkeiten, sich trotz der Enge der Zeit gut und vorteilhaft anzuziehen. . . . 'Mode' verkündet heute den Lebenswillen der Frau in einer schweren und ernsten Zeit, die durch unser Bemühen von einer leichteren und helleren abgelöst werden soll."

60 Ellie Tschauner, "Einmal ganz anders . . .!" *Die Frau von heute*, April no. 2, 1946: "[Der tiefste Sinn der Veranstaltung] lag nicht nur darin, der Frau zu zeigen, daß man auch in Notzeiten und behelfsmäßigen Mitteln seinen äußeren Eindruck pflegen kann,—denn er ist Spiegel der inneren Kultur!—, sondern in einem Notruf der Wirtschaft. Fünfzigtausend Menschen finden allein in der Berliner Bekleidungsindustrie ihr Auskommen. Hier gäbe es eine Anbahnung in die friedliche Welt, sobald die erforderlichen Rohstoffe zur Verfügung gestellt werden."

61 Gertrud Berger, "Frau Mode—entschleiert," *Die Frau von heute*, February no. 1, 1946.

62 R.Kn. "Anarchie im Reich der Mode," *Die Frau von heute*, March no. 3, 1946.

63 Erna Sommerfeldt, "Liebe Redaktion," *Für Dich*, November 17, 1946, 10.

64 Margarete Bechtinie, "Liebe Redaktion," *Für Dich*, November 24, 1946: "Für die modischen Anregungen sind Ihnen sicher alle Frauen sehr dankbar. Warum geben Sie aber keine Schnittmuster und Strickmuster dazu?"

65 See, for example, "Schnittmuster-Seiten der Nacht-Express," *Der Nacht-Express*, March 4, 1946.

Vignette 1

Epigraph. "Liebenswürdige Mode," *Berlins Modenblatt*, no. 3, March 1949: "Liebenswürdige Mode! Es ist so hübsch, wenn man das über die Mode schreiben kann! Und sie ist wirklich liebenswürdig, wie sie ich hier in einer Reihe von reizenden Kleidern präsentiert—liebenswürdig wir ihre Schöpferin Charlotte Glückstein. Sie weiß, was Frauen gern tragen, sie liebt keine Extravaganzen, für die ist immer die Forderung "schön und tragbar" maßgebend. Dabei wird der Rahmen weit gestreckt, jede Richtung der Mode kommt zu ihrem Recht und wird so 'transponiert,' daß die liebenswürdige Note und die graziöse Unauffälligkeit das Leitmotiv werden und zum Erfolg verhelfen."

[1] Erika Berneburg, "Wir sahen bei Charlott," *sie*, November 17, 1946, 10–11 (entire passage): "Dieser Salon 'Charlott' brachte den liebenswürdigen Beweis, wie geschmackvoll man die Nöte der Zeit meistern kann. Die modische Linie des Winters war bei allen Modellen mit großer Sorgfalt herausgearbeitet. Gleichzeitig aber bewies diese Schau, wie man mit wenig Stoffverbrauch Linie halten kann, und wie auch bescheidenes Material durch hübsche Stepp-Ornamente geschmückt und anspruchsvoll werden kann. Hinzu kamen auch nette Einfälle zum beliebten Thema des Verwandlungskleides, jener holden, aber zeitgemäßen Täuschung, wie man aus einem Kleid zwei machen kann, ohne eines davon verschwinden zu lassen. Diese Einschränkungen, durch den Materialmangel bedingt, beziehen sich jedoch nicht auf die schöpferische Phantasie der Gestalterin. Im Gegenteil, man hat hier den Eindruck, daß Mangel die Phantasie beflügelte. Die gelungene Arbeit verdient um so mehr Anerkennung, als die Inhaberin des Salons, Fräulein Charlotte Glückstein, zwei schwere Jahre im Konzentrationslager verbracht hatte."

[2] "Rundgang durch Berliner Modehäuser II," *Berlins Modenblatt*, no. 5, May 1947: "Schwere Jahre im Lager haben Charlotte Glückstein nichts von ihrer Freude am modischen Schaffen nehmen können,"

[3] On the return of Jews to Berlin in 1945, see Grossmann, *Jews, Germans, and Allies*, 2–3.

[4] The most detailed account of the role of Jewish fashion designers in Berlin and the process of Aryanization is found in Guenther, *Nazi Chic*; see also Loschek, "Contributions of Jewish Fashion Designers in Berlin"; Schallie, "Fashion Disappears from Germany"; see the interviews with Gerd Staebe and Detlev Albers in Westphal, *Berliner Konfektion und Mode*, 232–37.

[5] "Unser Interview: Heinz Oestergaard," *Illustrierter Telegraf*, March 25, 1948.

[6] See Züchner, *Der verbrannte Koffer*. Züchner touches on Glückstein's life as she reconstructs primarily the history of the Caro family. My account is partially based on Züchner's book and partially relies on information kindly provided by Gudrun Drechsler-Reichhardt, Charlotte Glückstein's daughter-in-law. I am thankful to Ms. Drechsler-Reichhardt, also a designer, now living in Düsseldorf, whom I interviewed by telephone and email in 2010 and 2011. She was not familiar with details about her mother-in-law's professional training and career before 1943, nor did she know the exact circumstances of Glückstein's survival, release, and return to Berlin. Additional helpful information about the fashion scene around the Kurfürstendamm in postwar Berlin was provided by Dagmar Hahn, the daughter of Ursula Oppenheimer, a fashion photographer for *Berlins Modenblatt* and *Der Tagesspiegel*. Ms. Hahn often served as a model for the children's fashion that her mother was photographing. I interviewed Ms. Hahn in December 2011.

[7] A commemorative brass cobblestone, a *Stolperstein*, on the sidewalk in front of Trautenaustraße 8 marks the last prewar Berlin address of Charlotte Glückstein

and Walter Caro—where they were arrested. See "Charlotte Glückstein," Stolpersteine in Berlin (website), www.stolpersteine-berlin.de/en/biografie/4419 (accessed February 1, 2018).

[8] Landesarchiv Berlin, B Rep. 042 no. 38538 Amtsgericht Berlin, Handelsregister, Firma Charlotte Glückstein (1946–52); Landesarchiv Berlin, B Rep. 042 no. 42024 Amtsgericht Berlin, Handelsregister, Firma Werner Caro (1946–75).

[9] Eva Braun's personal couturier, Annemarie Heise, who also provided glamorous costumes for half a dozen Nazi film productions between 1937 and 1942 (among them *La Habanera*), was featured in the traveling exhibition *Glanz und Grauen: Mode im Dritten Reich*, most recently mounted in Augsburg in the summer of 2017. See "So kleideten sich modebewußte Frauen in der NS-Zeit," *Die Welt*, May 10, 2017.

[10] "Das 'Friedenskleid' der Frau Hitler," *Der Nacht-Express*, March 11, 1946. In her last letter to her sister, in April 1945, Eva Braun gave her instructions to destroy business papers and sought to protect Heise's reputation for posterity. "On no account must Heise's bills be found," she wrote. Quoted in Görtemaker, *Eva Braun*, 86.

[11] See Wagner, "Das deutsche Mode-Institut 1933–1941," 174.

[12] See Elsa Herzog, "Londoner Mode-Cavalkade," *Berlins Modenblatt*, no. 8, August 1947; Joe Lederer, "London—ein Modebrief," *Mosaik*, November 1947.

[13] The stories of these individual businesses are told in detail in Guenther, *Nazi Chic*. See also the historical accounts, very similar in content, in Wagner, "Die Mode in Berlin," and Waidenschlager, "Modefürsten, Modekönige, Modezaren an der Spree," 20–23.

[14] B.E., "ADEFA—ein organisiertes Unrecht: Vorschläge zur Wiedergutmachung," *ITEX*, December 5, 1947.

[15] "Was passierte mit der Konfektion?," *ITEX*, March 20, 1949.

[16] Max Behling, "Bekleidungsindustrie oder Konfektion?" *ITEX*, April 24, 1949.

[17] Before the war, Hirschfeld had also been a contributor to *Die Textil-Woche*. See Mohr, *DOB Mode in Deutschland 1945 bis heute*, 148.

[18] Berneburg, "Wir sahen bei Charlott," 10–11.

[19] Another was the Berlin-based fashion photographer Norbert Leonhard (artistic pseudonym of Wilhelm Levy, 1913–71). A longtime contributor to *Die Mode* in the 1930s, Leonhard was arrested in 1941, sent to Auschwitz, and later assigned to do slave labor as a printer in a workshop for counterfeit currencies within the concentration camp Sachsenhausen. Like Glückstein, he returned to Berlin in 1946 and continued to work as a fashion photographer for a variety of magazines—*Heute*, *Film und Frau*, *Stern*, *Constanze*, and *Quick*). See Moderegger, *Modefotografie in Deutschland 1929–1955*, 180. Another such returnee I came across at the permanent exhibition of the Jewish Museum in Vienna was Hilde Ungar. She was one of the 34 survivors of the 5,000 Viennese Jews deported to Lodz and passed through several concentration camps. Upon returning to Vienna in 1946, she opened a dressmaking shop in the Eighth District, where she had worked as a seamstress prior to 1938.

[20] All of these designers were featured in *Berlins Modenblatt*'s regular series of articles "Rundgang durch Berliner Modehäuser," which appeared from 1946 to 1948. Helene Bornholdt, who had worked as an apprentice at the famous House Gerson before and after its Aryanization, opened her own salon in Berlin in 1946.

[21] Ursula Schewe was a young, independent, and upcoming fashion designer who established her first fashion salon in Berlin during the war and continued a stellar career throughout the late 1940s and the 1950s. In interviews with Irene Guenther, Schewe reminisces about her training in the Munich Meisterschule für Mode and her successful Berlin salon, Modewerkstätten. See Guenther, *Nazi Chic*, 6 and appendix 1. Heinz Oestergaard is the best known from that generation and has always enjoyed the greatest publicity. See Waidenschlager, *Heinz Oestergaard*.

[22] Berneburg, "Wir sahen bei Charlott": "[Das Konzept] des Verwandlungskleides, jener holden, aber zeitgemäßen Täuschung, wie man aus einem Kleid zwei machen kann, ohne eines davon verschwinden zu lassen."

[23] Ibid.

[24] Ibid.

[25] "Gut angezogen für den Alltag," *Chic*, November 18, 1947. On the practicality of her fashion designs, see also "Dominierendes Schwarz," *ITEX*, October 24, 1948. On the wide variety of the designs, see "So viele Kleider, so viele Stile," *Berlins Modenblatt*, no. 2, February 1949.

[26] See Manon, "Auf in die Schweiz. Berlin exportiert Mode," *Mosaik*, September 1948; "Deutsche Mode fürs Ausland," *sie*, October 24, 1948; "Berliner Modelle gefielen in der Schweiz," *sie*, December 12, 1948.

[27] On export to Switzerland, see "Herbst bei Charlott": *Berlins Modenblatt*, no. 10, October 1948. On the adaptability of Glückstein's designs, see "Aus zwei Meter Stoff—Sie haben die Wahl," *Berlins Modenblatt*, no. 1, January 1948.

[28] "Die Mode bei 'Charlott,'" *Berlins Modenblatt*, no. 11, November 1948: "So viele entzückende Einfälle und so geschicktes Anlehnen an die Weltmode, wie es die Kundinnen von Charlotte Glückstein erwarten. Aber wie geschmackvoll und klug ist alles ins Tragbare übersetzt. Und das scheint uns heute das Wichtigste zu sein!" See also "Aus zwei Meter Stoff—Sie haben die Wahl," and "Die ersten Herbst-Modelle bei Charlott," *Berlins Modenblatt*, no. 8, August 1949.

[29] "Charlotte zeigt die neuesten Modelle für Frühjahr und Sommer," *Berlins Modenblatt*, no. 6, June 1948: "Charlotte Glückstein hat unter den führenden Salons in Berlin ihre eigene Note geschaffen und bewahrt: jedes ihrer ganz reizenden—und dabei bis ins kleinste Detail durchdachten!—Modelle ist so, daß es die anwesenden Damen alle haben möchti. Hier ist belustigt-mokantes Lächeln, kein Resignieren in den Mienen der vielen, vielen Frauen zu lesen. Man sitzt froh, heiter und irgendwie beglückt da, wenn diese oft so einfachwirkenden Modelle vorüberziehen, die so viel Einfallsreichtum und technisches Können verraten. Lebensbejahend, wie ihre liebenswürdige Schöpferin selbst, sind sie! Frau Glückstein und ihre Helferin danken mit strahlendem Lächeln den Zuschauerinnen, die immer wieder versichern, 'Alles möchte man haben.'"

[30] See Maren Deicke, "Bilder vom Anfang," *Zeit Magazin*, November 21, 1980, 72, 74.

[31] "Modebarometer: steigend," *Heute*, June 15, 1947. See also A.W.P. [Anna Paula Wedekind-Pariselle, "Das Bild der Straße ist das Bild des Lebens," *Berlins Modenblatt*, no. 5, May 1947.

[32] See Gudrun Reichhardt, "Eine über 100jährige Geschichte der Berliner Textilfabrikanten Familie" (website), www.gudyx.de/html/indexa.html.

Chapter Three

Epigraph: "Es tut gut, wieder schöne Kleider zu sehen, auch wenn man sie noch nicht selbst tragen kann." The newsreel, produced by the British and American occupying forces, included commentary on the occasion of the "first spring fashion show" in Berlin, in February 1946.

[1] I use shortened titles, *Die Mörder* and *Der Himmel*, to refer to these films.

[2] Elizabeth Heineman's seminal essay on the clichéd images of women that dominated the West German media first prompted scholars to look for alternative paradigms for women's postwar experience. See Heineman, "Hour of the Woman."

[3] F.L. [Friedrich Luft], "Die Mörder sind unter uns," *Die Neue Zeitung*, October 18, 1946. Despite his enthusiasm for the revival of German film, Friedrich Luft, writing regularly for *Die Neue Zeitung*, was consistent in pointing out the lack of originality in rubble film and its aesthetic and stylistic continuities with Weimar and Nazi filmmaking.

[4] Schnurre, "Sammelrezension."

[5] For a summary of the public reactions, see Bergfelder, *International Adventures*, 28–29.

[6] "Stimmen aus Parkett und Rang: Man mag keine Ruinen," *Der Spiegel*, January 4, 1947.

[7] Pleyer, *Deutscher Nachkriegsfilm 1946–1948*, 68.

[8] See Brandlmeier, "Von Hitler zu Adenauer," 33–34.

[9] Greffrath, *Gesellschaftsbilder der Nachkriegszeit*," 430. The numbers quoted by Vogt, *Die Stadt im Kino*, 420, from a 1992 report in *Neues Deutschland*, are even higher, 6 million. Vogt also mentions that the film was exported to twenty-three countries. According to Rentschler, "The Place of Rubble in the *Trümmerfilm*," 13, *Die Mörder* became also the best-known *Trümmerfilm* internationally. See also a report on the successful US premiere of the film, "*Die Mörder sind unter uns* in Hollywood," *Spandauer Volksblatt*, December 4, 1947.

[10] Schnurre, "Sammelrezension," 174; this essay originally appeared in *Film-Rundschau*, no. 7, July 1948. After playing in Austria, . . . *und über uns der Himmel* premiered in New York in 1950 as *City of Torment*.

[11] Greffrath, *Gesellschaftsbilder der Nachkriegszeit*, 196.

[12] Given the loss of men during the war, women and adolescents made up 70 percent of cinema goers during the postwar years. On the Emnid survey of 1949, see Bergfelder, *International Adventures*, 31. See also Wortig, *Ihre Hoheit Lieschen Müller*, 15.

[13] Weckel, "*Die Mörder sind unter uns*," 105–15.

[14] The fashionable stocking seam is apparent in the scene in which Wallner finds a letter on the floor, an opportunity for the camera to zoom down to her legs and linger there.

[15] The costume designer for this film was Gertrud Recke, who worked on a number of wartime and postwar films. See entry in appendix 1.

[16] The costumes for *Der Himmel* were designed by Bessie Becker. See Berger, Reichmann, and Worschech, *Zwischen gestern und morgen*. See also entry for Bessie Becker in appendix 1.

[17] Uta Schwarz's studies of DEFA's *Der Augenzeuge* and West German newsreels foreground the preoccupation with fashion and "hedonistic consumption" on both sides of the ideological divide, especially in the early postwar years. See Schwarz, "Der blockübergreifende Charm dokumentarischer Bilder," 203–34, and Schwarz, *Wochenschau*, 73, 295–342.

[18] Prager, "Resemblances," 491.

[19] See Rentschler, "The Place of Rubble," 9.

[20] Andrews, "Film and History," 178. Andrews's comment is not new for film as a whole, but can be applied in a new way to rubble films.

[21] Baer, *Dismantling the Dream Factory*, 7.

[22] Baer, "*Film und Frau*," 152.

[23] In 1947, in an effort to alleviate clothes shortages, the Allies organized the so-called *Lumpenaktionen*, or rag initiatives. Theoretically, one could obtain a piece of new fabric in exchange for rags that weighed twelve times the weight of the new fabric. In reality the system was not very effective. See "Der Tausch—Lumpen gegen neue Textilwaren," *Spandauer Volksblatt*, June 14, 1947. See also F.B., "Fertigwaren gegen Lumpen: Sachliche Aufklärungen gegenüber unsachlichen Informationen," *Spandauer Volksblatt*, September 24, 1947. According to "Schwarzmarkt Preisliste" (Black-Market Pricelist), *sie*, February 22, 1948, a winter coat cost 1,000 to 5,000 cigarettes.

[24] On textile shortages, see Schubert, *Frauen in der Nachkriegszeit*, 199–200. See also repeated references to women consistently lacking warm clothing in Boehm, *A Woman in Berlin*, and in Friedrich, *Der Schattenmann*. For another account of how young women dealt with clothing shortages, see "Fünf Mädchen und ihr Wochenlohn," *sie*, March 31, 1946, 2–3.

[25] Guenther, *Nazi Chic*, 216.

[26] See Modemuseum im Münchner Stadtmuseum, *Aus 2 mach 1*. On the continuities between war and postwar practices of dealing with clothing shortages, see Hampicke, "Flotter Mangel, fesche Reste," 127–37.

[27] See, for example, Pinkert, *Film and Memory in East Germany*.

[28] Save the Children (Rettet die Kinder) was the biggest and most successful charitable action organized by the anti-fascist women's committees providing Berlin children in all four sectors with toys or clothing as Christmas presents in 1945. See Schmidt-Herzbach und Wald, "Rettet die Kinder," 59–66. See also Schmidt-Herzbach and Genth, "Die Frauenausschüsse," 47–74.

[29] Pinkert, *Film and Memory in East Germany*, 79.

[30] F.L. [Friedrich Luft], "Die Mörder sind unter uns," *Die Neue Zeitung*, October 18, 1946.

[31] Stacey, *Star Gazing*, 97 (emphasis added).

[32] "Frau Mode ist erfinderisch. Erste Modenschau im russischen Sektor," *Neue Zeit*, 2 April 1946: "Firma Schönwerk in Weißensee gab die erste Modenschau. Die Modelle waren hier wirklich Zauberwerke und wurden vom zahlreich versammelten Publikum begeistert beklatscht. Wie überall freuten sich auch hier die Frauen wieder am modischen Einfallsreichtum und Schönheit. Sie nahmen neue Anregungen mit und suchten zu Hause sicher nach Bettlacken, Sackstoff und Matratzendrell. Der Reinertrag wird der Aktion 'Rettet die Kinder' gegeben." See also "Für den Wiederaufbau deutscher Städte," *Berliner Zeitung*, November 20, 1945, which reports that the proceeds from a fashion show and a cabaret program in Neukölln were for Save the Children.

[33] Schnurre, "Sammelbesprechung."

[34] On the continuity and discontinuity of personnel in popular media over the 1930s and 1940s, see Lott-Almstadt, *Brigitte 1886–1986*, 148–75.

[35] A.P.W. [Anna-Paula Wedekind-Pariselle], "Unsere Mitarbeiterinnen stellen sich vor," *Berlins Modenblatt*, November 1946.

[36] Ingeborg Degenhardt, "Aus dem Familienalbum einer Modezeichnerin, 1946: das neue Kleid, von der Skizze zum Model," *Die Frau von heute*, March no. 2, 1946.

[37] "Modenschau hinter unseren Kulissen," *Mosaik*, no. 1–2, 1949, 12–13.

[38] G.G., "Modezeichnerinnen von Morgen," *Berlins Modenblatt*, no. 10, October 1948. See also "Mode-Graphikerinnen machen die Mode: Modelle der Hochschule für bildende Künste," *Berlins Modenblatt*, no. 7, July 1949.

[39] Anon., "Ich möchte Modezeichnerin werden. Was eine Neunzehnjährige zu sagen hat," *Mosaik*, July–August 1948. On the availability of fashion-related jobs, especially for young women, see Katharina Luthardt, "Jagd nach Arbeit," *Mosaik*, July–August 1948.

[40] "Ausdauernde Zuschauer" and "Filmzauber um Mitternacht," *Der Nacht-Express*, June 27, 1946.

[41] "Junges Mädchen im Vordergrund," *Der Nacht-Express*, June 27, 1946. For more on Knef's work as a graphic artist and fashion illustrator at UFA, see Lucas Lewalter, "In Seidenstrümpfen gross geworden. Der spannende Lebensroman einer Künstlerin," *Abendpost*, May 22, 1956.

[42] "Prominente gratulieren: Ein Jahr Berlins Modenblatt," *Berlins Modenblatt*, no. 10, October 1946, 3–4.

[43] "Von der Mode zum Film. Kleine Plauderei über Hildegard Knef," *Die neue Filmwoche*, August 23, 1947, 136.

[44] Ibid., 136. See also Schröder, *"Mir sollen sämtliche Wunder begegnen,"* 76–77.

[45] For more, see Trimborn, *Hildegard Knef*, 126–27. See also Tremper, *Meine wilden Jahre*, 249.

[46] See Trimborn, *Hildegard Knef*, 113–14.

[47] The irony was that earlier, at the very beginning of her career at UFA in 1942, Knef was helped out and promoted by the prominent Nazi film official Ewald von Demandowsky, with whom Knef had started an affair and whom she abandoned in 1946 after his arrest by the Allies. In her memoirs, she tried to cover up this affair.

[48] See Trimborn, *Hildegard Knef*, 116–17.

[49] Milde, *Berlin, Glienicker Brücke*, 336.

[50] Werner, *So wird's nie wieder sein*, 166.

[51] For more on the confluence of film and fashion stardom in the figure of Knef, see "Vignette 2."

[52] See Bodo Kochanowski, "Hoppla, jetzt komm' ich," *Berliner Morgenpost*, September 22, 1991. See also the analysis in Fisher, *Disciplining Germany*, 218–20.

[53] F.K., "Das war im Jahre 1854, als sich Herr Pommerenke die erste Nähmaschine kaufte: Heute gibt es wieder 12 000 Heimarbeiterinnen in Berlin," *Für Dich*, December 8, 1946: "Heute sind unsere Heimarbeiterinnen nicht mehr die Parias der Gesellschaft."

[54] E.K. ". . . und über uns der Himmel," *Der Tagesspiegel*, December 14, 1947.

[55] One photograph in the fashion section of the magazine *sie* stands out among the plentiful advice in the fashion media on how to transform common household fabrics into new dresses. It displays a dress by the designer Wolfgang Nöcker, made out of a curtain that looks almost identical to the one worn by Mizzi in this scene. See "Der Charme der Spitze," *sie*, August 4, 1946, 9.

[56] See Manon, "Taschen, die man selbst fertigt," *Spandauer Volksblatt*, October 17, 1946.

[57] In her senseless infatuation with fashion, Mizzi is remarkably similar to another, more marginal, female figure, Lissy Stenzel (played by Sonja Ziemann) in Gustav Fröhlich's first postwar film as a director, *Wege im Zwielicht* (1948). The young woman, who befriends one of the male protagonists, the troubled, homeless Peter Wille, is conspicuously fashionably dressed. As she appears at the workers' camp awkwardly balancing on high heels and with an elegant purse and hat, cheerful Lissy uses various English phrases such as "my dear" and "absolutely" to lure Peter to go with her to Hamburg and explore the night life there.

[58] Unlike others who have given the character of Mizzi only scant scholarly attention, Fisher presents a very detailed and persuasive analysis of her function in *Der Himmel*. See Fisher, *Disciplining Germany*, 224–33.

[59] "Fortuna kam im Citroen: Heidi will nicht Hedy sein," *Der Spiegel*, June 21, 1947, 20. The same issue of *Der Spiegel* features the actress on its cover with the headline "*Life* entdeckte Heidi Scharf" (*Life* discovered Heidi Scharf).

[60] The series by the war correspondent Walter Sanders appeared in *Life*, August 1, 1946.

[61] "Gefalle ich Dir?," *Die neue Filmwoche*, November 22, 1947, 218.

[62] Christa Rotzoll, ". . . und über uns der Himmel," *Der Kurier*, March 1, 1948.

[63] "Was sie gerne tragen," *Lilith*, August 18, 1948, 12–13. The other actresses featured were Winnie Markus, Joana Maria Gorvin, Karin Himbold, and Bruni Löbel.

Vignette 2

[1] Among the hundreds of richly illustrated articles that focused on Knef, her social appearances, her looks and clothes are "Apart—ohne Modediktat: Kleidsame Frisuren," *Film Revue*, 1949/7; Hans Schaller and Heinz Reinhard, "Hildegard Knef in Berlin," *Film Revue*, 1949/8 (offering the information that Knef's luggage contained twenty-five dresses, eight coats, and twenty pairs of shoes that she brought back from the United States); "Hildegard Knef wieder in Berlin," *Film Illustrierte*, July 6, 1949; "Interview ohne Hilde Knef," *Neue Filmwoche*, August 28, 1948; "In Hollywood: Bei Hilde Knef zu Besuch," *Neue Filmwoche*, November 18, 1948; "Hilde Knef erzählt: 'Meine Hüte kauft Marlene!',", *Constanze*, no. 24, November 1950; "Viele nette Leute in Berlin sind gut Freund mit der Knef," *Constanze*, no. 9, April 1950.

[2] Baer, *Dismantling the Dream Factory*, 57. See also von Moltke and Wulff, "Trümmer-Diva: Hildegard Knef," 304–16.

[3] Heinzelmeier, "Hildegard Knef: Das Trümmermädchen," 113–19, was among the first studies to establish the term *Trümmermädchen* and to trace the almost teleological line of gradual development from *Trümmermädchen* to femme fatale. See also Sieglohr, "Hildegard Knef: From Rubble Woman to Fallen Woman, 112–27.

[4] Von Moltke and Wulff, "Trümmer-Diva: Hildegard Knef," 311.

[5] Cover of *Der Spiegel*, May 10, 1947; "Von der Mode zum Film: Kleine Plauderei über Hildegard Knef," *Neue Filmwoche*, August 23, 1947.

[6] See Schröder, *Mir sollen sämtliche Wunder begegnen*, 28–29. See also Lucas Lewalter, "In 'Seidenstrümpfen' groß geworden: die Knef. Der spannende Lebensroman einer Künstlerin," *Abendpost*, May 23, 1956.

[7] Heinzelmeier, "Hildegard Knef: Das Trümmermädchen," 113–19.

[8] Knef's appearance on the cover of *Der Spiegel* is truly amazing given the fact that this spot was generally reserved for prominent political figures. See Schröder, *Mir sollen sämtliche Wunder begegnen*, 104.

[9] *Zwischen gestern und morgen* was filmed partly onsite in the ruins of Munich and partly in the Bavaria-Film studios in Geiselgasteig, outside Munich.

[10] "Kat, ein Mädchen unserer Zeit, gespielt von Hildegard Knef," *Der Spiegel*, May 10, 1947: "Der Stern unserer Zeit ist kein extravaganter Star. Natürliche Anmut bewundern wir an Hildegard Knef."

[11] "Hildegard Knef," *Der Stern*, August 1, 1948.

[12] Renn, "Personalien: Hildegard Knef," *Berliner Filmblätter*, December 21, 1948: "Hauptsache, Hilde bleibt wie sie ist. Unsere Hildemaus, Mädchen von heute. Madonnenprofil, goldgelbes Haar, widerspenstig ins Gesicht flatternd. Lange Hosen findet sie schick, blauer Dunst ist ihr lieber als Milchkakao."

[13] Riess, *Das gab's nur einmal*, 25.

[14] "Kat, ein Mädchen unserer Zeit,"19. That same year, Hildegard Knef became also the first German actress to be honored with three-page feature in *Life* magazine. There, too, the images captured by Walter Sanders revealed an elegant, almost glamorously dressed Knef both onstage and off, while the text emphasized her modesty and ingenuity as she was sharing the fate of many German women. It related the story of the actress's appearing on the stage of the Schloßparktheater in a dress she had made out of bed linen. See "New German Star: Hilde Knef Plays in Berlin Films backed by Russians and Americans," *Life*, May 19, 1947.

[15] Bessen, *Trümmer und Träume*, 205. For a discussion of the press's negative reviews of the film, see Shandley, *Rubble Films*, 67–69.

[16] Bessen, *Trümmer und Träume*, 204.

[17] See "Dirndl für die Welt," *Heute*, December 1, 1946, 28–29; "Wieder deutsche Mode," *Heute*, September 1, 1946, 34; Riederer, "Münchner Modebrief," 11; "Zieh Dir ein Dirndl an," *Die Frau von heute*, June no. 2, 1947; "Vorschlag für ein Winterdirndl," *Der Nacht-Express*, October 8, 1946; "Auch im Jahre 1948 ist das Dirndl große Mode: Bericht aus London," *Spandauer Volksblatt*, December 12, 1947.

[18] Schandley, *Rubble Film*, 160.

[19] Von Moltke, *No Place like Home*, 77.

[20] Baer, *Dismantling the Dream Factory*, 54.

[21] "Der Stern unserer Zeit ist kein extravaganter Star: Natürliche Anmut bewundern wir an Hildegard Knef," *Stern*, August 1, 1948.

[22] Trimborn, *Hildegard Knef*, 192.

[23] The script was written by Fritz Rotter in Los Angeles, potentially for a film to be made in Hollywood. After he failed to sell it in the United States, Rotter reworked it for a German audience with the help of Helmut Käutner and presented it to Erich Pommer, who ultimately became the producer of the film. See "Fernlastfahrer in der Broadway-Bar," *Die Zeit*, January 24, 1952.

[24] Trimborn, *Hildegard Knef*, 193. The press reviews of the film, and especially of Knef's performance, were extremely positive, among them: Felix Henseleit, "Schicksalskurve mit Schutzengeln," *Der Kurier*, February 19, 1952; D.F., "Guter deutscher Unterhaltungsfilm: erfolgreicher Start von 'Nachts auf den Straßen,'" *Telegraf*, February 20, 1952; W.Lg., "Nachts auf den Straßen," review, *Der Tagesspiegel*, February 20, 1952; Gerd Schulte, "Deutscher Film—ein Schritt nach Vorn!" *Hannoversche Allgemeine Zeitung*, January 19, 1952.

[25] "Der natürliche Lebenshunger," *Der Spiegel*, May 7, 1952. This was the second time that Knef graced a *Spiegel* cover, this time as a character in the Hollywood production *Decision before Dawn* (1952).

[26] See Fehrenbach, *Cinema in Democratizing German*, 240. In the end this plan was rejected due to the film's adult rating and protests from theater owners that such a screening would take money out of their pockets.

[27] In 1950 Knef promoted the new illustrated *Ford-Revue*. Several of the first issues of the magazine feature full-page images of Knef reading the magazine and

soliciting new subscriptions. See, for example, "Hildegard Knef und die Ford-Revue," *Ford-Revue*, no. 5, October 1950.

[28] "Hilde Knef erzählt: 'Meine Hüte kauft Marlene!'" The same issue features a two-page piece by Knef, "Meine Hüte kauft Marlene," in which she reminisces about her time in Hollywood and New York.

[29] "Ba," "Verlorene Illusionen: 'Illusion in Moll'—Hildegard Knef-Film in der Film-Bühne Wien," *Der Abend*.

[30] See "Mondän und temperamentvoll: Illusion in Moll in der Filmbühne Wien," *Telegraf*, February 4, 1953; A.T., "Drehbuch in Moll," *Volksblatt Berlin-Spandau*, February 4, 1953. On Knef's relationship to various designers, see Jaspers, "Schöne Hülle, verletzter Körper," 61–67. For more on Adlmüller's own star status and his work for Knef, see Bönsch, "Film- und Bühnenkostüme in Fallbeispielen," 98–109; Knef, *Der geschenkte Gaul*, 234. On Knef's personification of shifting West Berlin identities in the early 1950s, see Bach, "The Woman Between," 115–24.

[31] Rita Pesserl, "Illusion in . . . Dur," *Der Kurier*, February 3, 1953.

[32] Ibid.

[33] The film premiered in December 1953 in Berlin under the title *Gefährlicher Urlaub* (Dangerous Vacation). It was based on Walter Ebert's novel *Susanne in Berlin*, which appeared in serialized form in *Der Tagesspiegel* in 1951.

[34] For a discussion of Knef as the representative "Berlin woman" in this film, See Bach, "The Woman Between," 121–22.

[35] Heinz A. Schulze had been well known since the 1930s as a designer for film stars. When he opened his Berlin salon, Schulze-Bibernell, in partnership with Irmgard Bibernell, in 1934, Lilian Harvey, Renate Müller, Anny Ondra, Käthe von Nagy, Ilse Werner, Luise Ullrich, and Marianne Hoppe became his regular customers. After serving as a fashion consultant (*modischer Berater*) to a number of UFA films in the late 1930s and early 1940s, Schulze was appointed by Wolfgang Liebeneiner in 1943 as the chief costume designer of UFA, but he was soon sent to the front as punishment for his defiance and anti-Nazi stands. After the war Schulze settled in Munich and in 1947 opened a salon there. In 1949 his salon was renamed Schulze-Varell. For more, see Auer, *Der Couturier Heinz Schulze-Varell 1907–1985*, 92–93, 122–23.

[36] Sannwald, "Spröde Verführerin," 105–7.

[37] Jaspers, "Schöne Hülle," 62.

[38] Gundlach, *Die Pose als Körpersprache*, 5. "Ninotschka" refers to the lead role she played to great acclaim in the Broadway musical *Silk Stockings*, which was based on Lubitsch's film *Ninotschka* and featured songs by Cole Porter.

[39] Heidemarie Marzahn, "Hildegard Knef stellte ihre Modelinie 'Knef-Fashion' im Schweizerhof vor," *Der Tagesspiegel*, December 11, 1996, 12.

Chapter Four

Epigraphs: P.E., "'Martina,'" *Weltbühne*, no. 17, 1949: "Wohltuend ist es, neuen Gesichtern zu begegnen und nicht kostümierten, auf Trümmerfrau verkleideten

Stars"; Ulrike B., "Sommer in Berlin," *Mosaik*, July–August 1948: "Mode heute in Berlin heißt die Art und Weise, wie wir uns nicht kleiden."

[1] For some brief and explicitly negative reviews of *Straßenbekanntschaft*, see "Treffpunkt: Gesundheitsamt. Kennt ihr euch überhaupt?," *Der Spiegel*, April 17, 1948; *Wiesbadener Tageblatt*, film review, July 19, 1950. For biased, offhand remarks on *Martina*, see Hans Ulrich Eylau, "Martina und kein Ende: Eine betrübliche Filmbilanz," *Tägliche Rundschau*, September 30, 1949; N.P., "Schnellfabrikat *Martina*," *Vorwärts*, August 21, 1949.

[2] See Schittly, *Zwischen Regie und Regime*, 28–29. See also Brauerhoch, "Ästhetische Opposition/en in Peter Pewas' 'Strassenbekanntschaft,'" 139. See also Heimann, *DEFA, Künstler und SED-Kulturpolitik*.

[3] Schenk, "Zwischen den Zonen. 'Ehe im Schatten' und andere Filme zwischen Ost und West," *film-dienst*, no. 21, 1997.

[4] Pewas quotes distributors who qualified it as "the most dependable cash cow of the whole year" ("der kassensicherste Film des ganzen Jahres"; "der währungssicherste Film"). See Kurowski and Meyer, "Peter Pewas im Gespräch," in Kurowski and Meyer, *Der Filmregisseur Peter Pewas*, 47.

[5] For data on distribution in the West, see Benzenhöfer and Klatt, "Der DEFA-Film *Straßenbekanntschaft* (1948)," 17–26.

[6] See Greffrath, *Gesellschaftsbilder der Nachkriegszeit*, 231.

[7] Kurowski and Meyer, "Peter Pewas im Gespräch," 34.

[8] Mückenberger, "Zeit der Hoffnungen: 1946 bis 1949," 37.

[9] Ibid.

[10] See Brauerhoch, "Ästhetische Opposition/en in Peter Pewas' *Straßenbekanntschaft*."

[11] Kurowski and Meyer, *Der Filmregisseur Peter Pewas*, 7.

[12] F.V., "Film engage," *Münchner Allgemeine Zeitung*, December 13, 1950.

[13] Ibid.

[14] Quoted in Mückenberger and Jordan, *"Sie sehen selbst, Sie hören selbst. . .,"* 164. On the routine practice of renting the most fashionable costumes for film productions from leading designers in Berlin, see H.A., "Garderobiere in der heutigen Filmproduktion," *Die neue Filmwoche*, December 13, 1947.

[15] "Wie wir Frauen zu Hause gelebt haben, das weiß doch kaum einer von euch. Jeden Morgen in die Fabrik, spät abends nach Hause, hungrig, das kalte Zimmer, Alarm, dazu noch die Angst und die Hilflosigkeit. Ist es dann so unverständlich, dass man sich betäuben wollte. Was wollen wir denn: bißchen Wärme, satt werden, ein buntes Kleid, ein Kopftuch, ein bißchen Freude, damit wir endlich das Lachen lernen."

[16] Quoted in *Lilith*, January 1949.

[17] "Wer wird Martina?" *Illustrierter Telegraf*, October 7, 1948, 6.

[18] Ibid., 7.

[19] Schultze was among the first graduates of DEFA's fully state-funded Schauspielstudio für Bühne und Film, led by Werner Kepich and founded in 1947. See B., "Filmstudio auf neuen Wegen," *Film Illustrierte*, August 30, 1949. See also Hans Burgwalt, "Besuch bei Martina," *Film Illustrierte*, January 26, 1949.

20 "Die Hausfrauen spielen die Komparsen: Die Kamera zwischen Trockenkartoffeln und Mohrrüben," *Der Abend* (Berlin), March 5, 1949.

21 See G.W.W., "Die beiden Schwestern: Neue Gesichter im Film 'Martina,'" *Jugend-Telegraf,* March 18, 1949, for a detailed description of the conditions for filming in West Berlin during the Blockade.

22 See "Das 'Fräulein' ist noch einmal davongekommen," *Neue Zeit,* August 23, 1949; "*Martina*—Ein Gegenwartsfilm im Hans-Sachs-Filmtheater," *Nürnberger Nachrichten,* August 17, 1949; Wolfgang W. Parth, "*Martina,*" *sie,* August 26, 1949, 11. The film was especially well received in Vienna, and was counted among the "most interesting that German film producers have created since the war." See "*Martina,*" *Wiener Filmzeitung,* September 2, 1949.

23 For an incisive and extended discussion of the phenomenon of "Fräulein," see Brauerhoch, *Fräuleins und GIs.*

24 Wolfdietrich Schnurre, "Martina Marlitt," *Die Welt am Sonntag,* August 21, 1949. Schnurre, writing in the *Deutsche Rundschau,* November 1946, was critical of the fashionable costumes in *Die Mörder sind unter uns* as well: "After years in a concentration camp, it is not likely that one returns home to find in the closet three or four neatly ironed outfits" (Man habe "nach jahrelanger KZ-Haft nicht drei oder vier gebügelte Garderoben im Schrank"). Cited in Aurich, Becker, and Jacobsen, *Wolfdietrich Schnurre: Kritiker,* 104,

25 "Mode im Film," *Film Illustrierte,* April 6, 1949: "Die Mode spielt im Zeitfilm eine große Rolle. Die modernen Kleider der Darsteller ersparen uns den Besuch einer Modenschau. Der Einfluß des Films auf diesem Gebiete kann nicht genug eingeschätzt werden. Filme müssen 'echte' Kostüme zeigen. 'New Look' Kostüme zu entwerfen, erfordert Wissen, Können und Geschmack. Frl. Hartmann, bekannt aus führenden Modeblättern, muß mit dem Drehbuch vertraut sein, um Stimmung und Milieu kennenzulernen. . . . Sie entwirft die meisten Kostüme, aber oft müssen nur erreichbare Modesalons um Leihgaben angegangen sein."

26 Annedore Leber (1904–68) was married to a Social Democrat representative, Julius Leber, who was persecuted and ultimately executed by the Nazis in 1944. Annedore Leber had lived in Berlin since 1935, ran her own clothing store, and was an active member of the resistance. See Dertlinger, *Frauen der ersten Stunde,* 164.

27 Annedore Leber, "Brief an die Leser," *Mosaik,* Oktober 1947: "So wird es [das Monatsblatt] die nüchternen, harten und wenig bestechenden Farben der Gegenwart haben, die den Grundton unseres Lebens bilden. Doch die kleinen Glanzlichter der Illusion, des Heiteren, Liebeswerten, der menschlichen Wärme sollen die schweren und ernsten Töne unserer Nachkriegszeit aufhellen. Gemischt mit dem Schimmer der großen und fernen Welt wird es rufen zu dem Ziel, das erreicht werden muss."

28 See Parkins, *Poiret, Dior and Schiaparelli,* 111.

29 Ibid., 113.

30 Taylor, "Work and Function of the Paris Couture Industry, 34–44.

31 All of these shows were planned as charitable events with the proceeds split between German and French aid organizations. The Hamburg visit followed an

invitation of the influential women's magazine *Constanze*. Subsequent visits—in 1952 to Bad Godesberg and Düsseldorf and in 1953 to Munich, Essen, and Düsseldorf—were sponsored by the French high commissioner, André François-Poncet, and his wife and were considered important cultural-political events in the process of reconciliation between the two countries. See Rasche, "Fashion Shows Held by Christian Dior in Germany, 1949–1953."

[32] Gundlach and Richter, *Berlin en Vogue*, 139n104.

[33] *Chic*, a biweekly fourteen-page fashion newspaper, was launched in June 1947 with a license issued by the French military authorities. It was printed and distributed by Deutscher Verlag, formerly Ullstein. Erika Berneburg, since 1945 the fashion editor of *sie*, simultaneously took over as the editor in chief of *Chic*. Before the war Berneburg, a trained designer and graphic artist, had worked for various magazines produced by the Leipzig publisher Otto Beyer. She subsequently became the fashion editor for Ullstein in Berlin. See "Unsere Mitarbeiterinnen: Sieben Selbstporträts," *sie*, January 5, 1947.

[34] "Moderevolution des Jahres 1947: Diors 'New Look,'" *Heute*, August 15, 1947; "Revolution der Mode," *Heute*, November 1, 1947. See also "Von Kopf bis Fuß: The New Look," *Heute*, March 15, 1948. *Heute* seemed to be responding to a letter from a reader, Gerti Schmidt in Munich, who urged them to report more on the New Look from Paris: "You should publish fashion photos much more often. Of course we can't buy anything, but when we are remodeling an old dress, we want to make it a bit more fashionable and we need inspiration. Women are really happy, if you would show now and then a truly elegant dress, made out of fabrics that we don't have any more and to worn on an occasion that we would rarely have. Believe me, women like to see such things." ("Sie sollten viel öfter Modebilder bringen. Wir können uns zwar nichts kaufen, aber wenn wir ein Kleid ändern, so soll es doch ein bißchen modern werden, und da brauchen wir Anregung. Wenn Sie ab und zu ein wirklich elegantes Kleid zeigen, aus Stoffen, die wir nicht mehr haben, und zu Gelegenheit gedacht, die es für uns kaum noch gibt—, die Frauen freuen sich doch darüber. Glauben Sie mir, alle Frauen sehen sowas gern.") *Heute*, January 1, 1948. See also "New Look vom Lande," *Heute*, August 1, 1948.

[35] See E.W. [Ewa Lemke], "Beglücktsein durch Mode," *Chic*, June 17, 1947; Ewa Lemke, "Vier modische Begriffe," *Chic*, July 1, 1947; F.D., "Der gediegene Schneiderstil—eine 'neue Moderne'?," *Chic*, August 26, 1947; "Die repräsentative Linie," *Chic*, October 7, 1947; "Die Rocklänge ist kein Problem," *Chic*, October 14, 1947; "Gut angezogen für den Alltag," *Chic*, November 18, 1947; "Paris—hier einmal schlicht und einfach," *Chic*, February 1948, "Der Schöpfer des neuen Feminismus," *Chic*, March 9, 1948.

[36] Issi Puth, "Sind Beine unmodern?," *Mosaik*, November 1947, 10: "Der gesamte Schnitt, die gesamte Silhouette, das gesamte Drum und Dran mit Korsett, Federhütchen und Schleier: sehr kapriziöse und damenhafte Dinge sind es, die man in den französischen Modejournalen erblickt und die uns einem anderen Jahrhundert entnommen zu sein scheinen. Sie bedeuten den Anfang einer völligen Umgestaltung der Mode. Und sie werden allerorts noch manches Kopfzerbrechen bringen."

[37] See Wagner, "Everyone Is Talking about Dior."

[38] AWP [Anna Paula Wedekind-Pariselle], "Über kurz und lang. . ." *Berlins Modenblatt*, January 1948: "Ein Pariser Modeschöpfer, keiner von den Alten, mit geheiligter Tradition, sondern einer von den Jungen, Wagelustigen kommt auf die, sagen wir es ruhig, absurde Idee, die unkleidsamste Mode aufleben zu lassen, die jemals erdacht wurde, und hat einen Welterfolg! (den er vielleicht selbst nicht geahnt hat.) Er revolutioniert die Mode, er verwirft alles, was bisher als schön galt, er versucht sogar das Korsett wieder zu lancieren, es gelingt! Er verwischt die Korrektheit waagerecht sportlicher Schultern, er verwischt die knappen Umrisse der Gestalt und er verhüllt die Beine. In einem Zeitalter, das überall sich bemüht. der Frau die Gleichberechtigung zi erkämpfen, macht er aus Frauen hilflose, zarte Geschöpfe, deren Wespentaille wie einst aus einer Stoffhülle sondergleichen ganz schmal und fein aufsteigt. . . Paris hat die neue Linie begeistert aufgenommen, aus England hören wir, daß der lange Rock sich durchgesetzt hat und aus Amerika berichtet man über einen heftigen Widerstreit der Meinungen. Über "kurz oder lang" wird auch bei uns heftig disputiert, aber mehr in rhetorischer Form."

[39] "Berlin, April 1948," *Chic*, April 6, 1948: "Unsere jungen deutschen Mädchen haben heute ganz besonders stark den Wunsch nach Leben und Jung-sein-dürfen. . . . Sie gehen tanzen, und wenn es auch inmitten der Trümmern ist, sie wollen genießen. . . . Sie gehen gern ins Kino und Theater und interessieren sich für Mode." See also "Berliner Modeschöpfer zeigen ihre neuesten Modelle, *sie*, April 17, 1948.

[40] See I.K., "Ich bin 21 Jahre alt," *Die Frau von heute*, April no. 2, 1947.

[41] See Philine, "Die Mode diktiert, die Mode fordert und bestimmt," *Die Frau von heute*, June no. 1, 1948.

[42] Ursula Schewe designed for film as well. She provided all the fashionable attire for the 1951 film *Unschuld in tausend Nöten* (Das Mädel von der Konfektion, directed by Carl Boese), which is set, notably, in a Berlin fashion salon and whose protagonist, Eva (played by Hannelore Schroth) is the rising model in this salon, specializing in presenting Paris designer dresses. See W.V., "Das Mädel aus der Konfektion," *Die Neue Zeitung*, May 29, 1951. For more on Schewe, see appendix 1.

[43] "Ue.," "Blick in zwei Kollektionen," *Die Frau von heute*, January no. 2, 1948: "So wie es möglich ist, unsere Frisur der Linie der Pariserin oder Amerikanerin anzugleichen, so könnten wir auch aus einem Modediktat, das wir im Prinzip ablehnen, für uns durchaus brauchbare Anregungen entnehmen. Die Modehäuser Hanni Christ und Ursula Schewe haben bei der Schöpfung ihrer Modelle eine glückliche Lösung gefunden: ihre Modelle folgen zwar dem Stil der neuen Mode, ohne der Trägerin voll und ganz das Modediktat des New Looks aufzudrängen. Sie überlassen es der Trägerin, die ihr am meisten zusagenden Anregungen für sich zu verwerten. Die gezeigten Modelle sind für den Export gedacht, wenn es auch meist nur ein 'Export' innerhalb der Stadtmauern von Berlin ist. Das ist auch der Grund, weshalb die beiden Modehäuser hier und da dem Modediktat einen höheren Tribut zahlen, als wir es für richtig halten."

[44] H.K., "Die Leipziger Messe mit den Augen einer Frau," *Die Frau von heute*, March no. 2, 1948: "Der New Look ist da—nicht pariserisch, nicht englisch

und amerikanisch, sondern deutsch. Daß er auch gefällt, beweisen die vielen ausländischen Aufträge." See also "Leipziger Moden," *ITEX*, March 21, 1948; "Nocheinmal Leipzig: Querschnitt durch das Modeschaffen aller Zonen," *ITEX*, March 28, 1948. Fashion shows at the Leipzig Trade Fair in 1948 were covered in *sie*, and the journalist Erika Berneburg came to the same conclusion: "Not the most extravagant, but the most wearable outfits of the New Look won both the jury's prize and the most audience applause. They were designed by Berlin couturier Oestergaard." See E.B. [Erika Berneburg], "Beifall für schlichte Eleganz," *sie*, March 28, 1948.

[45] See "CARE Packages Arrive in Berlin," *New York Times*, February 20, 1947; "Mode streckt sich nach der Decke," *Heute*, June 1, 1947.

[46] A special fashion show took place in New York on February 3, 1947, when these models had their public premiere. See Virginia Pope, "Blankets Turned into Modish Garb," *New York Times*, February 4, 1947; "Blanket Fashions," *Life*, February 17, 1947. I am grateful to Rebecca Jumper Matheson for elucidating the connection between CARE and the New York Dress Institute in her presentation "Austerity and Charity: New York Designers and the United States Army Surplus CARE Packages," at the "The Look of Austerity," a conference at the Museum of London, September 11–12, 2015.

[47] "Mode streckt sich nach der Decke"; see also "CARE-Wolle: CARE Paket zum Stricken," *Heute*, December 1, 1947; "Das Berliner CARE-Committee," *sie*, August 10, 1947. On the importance of the CARE packages during the Berlin Blockade, see Werner Koch, "Wo bleibt mein Carepaket?" *sie*, November 21, 1948.

[48] See "Made in Berlin," and "Stoffe über die Luftbrücke," *ITEX*, March 6, 1949; "Blockadehilfe für Berlin," *ITEX*, April 10, 1949; "Berliner Modelle gefielen in der Schweiz," *sie*, December 12, 1948. "Berliner Mode trotz Blockade," *sie*, March 20, 1949; "U.S. Aid to Berlin Rises: Increase Is Noted in Number of CARE Blanket Packages Ordered," *New York Times*, June 27, 1948. According the *New York Times* report, an average of 25,000 to 30,000 CARE packages purchased by Americans were being distributed to Berliners per month. For a detailed account of fashion practices during the Berlin Blockade, see Ganeva, "'Stoffe über die Luftbrücke.'"

[49] "Feuilleton entzückend anzusehen."

[50] Kieselbach, like Recke and other costume designers, worked for both DEFA and West German films until 1950, when he accepted a permanent position with DEFA.

[51] "Martinas vor die Kamera!," *Berliner Filmblätter*, August 12, 1949.

[52] See "Es waren vier herrliche Wochen," *Film Illustrierte*, March 16, 1949.

[53] "Apart—ohne Modediktatur," *Film-Revue*, no. 17, 1949. This was also the first issue of *Film-Revue* in which a page was dedicated to beauty and fashion, themes of interest to female readers: "Beginnend mit dieser Nummer bringt die 'Film-Revue' in jeder Ausgabe eine Seite für die Dame, die Anregungen auf dem Gebiete der Mode, der Körperpflege und allen Fragen des persönlichen Geschmacks geben wird."

[54] Ibid.

[55] "Cornell Borchers: klug und schön," *Film Illustrierte*, February 23, 1949; "Sie spielt die Knef-Rolle," *Film-Revue*, 1949.

[56] See "Gisela Trowe," *Neue Film-Welt*, no. 4, 1949; "Heidi Scharf," *Neue Film-Welt*, no. 2, 1947. Gisela Trowe's next role was in the West German film *Die Zeit mit Dir* (1948, directed by Georg Hurdalek), where she was cast as a fashionable hat maker, before appearing in DEFA's *Affäre Blum* (1948, directed by Erich Engel) and in the West German film *Der Verlorene* (1951, directed by Peter Lorre).

[57] All of the filmmakers mentioned here eventually moved to the West. Later in his career, Peter Pewas produced in West Berlin a series of short documentaries and longer advertising films (*Werbefilme*) centered around fashion: *Verliebt in Kleider* (1951, 13 min.) and *Der Modespiegel* (part 1 in 1954, 12 min.; part 2 in 1955, 12 min., and part 3 in 1956, 13 min.).

Chapter Five

[1] "Modell Bianka," press release for *Modell Bianka*, Deutsche Kinemathek, Schriftgutarchiv, item no. 3725.

[2] See "Zulassungsprotokolle 4115/1979," Bundesarchiv/Filmarchiv, Berlin; Horst Knietzsch, "Erzählungen über Glück und Selbstbestätigung: DEFA Retrospektive zum 30. Jahrestag der DDR," *Neues Deutschland*, January 24, 1979.

[3] Knietzsch, "Erzählungen über Glück und Selbstbestätigung."

[4] Wildt, "Changes in Consumption as Social Practice in West Germany During the 1950s," *Getting and Spending: European and American Consumer Societies in the Twentieth Century*, ed. Susan Strasser, Charles McGovern, and Matthias Judt (Cambridge: Cambridge University Press, 1998), 301–16.

[5] Wildt, "Changes in Consumption," 303.

[6] Other consumption excesses in the 1950s included a *Fresswelle*, "gorging wave," and *Urlaubswelle*, "travel wave." See Wildt, "Changes in Consumption," 303.

[7] See Beier, *Der Demonstrations- und Generalstreik vom 12. November 1948.*

[8] For more concrete data and numbers, see Wildt, "Changes in Consumption," 305.

[9] For a detailed analysis of the problems with clothing supply that were due to reparations, lack of resources, and dismantling of the industrial facilities by the Soviet authorities, see hs., "Bekleidungsprobleme in der Ostzone," *Der Kurier*, February 21, 1947. For more of the rise of sophisticated consumer expectations in the GDR in the 1948–51 period, see Stitziel, *Fashioning Socialism*, 49–52.

[10] For an excellent discussion of the launch of the HO stores, see Pence, "Building Socialist Worker-Consumers."

[11] See Groschopp, "Faszination Film."

[12] Groschopp, "Heitere Filme," 55: "Der Ruf der Bevölkerung nach lustigen Filmen bricht nicht ab. Aber . . . lustige Filme für unsere neuen Menschen zu

schaffen ist eine ernsthafte, schwere und verantwortungsvolle Aufgabe. Nirgends ist die Suche nach neuen Wegen notwendiger aber auch komplizierter als bei der leichten Filmgattung."

13 Ibid., 56.

14 Ibid., 34.

15 Ibid.

16 Ibid., 57.

17 P.L., "Verwandlungswunder Bianka: In Johannisthal dreht die DEFA einen heiteren Spielfilm aus der Gegenwart," *Berliner Zeitung*, May 11, 1951.

18 See Herman Müller, "Ein mißglücktes Modell," *Neues Deutschland*, June 23, 1951; "-ach," "Ein Modell mit Schönheitsfehlern," *Union*, June 30, 1951; "-d-," "Modell Bianka—etwas zu leicht," *Sonntag*, no. 25, 1951.

19 For accounts of the public's enthusiastic reaction at the premiere and later screenings, see E.k., "Liebe und Wettbewerb," *Der Morgen*, June 17, 1951. Herrmann Barkhoff, in "Um ein Modellkleid: Der lustige DEFA-Film vom friedlichen Wettbewerb," *Neue Film-Welt*, no. 4, 1951, wrote, "The film derives its content from our time and draws a picture of the consciousness of our people. The DEFA production is marked by lively realism, seriousness, and the humor of our daily life." ("Der Film schöpft seinen Inhalt aus unserer Zeit und zeichnet das neue Bewußtsein unserer Menschen. Lebendige Wirklichkeit, Ernst und Humor des täglichen Lebens sind das Zeichen dieses DEFA-Films" [22–23].)

20 See "Modenschauen in der Kastanienallee," announcement in *Die Weltbühne*, June 13, 1951.

21 Groschopp, "Faszination Film," 35.

22 "Bitterer Lorbeer," *Der Spiegel*, February 13, 1952 (complete text of passage): "Dabei ist die Nachfrage nach solchen unproblematischen Fabrikaten im arbeitsgrauen Osten sehr groß, wie sich unschwer am Beispiel des anspruchslosen Filmchens "Modell Bianka," das von volkseigener Kleiderkonfektion, Pulverschnee und Liebe handelt, erkennen läßt. Dieser Film spielte entgegen allen Erwartungen der DEFA sehr rasch seine Kosten ein."

23 H.U.E., "Mode, Mädchen, Modelle," *Berliner Zeitung*, June 17, 1951.

24 Mb., "Welche Filme wollen die Frauen sehen?" *Neue Zeit*, July 15, 1951.

25 According to Bartlett, *Fashion East*, 109, developments in the GDR were typical of those throughout Eastern Europe. Following the Communist takeovers in 1948, all states were forced to adopt the same centralized model of garment production. The textile and clothing industries and their prewar fashion salons were gradually nationalized, and central clothing institutions, based on Moscow's Dom Modelei (House of Fashion), were set up to coordinate the activities of these industries and to design new dresses.

26 See Pence, "'You as a Woman will understand.'" For examples of public criticism and photographs of low-quality or even disastrous fashion designs produced by VEB Fortschritt, see "Von 'Übergrößen' und 'Flicken hinter Gittern,'" *Die Frau von heute*, January no. 2, 1952.

27 Luise Ermisch was a founder and leader of a "quality brigade" ("Qualitätsbrigade") at a Halle clothing factory (VEB Hallesche Kleiderwerke) in 1949. She received prestigious national awards and was promoted from a seamstress to a director of VEB Bekleidungswerk Mühlhausen in 1951. See "Jedes Produktionsstück—ein Qualitätsstück," *Neues Deutschland*, September 20, 1949.

28 Luise Ermisch, "Kollegen, produziert Qualitätskleidung!" *Neues Deutschland*, July 4, 1951: "Eine Modeschau ist nicht nur eine unterhaltende Veranstaltung. In noch stärkerem Maße in unseren volkseigenen Betrieben veranstaltet, würde die Modeschau als Wettbewerb zwischen den einzelnen Bekleidungswerken durch die Kritik unserer Werktätigen in den Betrieben entscheidend bereichert werden."

29 The state-owned VEB Fortschritt was the successor to a large textile company in Berlin-Lichtenberg that had been founded in 1907, owned for some periods of time by Peek & Cloppenburg, expropriated by the Soviet occupation authorities in 1945, and merged with seventeen smaller Berlin-based clothing companies (*Konfektionsfirmen*) that had been nationalized. It comprised several production sites in Berlin: Fortschritt, Werk I (the main one) in the Möllendorffstraße; Fortschritt, Werk II, in Greifswalder Straße; and Fortschritt III, IV, V and VI. See "Herrenbekleidung 'Fortschritt,'" based on Landesarchiv Berlin C Rep. 470-02, at www.modernruins.de//index.php?option=com_content&view=article&id=64&Itemid=92.

30 For a story on a fashion show in Fortschritt see "Darauf haben wir gewartet: Das Schönste, was auf der Punktkarte gibt," *Die Frau von heute*, February no. 2, 1949. See also "Fortschritt: Ein Betrieb, der seinem Namen Ehre macht," *Die Frau von heute*, March no. 1, 1949; "Fortschrittliches für den Herbst," *Neue Berliner Illustrierte*, 1952/31; "Fortschritt Werk III zeigt," *Die Frau von heute*, October 30, 1953. See also Edith Höding, "Eine Modenschau für die werktätige Berlinerin: Arbeiterkorrespondenz," *Neues Deutschland*, December 14, 1948; Rosemarie Rehahn, "Die Zeit der formlosen Kleidchen ist vorbei. Schöne Modelle für die werktätige Frau," *Neues Deutschland*, October 21, 1950; "Das volkseigene Bekleidungswerk Fortschritt zeigt eine Modeschau in zehn Berliner Großbetrieben," *Neues Deutschland*, September 30, 1950; U.S., "'Uschi' macht das Rennen: Berliner Modeausschuss und 'Fortschritt' Hand in Hand," *Neues Deutschland*," July 7, 1949.

31 This focus on the subway sign also directs audiences' attention to the fact that this station was among the first in East Berlin to be restored to its historical beauty. Numerous articles in the East German press proudly announced the reopening of the subway station in 1950 and the ongoing rebuilding of the area, for example, "Berlins schönster Bahnhof fertig gestellt," *Neues Deutschland*, January 8, 1950; "Alter Bahnhof—neuer Glanz," *Berliner Zeitung*, January 8, 1950; "Berlin kommt wieder!" *Neues Deutschland*, January 26, 1950.

32 There was such an administration housed on Hausvogteiplatz, but the magnificent building the viewers see is actually that of the VEB Fortschritt in Berlin-Lichtenberg.

33 G.L., "Hausvogteiplatz," *Neue Zeit*, January 12, 1950. See also L.Z., "Umbau im Berliner Handelsapparat," *Neue Zeit*, May 17, 1950.

[34] For similar images of supply rooms full of fabrics, see "Karriert, gestreift, gefältet, geglockt," *Neue Berliner Illustrierte*, 1951/5; "Es gibt viel Karostoffe," *Die Frau von heute*, April no. 2, 1949.

[35] See "Brief an Frau Groschopp," Bundesarchiv, file 117/32505, a letter from the director of production, Adolf Hannemann, to Frau Groschopp, cc'd to the head DEFA's costume department, Herr Michieli, expressing gratitude for her generosity in providing some of her own clothes for the film.

[36] *Die Frau von heute* reported often on fashion shows that took place at industrial facilities such as the steel factory in Hennigsdorf, for example, where the female workers evaluated the designs presented by nonprofessional models of different ages, especially middle-aged women. See, for example, "Werkstätige bestimmen die Mode," *Die Frau von heute*, 1951/7. Edith Höding, "Eine Modenschau für die werktätige Berlinerin," *Neues Deutschland*, December 14, 1948, makes the same point in a story about a big fashion show presented by and for female workers in Fortschritt III in Lichtenberg.

[37] See "Hier geht es um ein Modellkleid." *Der Nacht-Express*, February 11, 1951.

[38] Groschopp, "Heitere Filme—ernste Sache."

[39] See "Production Protocol," Bundesarchiv, file 117/32505.

[40] Most likely he used documentary material he had filmed himself in Leipzig for *Der Augenzeuge*.

[41] In reality, continuous problems with the production of consumer goods in the East caused problems at the Leipzig Fair as well. The spring fairs were canceled from 1952 to 1954 as the GDR economy went through a difficult period. The crisis culminated in the June 17, 1953, uprising. For an illuminating historical account, see Pence, "'A World in Miniature,'" 21–50.

[42] See Stitziel, *Fashioning Socialism*, 64–65.

[43] Numerous newspaper articles report on the fashion shows during the trade fair. See, for example, "rt," "Die Messe im Urteil der Berliner Aussteller," *Berliner Zeitung*, March 12, 1947; "Im Spiegel der Leipziger Messe," *Berliner Zeitung*, August 22, 1947; S.G., "Wir sahen die Sommermode in Leipzig: Täglich zwei Messemodeschauen," *Berliner Zeitung*, March 12, 1950.

[44] PL, "Verwandlungswunder Bianka," *Berliner Zeitung*, May 11, 1951, a preview of the film, provides a detailed description for its curious readers: "Transformation number one: the jacket is taken off and one sees a sport's dress with a wide collar covering the shoulders. The collar is removed, reversed, and attached around the hips; the long sleeves are detached with one quick pull down, and here comes the second transformation: an elegant afternoon dress. All of a sudden more layers peel off. The shoulders are laid bare, the upper part of the dress folds down and releals a fine silk fabric. The modell wraps around her hips an ankle-long skirt that is made of the same material. This is transformation number three: a breath-taking evening gown. A dream made of gauze and lace"("Erste Verwandlung: die Jacke wird ausgezogen, zum Vorschein kommt ein sportliches Kleid mit sehr breitem Schulterkragen. Dieser läßt sich ablegen, wenden und um die Hüfte knüpfen, die langen Ärmel können mit einem Griff abgestreift werden, und zum Vorschein kommt, als zweite Verwandlung: ein elegantes Nachmittagskleid. Plötzlich fallen

weitere Hüllen. Die Schultern der Vorführdame werden freigelegt, das Oberteil des Kleides klappt nach unten und läßt zartere, seidige Gewebe erkennen. Ein knöchellanger Rock aus dem gleichen Material wird umgebunden: fertig ist Verwandlung Nummer drei, ein berauschendes Abendkleid. Traum aus Tüll und Spitzen").

[45] U.S.,"'Uschi,' das Verwandlungskleid, macht das Rennen: Berliner Modeausschuß und 'Fortschritt' Hand in Hand" *Neues Deutschland*, July 7, 1949.

[46] K.B., "Eine Modeschau im Betrieb," *Neues Deutschland*, September 4, 1951: "Die größte Überraschung waren Jedoch die Verwandlungskleider. Mit Hilfe einiger Stoffreste, so erklärten die Fachleute, läßt sich ein Kleid in vier bis fünf verschiedene Anzüge verwandeln."

[47] S.G., "Wir sahen die Sommermode in Leipzig," *Berliner Zeitung*, March 12, 1950: (complete text of passage): "Es wurde einem fast schon schwindelig von den vielen Verwandlungskleidern, die nach öfterem An- und Ausziehen von Boleros und kurzen Jäckchen ein schulterfreies Nachmittagskleid oder Sonnenkleid hervorbrachten. Sie wurden beifällig aufgenommen."

[48] Groshopp, "Faszination Film," 35. The fact that the acclaimed Walter Schulze-Mittendorff designed the *Verwandlungskleid* was also advertised in a preview of the film, about a month before the premiere. See "Verwandlungswunder Bianka: In Johannisthal dreht die DEFA einen heiteren Spielfilm aus der Gegenwart," *Berliner Zeitung*, May 11, 1951. However, Schulze-Mittendorff's name was not included in the credits; only Gerhard Kaddatz, who was responsible for the rest of the costumes, was mentioned. Walter Schulze-Mittendorff (1893–1976) was a legendary artist and set designer who had worked on the costume and set designs for several Fritz Lang films in the 1920s and on close to twenty UFA film productions in the 1930s. In 1946, he signed a contract with DEFA, where he was soon promoted to a chief costume designer. He designed the costumes for almost thirty-six films made in the GDR, mostly historical costume dramas. After the Berlin Wall went up, Schulze-Mittendorff, a native West Berliner, remained in the Western part of the city. For a detailed account of Schulze-Mittendorff's career as costume designer and his high reputation at DEFA, see Hilde R. Lest, "Kostüme haben Charakter," *Die neue Filmwoche*, no. 1, 1948. See also appendix 1.

[49] See Müller, "Ein mißglücktes Modell": "In jedem Konsumladen kann man feststellen, daß die VEB- Bekleidungsindustrie trotz mancher Mängel bedeutend phantasievoller, geschmackvoller ist und keine Schabracken von 'Modellen' ausknobelt, die eine Frau niemals anziehen würde."

[50] See "Friedlich-hohe Modekonkurrenz," *Neue Berliner Illustrierte*, 1951/38; "Mode mit Verstand: praktische Vorschläge der tschechoslowakischen Bekleidungsindustrie," *Neue Berliner Illustrierte*, 1951/23; "Budapester Stil," *Neue Berliner Illustrierte*, 1951/15; "Das schöne Ende kommt nach: der deutschtschechoslowakische Wettbewerb," *Neue Berliner Illustrierte*, 1951/12.

[51] The rationing of basic foods and consumer goods other than clothes, shoes, and textiles in the GDR did not end until 1958. Traditionally, as numerous historians have pointed out, the clothing sector was of particular importance to the German consumer, both East and West, even during the Nazi years and the wartime period. In the first half of the 1950s, East German consumers increased their

spending for clothes from 16 percent to 19 percent of their income. Thus, priority was given to lifting the rations at least for some apparel and textiles by 1951. See Sywottek, "Zwei Wege in die 'Konsumgesellschaft,'" 271; Roesler, "Privater Konsum in Ostdeutschland 1950–1960," 285–86. For an overview of the continuing rationing in the GDR till 1958, see Landsman, *Dictatorship and Demand.*

52 U.S., "Ab 25. Januar Belieferung der Punktkarte," *Neues Deutschland*, January 10, 1949.

53 U.S., "Wiedergeburt seiner Majestät des Kunden," *Neues Deutschland*, January 10, 1949. See also "Punkte, Punkte, Punkte," *Neues Deutschland*, January 30, 1949, a report on the sale of about 1,800 outfits directly from the company store of Fortschritt in Gertraudenstraße. In February a fashion show was organized in the Friedrichstadt-Palast, in which workers from Fortschritt modeled their company's new designs, priced to fit the new ration card. See U.S., "Modell 'Hedi' kostet 48 Punkte," *Neues Deutschland*, February 22, 1949.

54 "Modelle auf die Punktkarte," *Die Frau von heute*, January no. 2, 1949.

55 See Bartlett, *Fashion East*, 99.

56 For more on the discrepancy between the spectacle of the Leipzig Fair and the frustration of the average consumer, see Pence, "'A World in Miniature,'" 32–36.

57 In addition to the postwar DEFA production *Unser täglich Brot* (1949), Slatan Dudow directed an avant-garde film with a script by Bertolt Brecht, *Kuhle Wampe: oder wem gehört die Welt?* (Kuhle Wampe: or Who Owns the World, 1932, released in English as *To Whom Does the World Belong*), with which it shares some motifs and even characters. On the appropriation of some stylistic features of *Kuhle Wampe* in *Frauenschicksale*, see Mittman, "Fashioning the Socialist Nation," 23–24; 28–44. Kuhle Wampe is a location outside Berlin whose name can be translated literally as "Hollow Belly."

58 The first DEFA production in color was *Das kalte Herz* (1950, directed by Paul Verhoeven), an adaptation of a fairy tale, on the heels of the first West German color film, *Schwarzwaldmädel* (Black Forest Girl, 1950, directed by Hans Deppe).

59 See Reinhard Klassen, "Betriebspremiere des DEFA-Farbfilms Frauenschicksale im Bekleidungswerk Mühlhausen," *Das Volk* (Jena), June 19, 1952.

60 The World Youth Festival was held in East Berlin in August 1951. Approximately 2 million German youths from both parts of Germany and 26,000 delegates from 104 countries participated in a range of political, cultural, and sports events. In its final sequence, Dudow's film incorporates documentary footage from this event, but in *Forrest Gump*–fashion, several characters from the film are seen taking part in the festivities. For more on the youth festival, see Ruhl, *Stalin-Kult und Rotes Woodstock.*

61 For more on the troubles of filming in color and UFA's ultimate success with *Frauen sind doch bessere Diplomaten*, see Kreimeier, *Die UFA-Story*, 329. See also "Frauen sind doch bessere Diplomaten," *Filmwelt: Das Film- und Foto-Magazin*, November 12, 1941, 928.

62 Rother, "Der Weg in ein neues Leben," 174–89.

63 Fortschritt II was at 212–213 Greifswalder Straße. A photograph in the Bundesarchiv shows numerous young women leaving the factory at the end of

the workday. See "Bundesarchiv Bild 183-09061-0002, Berlin, Greifswalder Straße, Feierabend," Wikimedia, https://commons.wikimedia.org/wiki/File:Bundesarchiv_Bild_183-09061-0002,_Berlin,_Greifswalder_Stra%C3%9Fe,_Feierabend.jpg. This branch of VEB Fortschritt became one of the sites affected by the workers' uprising in June 1953, when twenty people are wounded in a street fight near the building.

64 A. Künnemann, "Frauenschicksale—zu wenig motiviert," *Neues Deutschland*, September 17, 1952.

65 Slatan Dudow, "Zur Diskussion über den Film 'Frauenschicksale': Antwort an den Demokratischen Frauenbund Deutschlands," *Neues Deutschland*, November 21, 1952.

66 See Strauß, *Frauen im deutschen Film*, 52–53.

67 *Fürst von Pappenheim* (1952) is a light opera (*Operettenschwank*), a remake of the eponymous silent comedy from 1927, with Curt Bois in a hilarious cross-dressing role. Bobby Lüthge, a prolific scriptwriter—*Drehbuchfabrikant*—placed the story in contemporary times and changed the plot significantly.

68 In "Libbe, Erijotik und Zoff," *Der Spiegel*, April 16, 1952, a reviewer wrote: "In the lingo of the specialists, this is a 'remake,' which in German means 'Make new out of old.' Or using film terminology: Clothes always sell. Lüthge demonstrated again and again the effectiveness of his recipe during the lean postwar years of German film." ("Dieses Rezept heißt im Fachjargon auf gut englisch: 'Remaking'—zu deutsch: 'Aus alt mach neu,' oder filmphilosophisch ausgedrückt: Klamotte geht immer. Die Wirksamkeit seines Rezepts hat Lüthge in den mageren Nachkriegsjahren des deutschen Films immer wieder und überzeugend demonstriert.")

69 For more on the image of the industrialist in popular film, see Wiesen, *West German Industry and Challenge of the Nazi Past 1945–1955*.

70 On the return of Hannelore Schroth, a film idol from UFA times, to the postwar screen, see Huwe, "Wandlungen einer komödiantischen Begabung."

71 "Modenschau bei Pappenheim," *Film- und Mode-Revue*, no. 14, 1952.

72 For a preview of the film see "In Berlin schnurrt wieder die Kamera," *Der Tag*, April 12, 1951.

73 See Ch.St., "Draufgängerpossen: 'Fürst von Pappenheim' in Marmorhaus," *Die Neue Zeitung*, June 25, 1952; W.V., "Wieder Film im Freien," *Die Neue Zeitung*, May 29, 1951.

74 See Ganeva, "Miss Germany, Miss Europe, Miss Universe," 111–29.

75 The first postwar pageant was held in Wiesbaden in 1948. Its organizer, Karl-Heinz Ronke, founded the Deutsche Modeschau-Gesellschaft (German Fashion Show Society), which launched the Miss Germany competition the following year. See "Die Schönste im ganzen Land: Frau nach Maß," *Der Spiegel*, August 28, 1948. Smaller-scale regional pageants also proliferated. The newsreel *Blick in die Welt*, no. 32, 1949, reported in a cheery tone on the first postwar "pageant on the beach," in Wannsee, where Helga Schröder was selected *Strandkönigin* (queen of the beach).

[76] Heinz Friedrich, "Der bunte Traum," review, *Die Zeit*, March 6, 1951. Such cinematic entertainment extravaganzas incurred enormous production costs (2.5 million marks for *Der bunte Traum*, over 1 million for *Johannes und die 13 Schönheitsköniginnen*) and often provoked very critical reviews, but still were considered hits (*Publikumstreffer*). For negative reviews see "Neu in Deutschland: Johannes und die 13 Schönheitsköniginnen," *Der Spiegel*, October 3, 1951; Gunter Groll, "Grenzen des Geschmacks: Dreizehn Schönheitsköniginnen," *Süddeutsche Zeitung*, September 28, 1951, in Groll, *Magie des Films*. *Johannes und die 13 Schönheitsköniginnen* was written by the notoriously prolific "script-manufacturer" Bobby E. Lüthge and produced by the same team at Berolina-Film that was responsible for the success of *Grün ist die Heide* (1951) and *Schwarzwaldmädel* (1950), two *Heimatfilme*. The plot revolves around the transportation of thirteen charming but unruly beauty queens from different nationalities to Nice, in order to participate in a Miss Europe competition.

[77] Katja von Glinski, "Gekrönte Schönheit," *sie*, April 24, 1949. Thea Tell won the Miss Berlin title in 1949, in the Titania-Palast as one of forty candidates and was featured on the cover of *Illustrierter Telegraf*. See "Berlins Schönste," *Illustrierter Telegraf*, April 17, 1949. Inge Löwenstein, Miss Frankfurt, became the first Miss Germany in 1949, a few months before the founding of the Federal Republic.

[78] Susanne Erichsen's autobiography details her serendipitous transitions from prisoner in a Soviet camp to film cutter in the film industry to model in Munich, Berlin, and New York, in a way that is remarkably similar to that of the fictional character Ingrid. See Erichsen and Hansen, *Ein Nerz und eine Krone*.

[79] After winning the Miss Germany title Erichsen became a sought-after model for the exquisite Berlin salon Gehringer & Glupp. Her photographs often appeared in and on the covers of *Film und Frau*, *Heute*, and other illustrated magazines. In 1952 she accepted an invitation to the United States as a *Botschafterin der Eleganz* (ambassador of elegance) where she lived and worked intermittently for six years without giving up her commitment to Gehringer & Glupp in Berlin. See ibid., 169–211.

[80] See K.Nf. [Karena Niehoff], "'Ingrid, Die Geschichte eines Fotomodells' im Kiki," *Der Tagesspiegel*, January 23, 1955. On *Ingrid* as an "effective film report" and "unusual work," see Karl-Heinz Krüger, ". . .Was man so Glück nennt: 'Ingrid, Die Geschichte eines Fotomodells' im Kiki," *Der Abend* (Berlin), January 22, 1955. Numerous positive reviews include cro, "Hanna Matz—entzuckert," *Die Welt*, January 24, 1955; Klaus Hebecker, "Ingrid, Die Geschichte eines Fotomodells," *Der neue Film* (Wiesbaden), January 31, 1955.

[81] Erichsen, *Ein Nerz und eine Krone*, writes, "Gehringer liked to call us models his muses. All of the dresses were designed and cut individually on the model" ("Gehringer nannte uns Mannequins gern seine Musen. Alle Kleider wurden uns individuell auf den Leib geschneidert" (171).

[82] For an account of the film's overall success with the critics and its dismal performance at the box office, see Sobotka, *Die Filmwunderkinder*, 144–45.

Epilogue

[1] Although it is not clear who commissioned the production, the short documentary was evaluated "wertvoll" by the Film Assessment Office (Filmbewertungsstelle, or FBW), which according to the new Entertainment Tax Law (Vergnügungssteuergesetz) enacted in 1947 qualified it to be bundled with a feature film and shown in theaters. The addition of a culture film to the main feature ensured lower distribution fees. See Lehnert, *Wochenschau*, 86–87. See also Roeber and Jacoby, *Handbuch der filmwissenschaftlichen Bereiche*, 255.

[2] Unlike other DEFA productions, *Besondere Kennzeichen: keine* was free of direct propaganda and was highly praised in the West German press for its refreshing and convincing realism, aimed at portraying the everyday postwar lives of ordinary Germans. Leading film trade publications in the Federal Republic such as *Filmblätter* and *Deutsche Film-Korrespondenz* lobbied hard—but in vain—for the release of this film to West German audiences. See Heimann, *DEFA, Künstler und SED-Kulturpolitik*, 161.

[3] Klaus Wischnewski, "Auch das Alltägliche ist ein Besonderes: Zum DEFA-Film *Besondere Kennzeichen: keine*," *Deutsche Filmkunst*, April 1956, 100–103.

[4] Kaes, *From Hitler to Heimat*, x.

Appendix 1. Principal Costume and Fashion Designers: Biographical Notes

[1] Ackermann, *Couture in Deutschland*, 71–76; Leoni Holz, "Bessie Becker," *Berlin im Spiegel*, no. 2, 1960, 33.

[2] "Hinter den Kulissen," *Die Mode*, February 1941; "Berlin zeigt," *Die Mode*, August–September 1941; "Bei Schulze-Bibernell," *Die Mode*, March 1942; "Irmgard Bibernell," *Constanze*, no. 13, June 1951, 27; "Irmgard Bibernell gestorben," *Hamburger Abendblatt*, February 26, 1999.

[3] Alfred Bücken, "Vor der Idee bis zur Uraufführung: Der Punkt auf dem i—ohne Punkte," *Die Filmwelt*, no. 41–42, 1942; Hans Traub, "Mode und Kostüm im Film," *Die Mode*, April 1942.

[4] Source: Galerie Bernd Dürr, *Ilse Fehling: Bauhaus, Bühne, Akt, Skulptur 1922–1967*; Charlotte Till, "Fantasien in Farbe und Form," *Die Koralle*, May 28, 1944.

[5] Till, "Fantasien in Farbe und Form"; Anneliese Maurer, "Frauenberufe rund um den Film," *Filmwelt: das Film- und Foto-Magazin*, no. 50–51, December 1936; Manon Hahn, "'Boccaccio' aus der Kleiderperspektive," *Filmwelt: das Film- und Foto-Magazin*, 1936/23.

[6] Hans Martin Cremer, "Die Kostümberaterin und ihr Aufgabenfeld," *Film-Kurier*, November 16, 1940; "Margot Hielscher ist tot," *Der Spiegel*, August 22, 2017; "Margot Hielscher," filmportal.de.

[7] Eva Lemke, "Aus einer Werkstatt für Film-Mode" *Die Mode*, April 1942; report of the NSDAP Gauleitung Berlin, Landesarchiv Berlin, Personalakte Nr. 18460 (microfilm); Eva Lemke, "Modezeichnerinnen von morgen," Eva Lemke, *Berlins*

Modenblatt, no. 10, October 1948; Eva Lemke, "Modegraphikerinnen machen Mode," *Berlins Modenblatt*, no. 7, July 1949.

[8] "Gerda Leopold," filmportal.de.

[9] "Filmberuf: Der Kostümbildner (DEFA-Kostümbildnerin Vera Mügge)," *Neue Film-Welt*, 1951/4.

[10] Thomas Staedeli, "Porträt der Kostümbildnerin Ilse Naumann"; "Ilse Naumann," www.cyranos.ch/smnaum-d.htm; Dimic, "Ilse Naumann: Modezeichnerin und Kostümbildnerin."

[11] "Hildegard Ordnung," Personalakte A234-03, Landesarchiv Berlin.

[12] Lise Peck, "Eine Kostümberaterin erzählt: Frau Pommer-Pehl über ihre Arbeit für den neuen Bavaria-Film 'Komödianten,'" *Film-Kurier*, February 24, 1941.

[13] Ackermann, *Couture in Deutschland*, 71–76; "Besuch in Berliner Ateliers: III. Rudow," *Elegante Welt*, no. 5, February 1950, 8–9; "Die Mode und ihre Schöpfer," *Film und Frau*, no. 25, 1949, 18–19; "Sinaida Rudow," Registerakte B Rep. 042 Nr. 33916, Landesarchiv Berlin, Amtsregister Charlottenburg.

[14] Guenther, *Nazi Chic*; Sridhar, *Candlelight in a Storm*, 75–76; Tödt, *Der Mann im Hintergrund*; "Ursula Schewe," *Berlin im Spiegel*, no. 1, 1960; "Aus einer Modenschau: Ursula Schewe," *Die Frau von heute*, June no. 1, 1946.

[15] "Walter Schulze Mittendorff," www.walter-schulze-mittendorff.com; "Walter Schulze Mittendorff," www.filmportal.de.

[16] Aschke, "Die geliehene Identität," 256; Hete Nebel, "Film macht Mode," *Der deutsche Film*, 1939/9; "Film und Mode," *Der deutsche Film*, 1941/2–3.

[17] Siebenbrodt and Schöbe, *Bauhaus 1919–1933 Weimar-Dessau-Berlin*.

Bibliography

Periodicals

Abendpost (Frankfurt am Main)
Berlin am Mittag
Berlin im Spiegel
Berliner Filmblätter
Berliner Lokal-Anzeiger
Berliner Zeitung
Berlins Modenblatt
Chic: die neue Modenzeitung
Constanze
Daily Mail
Das Reich: deutsche Wochenzeitung (Munich)
Das Volk (Jena)
Der Abend (Berlin)
Der Berliner: Nachrichtenblatt der britischen Militärbehörde
Der deutsche Film
Der Kurier (Berlin)
Der Morgen
Der Nacht-Express
Der neue Film (Wiesbaden)
Der Silberspiegel
Der Spiegel
Der Tag (Berlin)
Der Tagesspiegel
Deutsche Filmkunst
Deutsche Film-Rundschau
Deutsche Rundschau
Deutsche Werbung
Die Frau von heute (Leipzig)
Die Koralle
Die Mode
Die neue Filmwoche
Die Neue Zeitung
Die Welt
Die Welt am Sonntag
Die Weltbühne
Die Zeit
Elegante Welt
Film Illustrierte

Film Revue
Film und Frau
Film- und Mode-Revue
film-dienst
Film-Echo
Film-Kurier
Film-Rundschau
Filmwelt: das Film- und Foto-Magazin
Ford-Revue: eine kulturelle Monatszeitschrift
Für Dich: Die neue illustrierte Frauenzeitung
Hannoversche Allgemeine Zeitung
Heute: die Amerikanisch-deutsche Illustrierte
Illustrierter Telegraf
ITEX: illustrierte Fachzeitschrift für die gesamte Textil- und Bekleidungswirtschaft
Jugend-Telegraf
Life
Lilith: die Zeitschrift für junge Mädchen und Frauen
Mosaik: das Weltbild der Frau
Münchner Allgemeine Zeitung
Münchner neueste Nachrichten
Neue Berliner Illustrierte
Neue Film-Welt
Neue Zeit
Neues Deutschland
New York Times
Nürnberger Nachrichten
sie: Wochenzeitung für Frauenrecht und Menschenrecht
Sonntag
Spandauer Volksblatt
Stern (Hamburg)
Tägliche Rundschau
Telegraf
The Economist
Union
Vogue (London)
Volksblatt Berlin-Spandau
Vorwärts
Wiener Filmzeitung
Wiesbadener Tageblatt

Primary and Secondary Sources Cited

Ackermann, Susa. *Couture in Deutschland: Streiflichter aus dem deutschen Mode-schaffen*. Munich: Perlen-Verlag, 1961.

Albrecht, Gerd. "Kino am Abgrund: Film im Dritten Reich zum Jahreswechsel 1944/45." *Unser Jahrhundert im Film und Fernsehen: Beiträge zu zeitge-schichtlichen Film- und Fernsehdokumenten*. Konstanz: UVK Medien, 1995.

Altman, Wolfgang. "A Spirit of Optimism." In *German Fashion Design 1946–2012*, edited by Nadine Barth. Berlin: Distanz, 2011.

Aly, Götz. *Hitler's Beneficiaries: Plunder, Racial War, and the Nazi Warfare State*. Translated by Jefferson Chase. New York: Henry Holt, 2008.

Andrews, Dudley. "Film and History." In *Film Studies: Critical Approaches*, edited by John Hill and Pamela Church Gibson, 174–87. Oxford: Oxford University Press, 2000.

Arendt, Hannah. "The Aftermath of the Nazi Rule: Report from Germany." *Essays in Understanding 1930–1954*, edited and with an introduction by Jerome Kohn, 248–69 (New York: Harcourt Brace, 1993). Originally published in *Commentary*, October 1950.

———. *Essays in Understanding, 1930–1950*, edited and with an introduction by Jerome Kohn. New York: Harcourt Brace, 1993.

Aschke, Katja. "Die geliehene Identität: Film und Mode in Berlin 1900–1990." In *Berlin en Vogue: Berliner Mode in der Photographie*, edited by F. C. Gundlach and Uli Richter, 233–76. Berlin: Ernst Wasmuth, 1993.

Auer, Anita. *Der Courturier Heinz Schulze-Varell (1907–1985): Entstehung und Entwicklung einer Haute Couture in Deutschland*. Konstanz: Horte-Gorre, 1993.

Aurich, Rolf, Jörg Becker, and Wolfgang Jacobsen, eds. *Wolfdietrich Schnurre: Kritiker*. Munich: edition text + kritik and Deutsche Kinematek, 2010.

Bach, Ulrich. "The Woman Between: Hildegard Knef's Movies in Cold War Berlin." In *Berlin, Divided City 1945–1989*, edited by Philip Broadbent and Sabine Hake, 115–24. New York: Berghahn Books, 2010.

Baer, Hester. *Dismantling the Dream Factory: Gender, German Cinema and the Postwar Quest for a New Film Language*. New York: Berghahn, 2009.

———. "*Film und Frau* and the Female Spectator in 1950s West German Cinema," In *Framing the Fifties: Cinema in a Divided Germany*, edited by John E. Davidson and Sabine Hake, 151–65. New York: Berghahn, 2007.

Bartlett, Djurdja. *Fashion East: The Spectre That Haunted Socialism*. Cambridge, MA: MIT Press, 2010.

Bauer Alfred, *Spielfilm Almanach, Band 2: 1945–1955*. Munich: Filmbuchverlag Winterberg, 1981.

Beier, Gerhard. *Der Demonstrations- und Generalstreik vom 12. November 1948*. Frankfurt am Main: Europäische Verlagsanstalt, 1975.

Benzenhöfer, Udo, and Gunnar Klatt. "Der DEFA-Film *Straßenbekanntschaft* (1948): Mit Bemerkungen zu seinem Einsatz bei der Geschlechtskrankheitenbekämpfung in der sowjetischen Besatzungszone und in Niedersachsen." In *Medizin im Spielfilm der fünziger Jahre*, edited by Udo Benzendörfer, 17–26. Pfaffenweiler: Centaurus, 1993.

Berger, Jürgen, Hans P. Reichmann, and Rudolf Worschech, eds. *Zwischen gestern und morgen: Westdeutscher Nachkriegsfilm 1946–1962*. Frankfurt am Main: Deutsches Filmmuseum, 1989.

Bergfelder, Tim. *International Adventures: German Popular Cinema and European Co-Productions of the 1960s*. New York: Berghahn, 2005.

Berghoff, Hartmut. "Konsumpolitik im nationalsozialistischen Deutschland." In *Die Konsumgesellschaft in Deutschland 1890–1990*, edited by Heinz-Gerhard Haupt and Claus Torp, 268–88. Frankfurt am Main: Campus, 2009.

Berlin Municipal Council. *Das erste Jahr: Berlin im Neuaufbau, ein Rechenschaftsbericht des Magistrats der Stadt Berlin.* Berlin: Das neue Berlin, 1946.

Bessen, Ursula. *Trümmer und Träume: Nachkriegszeit und fünfziger Jahre auf Zelloid.* Bochum: Studienverlag Dr. N. Brockmeyer, 1989.

"Bilder vom ersten Friedens-Modentee." Staatliche Museen zu Berlin, Kunstbibliothek, Collection Lipperheide, Lipp OZ 148.

Boehm, Philip, trans. *A Woman in Berlin: A Diary.* New York: Henry Holt, 2005.

Bönsch, Annemarie. "Film- und Bühnenkostüme in Fallbeispielen." In *W. F. Adlmüller: Mode, Inszenierung und Impuls,* edited by Elisabeth Frottier and Gerald Bast, 98–109. Vienna: Springer, 2009.

———. "Kleidung nach dem Krieg." In *Menschen nach dem Krieg: Schicksale 1945–1955,* edited by Gerhard Jagschitz and Stefan Karner, 96–107. Vienna: Ausstellung Schloß Schallaburg, 1995.

Borgelt, Hans. *Das war der Frühling von Berlin: eine Chronik.* Munich: Schneekluth, 1980.

Borneman, John. *Belonging in the two Berlins: Kin, State, Nation.* New York: Cambridge University Press, 1992.

Brandlmeier, Thomas. "Von Hitler zu Adenauer: Deutsche Trümmerfilme." In *Zwischen Gestern und Morgen: Der deutsche Nachkriegsfilm 1946–1962,* edited by Jürgen Berger, Hans P. Reichmann, and Rudolf Worschech, 33–60. Frankfurt am Main: Filmmuseum, 1989.

Brauerhoch, Annette. "Ästhetische Opposition/en in Peter Pewas' *Straßenbekanntschaft.*" In *Demokratisierung der Wahrnehmung? Das westeuropäische Nachkriegskino,* edited by Hermann Kappelhoff, Bernard Gross, and Daniel Illger, 135–47. Berlin: Vorwerk 8, 2010.

———. *Fräuleins und GIs: Geschichte und Filmgeschichte.* Frankfurt am Main: Stroemfeld, 2006.

Bruns, Jana. *Nazi Cinema's New Women.* Cambridge, UK: Cambridge University Press, 2009.

Bundeszentrale für politische Bildung. *Neubeginn und Wiederaufbau 1945–1949.* Bonn: Bundeszentrale für politische Bildung, 1997.

Carter, Erica. *How German Is She? Postwar West German Reconstruction and the Consuming Woman.* Ann Arbor: University of Michigan Press, 1997.

Chamberlin, Brewster S. *Kultur auf Trümmern: Berliner Berichte der amerikanischen Information Control Section Juli–Dezember 1945.* Stuttgart: Deutsche Verlags-Anstalt, 1979.

Charman, Terry. *The German Home Front 1939–45.* New York: Barrie & Jenkins, 1989.

Confino, Alon. *Germany as a Culture of Remembrance: Promises and Limits of Writing History.* Chapel Hill: University of North Carolina Press, 2006.

Davidson, John E. "Working for the Man, Whoever That May Be: The Vocation of Wolfgang Liebeneiner." In *Cultural History through a National Socialist Lens,* edited by Robert C. Reimer, 240–67. Rochester, NY: Camden House, 2000.

De Grazia, Victoria. *Irresistible Empire: America's Advance through Twentieth-Century Europe.* Cambridge, MA: Harvard University Press, 2005.

Dertlinger, Antje. *Frauen der ersten Stunde: Aus den Gründerjahren der Bundesrepublik.* Berlin: J. Latka, 1989.

Dimic, Natalie. "Ilse Naumann: Modezeichnerin und Kostümbildnerin." In *Glanz und Grauen: Mode im Dritten Reich*, edited by Claudia Gottfried. Ratingen: LVR Industriemuseum, 2012.

Ehrlich, Curt. "Die PuC Werkstätten. Ein Werbeargument erst recht in Kriegszeiten." *Deutsche Werbung* 33, no. 5–6 (March 1940): 140–42.

Epp, Sigrid. *Kleider machen Münchner: Die Geschichte der Mode in München 1945–2000*. Munich: Buchendorfer Verlag, 2001.

Erichsen, Susanne, and Dorothée Hansen. *Ein Nerz und eine Krone: Die Lebenserinnerungen des deutschen Fräuleinwunders*. Munich: Econ, 2003.

Fay, Jennifer. *Theaters of Occupation: Hollywood and the Reeducation of Postwar Germany*. Minneapolis: University of Minnesota Press, 2008.

Fehrenbach, Heide. *Cinema in Democratizing Germany: Reconstruction of National Identity after Hitler*. Chapel Hill: University of North Carolina Press, 1995.

Feike, Birgit. *Vom Vorhangkleid zur Dreamline: Mode in Österreich von 1945 bis zum Ende der 1950er Jahre*. Vienna: Universitätsverlag, 1996.

Fisher, Jaimey. *Disciplining Germany: Youth, Reeducation, and Reconstruction after the Second World War*. Detroit: Wayne State University Press, 2007.

Freiß, Lisbeth. *Die Strickjacke: Mode- und Mediengeschichte und Semiologie im deutschsprachigen Spielfilm der 1930er bis 1950er Jahre*. Vienna: Löcker, 2013.

Friedrich, Karin. *Zeitfunken: Biographie einer Familie*. Munich: C. H. Beck, 2010.

Friedrich, Ruth Andreas. *Der Schattenmann: Tagebuchaufzeichnungen 1938–1948*. Frankfurt am Main: Suhrkamp, 2000.

Frisch, Max. "Notizen aus Berlin und Wien." In *Städte 1945: Berichte und Bekenntnisse*, edited by Ingeborg Drewitz, 183–89. Düsseldorf: Eugen Diederich Verlag, 1970.

Frottier, Elisabeth, and Gerald Bast. *W. F. Adlmüller.Mode: Inszenierungen + Impulse*. Vienna: Springer, 2009.

Ganeva, Mila. "Fashion amidst the Ruins: Revisiting the Early Rubble Films *And the Heavens Above* (1947) and *The Murderers Are among Us* (1946)." *German Studies Review* 37, no. 1 (2014): 61–85.

———. "Miss Germany, Miss Europe, Miss Universe: Beauty Pageants in the Popular Media of the Weimar Republic." In *Globalizing Beauty: Consumerism and Body Aesthetics in the Twentieth Century*, edited by Hartmut Berghoff and Thomas Kühne, 111–30. New York: Palgrave Macmillan, 2013.

———. "Die Modeschriftstellerin Helen Hessel." In Helen Hessel, *Ich schreibe aus Paris: Über die Mode, das Leben und die Liebe*, edited by Mila Ganeva, 327–51. Wädenswil am Zürichsee: Nimbus, 2014.

———. "'Stoffe über die Luftbrücke': Film und Mode trotz der Blockade." In *Die Berliner Luftbrücke: Erinnerungsort des Kalten Krieges*, edited by Corinne Defrance, Bettina Greiner, and Ulrich Pfeil, 253–70. Berlin: Christoph Links Verlag, 2018.

———. "Vicarious Consumption: Fashion in German Media and Film during the War Years 1939–1943." In *The Consumer on the Home Front: Second World War Civilian Consumption in Comparative Perspective*, edited by Felix Römer, Jan Logermann, and Hartmut Berghoff, 199–221. Oxford, UK: Oxford University Press, 2017.

Gemünden, Gerd. *Foreign Affair: Billy Wilder's American Films.* New York: Berghahn, 2008.

Glaser, Hermann. *The Rubble Years: The Cultural Roots of Postwar Germany 1945–1948.* Translated by Franz Feige and Patricia Gleason. New York: Paragon, 1986.

Goos, Manuela, and Brigitte Heyde. "Kleider machen Frauen." Brochure for an exhibit *Women in the Charlottenburg Fashion Industry after 1945 7.11.1990–13.01.1991.* Heimatmuseum Charlottenburg, November 7, 1990–January 13, 1991. Berlin: Heimatmuseum Charlottenburg, 1991.

Görtemaker, Heike B. *Eva Braun: Life with Hitler.* New York: Alfred Knopf, 2011.

Greffrath, Bettina. *Gesellschaftsbilder der Nachkriegszeit: Deutsche Spielfilme 1945–1949.* Pfaffenweiler: Centaurus, 1995.

Groll, Gunter. *Magie des Films: Kritische Notizen über Film, Zeit und Welt.* Munich: Süddeutscher Verlag, 1953.

Groschopp, Richard. "Faszination Film. Ein Gespräch, aufgezeichnet von Ralf Schenk." *Theorie und Praxis des Films: Betriebsschule des VEB DEFA Studio für Spielfilme,* no. 3 (1987): 23–173.

———. "Heitere Filme—ernste Sache." *DEFA-Pressedienst,* no. 5 (1951).

Groß, Bernhard. *Die Filme sind unter uns: Zur Geschichtlichkeit des frühen deutschen Nachkriegskinos: Trümmer-, Genre-, Dokumentarfilm.* Berlin: Vorwerk 8, 2015.

Grossmann, Atina. *Jews, Germans, and Allies: Close Encounters in Occupied Germany.* Princeton, NJ: Princeton University Press, 2007.

Guenther, Irene. *Nazi Chic: Fashioning Women in the Third Reich.* Oxford: Berg, 2004.

Gundlach, F. C. *Die Pose als Körpersprache.* Cologne: König, 2001.

Gundlach, F. C., and Uli Richter, eds. *Berlin en Vogue: Berliner Mode in der Photographie.* Tübingen: Wasmuth, 1993.

Hake, Sabine. *Popular Cinema of the Third Reich.* Austin: University of Texas Press, 2002.

Hampicke, Evelyn. "Flotter Mangel, fesche Reste: Vom pfiffigen Film-Kampf mit Versorgungsengpässen." In *Im Banne der Katastrophe: Innovation und Tradition im europäischen Film 1940–1959,* edited by Johannes Roschlau, 127–37. Munich: edition text + kritik, 2010.

Hanisch, Michael. *"Um 6 Uhr abends nach Kriegsende" bis "High Noon": Kino und Film in Berlin der Nachkriegszeit 1945–1953.* Berlin: DEFA-Stiftung, 2004.

Harsch, Donna. *Revenge of the Domestic: Women, the Family, and Communism in the German Democratic Republic.* Princeton, NJ: Princeton University Press, 2007.

Hartung, Gert. "Wer in der Mode lebt, lebt im Heute und im Morgen, aber nicht im Gestern." In *Stoff zum Träumen: Wie Heinz Oestergaard Mode machte,* edited by Margit Vogel, 46–64. Berlin: edition q, 1996.

Hauptamt für Statistik von Groß-Berlin. *Berlin in Zahlen 1946–1947.* Berlin: Hauptamt für Statistik von Groß-Berlin, 1947.

Heimann, Thomas. *DEFA, Künstler und SED-Kulturpolitik: zum Verhältnis von Kulturpolitik und Filmproduktion in der SBZ/DDR 1945 bis 1959.* Berlin: VISTAS, 1994.

Heineman, Elizabeth. "The Hour of the Woman: Memories of Germany's 'Crisis Years' and West German National Identity." *American Historical Review* 101, no. 2 (1996): 354–95.

Heinzelmeier, Adolf. "Hildegard Knef. Das Trümmermädchen." In *Die Unsterblichen des Kinos: Glanz und Mythos der Stars der 40er und 50er Jahre,* edited by Adolf Heinzelmeier, Berndt Schulz, and Karsten Witte, 113–19. Frankfurt am Main: Fischer, 1980.

Hermand, Jost. *Kultur im Wiederaufbau: Die Bundesrepublik Deutschland 1945–1965.* Munich: Nymphenburger, 1986.

Höhn, Carola. *"Fange nie an aufzuhören..."*: *Erinnerungen.* Koblenz: Kettermann & Schmidt, 2003.

Howell, Geraldine. *Wartime Fashion: From Haute Couture to Homemade 1939–1945.* London, New York: Berg, 2012.

Industrie- and Handelskammer zu Berlin. *Die Wirtschaft Westberlins 1945–1955.* Berlin: Industrie- and Handelskammer, 1955.

Janke, Willi. "Bekleidungs- und Mode-Metropole Berlin." In *Berlin, am Kreuzweg Europas, am Kreuzweg der Welt,* edited by Ernst Lemmer, 61–64. Berlin: Eschen, 1959.

Jaspers, Kristina. "Schöne Hülle, verletzter Körper: Alltagsmode und Haute Couture." In *Hildegard Knef: Eine Künstlerin aus Deutschland,* edited by Daniela Sannwald, Kristina Jaspers, and Peter Mänz, 61–67. Berlin: Bertz & Fischer, 2005.

Kaes, Anton. *From Hitler to Heimat: The Return of History as Film.* Cambridge, MA: Harvard University Press, 1989.

Kessemeier, Gesa. "Die Mode erobert den Kurfürstendamm: Mode und Modellhäuser im Berlin der 1950er und 1960er Jahre." In *Heimweh nach dem Kurfürstendamm: Geschichte, Gegenwart und Perspektiven des Berliner Boulevards,* edited by Michael Zajonz and Sven Kuhrau, 149–59. Petersberg: Michael Imhof Verlag, 2010.

Kirkham, Pat. "Fashion, Femininity and 'Frivolous' Consumption in World-War-Two Britain." In *Utility Reassessed: The Role of Ethics in the Practice of Design,* edited by Judy Attfield, 145–55. Manchester: St. Martin's Press, 1999.

———. "Keeping Up Home Morale: 'Beauty and Duty' in Wartime Britain." In *Wearing Propaganda: Textiles on the Home Front in Japan, Britain and the United States, 1931–1945,* edited by Jacqueline M. Atkins, 205–26. New Haven, CT: Yale University Press, 2005.

Klaus, Ulrich J. *Deutsche Tonfilme,* vol. 12. Berlin: Klaus-Archiv, 2001.

Knef, Hildegard. *Der geschenkte Gaul: Bericht aus einem Leben.* Berlin: Edel, 2008, 234.

Koch, Gertrud. "Nachstellungen: Film und historischer Moment." In *Die Gegenwart der Vergangenheit: Dokumentarfilm, Fernsehen und Geschichte,* edited by Eva Hohenberger and Judith Keilbach, 216–29. Berlin: Vorwerk 8, 2003.

Kreimeier, Klaus. *Die UFA-Story.* Munich: Hanser, 1992.

Kremer, Roberta S., ed. *Broken Threads: The Destruction of the Jewish Fashion Industry in Germany and Austria.* Oxford: Berg, 2007.

Kurowski, Ulrich, and Andreas Meyer, eds. *Der Filmregisseur Peter Pewas: Materialien und Dokumente*. Berlin: Volker Spiess, 1981.

Landsman, Mark. *Dictatorship and Demand: The Politics of Consumerism in East Germany*. Cambridge, MA: Harvard University Press, 2005.

Lange, Gabriele. *Das Kino als moralische Anstalt: Soziale Leitbilder und die Darstellung gesellschaftlicher Realität im Spielfilm des Dritten Reichs*. Frankfurt am Main: Peter Lang, 1994.

Lant, Antonia. *Blackout: Reinventing Women for Wartime British Cinema*. Princeton, NJ: Princeton University Press, 1991.

Lehnert, Sigrun. *Wochenschau und Tagesschau in den 1950er Jahren*. Munich: UKV Verlagsgesellschaft Konstanz, 2013.

Lennox, Sara. "Constructing Femininity in the Early Cold War Era." In *German Pop Culture: How American Is It?*, edited by Agnes C. Mueller. Ann Arbor: University of Michigan Press, 2004.

Loschek, Ingrid. "Contributions of Jewish Fashion Designers in Berlin." In *Broken Threads: The Destruction of the Jewish Fashion Industry in Germany and Austria*, edited by Roberta S. Kremer, 48–74. Oxford: Berg, 2007.

Lott-Almstadt, Sylvia. *Brigitte 1886–1986: Die ersten hundert Jahre, Chronik einer Frauenzeitschrift*. Hamburg: Gruner & Jahr, 1986.

———. *Die Frauenzeitschriften von Hans Huffzky und John Jahr: Zur Geschichte der deutschen Frauenzeitschrift zwischen 1933 und 1970*. Berlin: Volker Spiess, 1985.

Metzger, Karl-Heinz, and Ulrich Dunker. *Der Kurfürstendamm: Leben und Mythos des Boulevards in 100 Jahren deutscher Geschichte*. Berlin: Konopka, 1986.

Meyer, Ulfilas. "Trümmerkino." In *So viel Anfang war nie: Deutsche Städte 1945–1949*, edited by Herman Glaser, Lutz von Putendorf, and Michael Schöneich, 258–69. Berlin: Siedler, 1989.

Milde, Maria. *Berlin, Glienicker Brücke: Babelsberger Notizen*. Berlin: Universitas, 1978.

Mittman, Elizabeth. "Fashioning the Socialist Nation: The Gender of Consumption in Slatan Dudow's *Destinies of Women*." *German Politics and Society*, Winter 2005, 28–44.

Modemuseum im Münchner Stadtmuseum. *Aus 2 mach 1: Mode der Kriegs- und Nachkriegszeit*. Catalogue for exhibition, July 27 to October 15, 1995. Munich: Modemuseum im Münchner Stadtmuseum, 1995.

Moderegger, Johannes Christoph. *Modefotografie in Deutschland 1929–1955*. Norderstedt: Libri Books, 2000.

Mohr, Heinz. *DOB Mode in Deutschland 1945 bis heute*. Cologne: Verband der DOB, 1982.

Moritz, Cordula. *Die Kleider der Berlinerin: Mode und Chic an der Spree*. Berlin: Haude & Spenersche Verlagsbuchhandlung, 1972.

Mückenberger, Christiane. "Zeit der Hoffnungen: 1946 bis 1949." In *Das zweite Leben der Filmstadt Babelsberg: DEFA-Spielfilme 1946–1992*, edited by Ralf Schenk, 8–49. Berlin: Henschel, 1994.

Mückenberger, Christiane, and Günter Jordan. *'Sie sehen selbst, Sie hören selbst. . .': Die DEFA von ihren Anfängen bis 1949*. Marburg: Hitzeroth, 1994. ,

Munich, Adrienne, ed. *Fashion in Film*. Bloomington: Indiana University Press, 2011.

O'Brien, Mary-Elizabeth. *Nazi Cinema as Enchantment: The Politics of Entertainment in the Third Reich*. Rochester, NY: Camden House, 2003.

Oberschernitzki, Doris. *"Der Frau ihre Arbeit!" Lette-Verein, zur Geschichte einer Berliner Institution 1866 bis 1986*. Berlin: Edition Hentrich, 1987.

Parkins, Ilya. *Poiret, Dior and Schiaparelli: Fashion, Femininity and Modernity*. New York: Berg, 2012.

Pence, Katherine. "Building Socialist Worker-Consumers: The Paradoxical Construction of the Handelsorganisation—HO, 1948." In *Arbeiter in der SBZ—DDR*, edited by Peter Hübner and Klaus Tenfelde, 497–525. Essen: Klartext, 1999.

———. "'A World in Miniature': The Leipzig Trade Fairs in the 1950s and East German Consumer Citizenship." In *Consuming Germany in the Cold War*, edited by David F. Crew, 21–50. Oxford: Berg, 2003.

———. "'You as a Woman Will Understand': Consumption, Gender, and the Relationship between State and Citizenry in the GDR's June 17, 1953 Crisis." *German History*, no. 19 (2001): 218–52.

Pinkert, Anke. *Film and Memory in East Germany*. Bloomington: Indiana University Press, 2008.

Pleyer, Peter. *Deutscher Nachkriegsfilm 1946–1948*. Münster: C. J. Fahle, 1965.

Prager, Brad. "Resemblances: Between German Film Studies and History." *German Studies Review* 35, no. 3 (October 2012): 490–94.

Prinz, Friedrich, ed. *Trümmerzeit in München: Kultur und Gesellschaft einer deutschen Großstadt im Aufbruch 1945–1949*, edited by Friedrich Prinz. Munich: C. H. Beck, 1984.

Prommer, Elisabeth. *Kinobesuch im Lebenslauf: Eine historische und medienbiographische Studie*. Konstanz: UVK Medien, 1999.

———. "Das Kinopublikum im Wandel." In *Das Kulturpublikum: Fragestellungen und Befunde der empirischen Forschung*, edited by Patrick Glogner and Patrick S. Föhl, 195–237. Wiesbaden: VS Verlag für Sozialwissenschaften, 2010.

Rasche, Adelheid. "Fashion Shows Held by Christian Dior in Germany, 1949–1953." In *Christian Dior and Germany: 1947 to 1957*, edited by Adelheid Rasche with Christina Thomson, 206–29. Stuttgart: Arnoldsche, 2007.

Reiche, Jürgen. "Berlin: Zukunft nach dem Ende." In *So viel Anfang war nie: Deutsche Städte 1945–1949*, edited by Hermann Glaser, Lutz von Putendorf, and Michael Schöneich, 36–49. Berlin: Siedler, 1989.

Rentschler, Eric. *The Ministry of Illusion: Nazi Cinema and Its Afterlife*. Cambridge, MA: Harvard University Press, 1996.

———. "The Place of Rubble in the *Trümmerfilm*." *New German Critique* 37, no. 2 (Summer 2010): 9–30.

Riederer, Marietta. *Wie Mode Mode wird*. Munich: Bruckmann, 1962.

Riess, Curt. *Berlin! Berlin! 1945–1953*. Berlin: Non Stop-Bücherei, 1953.

———. *Das gab's nur einmal: Der deutsche Film nach 1945*. Hamburg: Nannen, 1977.

Roeber, Georg, and Gerhard Jacoby. *Handbuch der filmwissenschaftlichen Bereiche: die wirtschaftlichen Erscheinungsformen des Films auf den Gebieten der Unterhaltung, der Werbung, der Bildung und des Fernsehens.* Pullach/ Munich/: Verlag der Dokumentation, 1973.

Roesler, Jörg. "Privater Konsum in Ostdeutschland 1950–1960." In *Modernisierung im Wiederaufbau: Die westdeutsche Gesellschaft der 50er Jahre*, edited by Axel Schildt and Arnold Sywottek. 290–303. Bonn: Dietz, 1998.

———. "Der Wiederaufbau der Berliner Industrie 1945–1947." *Jahrbuch für Geschichte* 35 (1987): 486–538.

Rother, Hans-Jörg. "Der Weg in ein neues Leben: Der DEFA-Regisseur Slatan Dudow. Eine Spurensuche." In *apropos: Film 2004, Das 5. Jahrbuch der DEFA-Stiftung*, edited by Ralf Schenk, Erika Richter, and Claus Löser. Berlin: Bertz & Fischer, 2004.

Ruhl, Andreas. *Stalin-Kult und Rotes Woodstock: Die Weltjugendfestspiele 1951 und 1973 in Ostberlin.* Marburg: Tectum, 2009.

Sachsse, Rolf. "Im Schatten der Männer: Deutsche Fotografinnen 1940 bis 1950." In *Frauenobjektiv: Fotografinnen 1940 bis 1950*, edited by Hermann Schäfer, 12–25. Cologne/Bonn: Wienand, 2001.

Sannwald, Daniela. "Spröde Verführerin." In *Traumfrauen: Stars im Film der fünfziger Jahre*, edited by Gabriele Jatho and Hans Helmut Prinzler, 105–7. Berlin: Bertz & Fischer, 2006.

Saryusz-Wolska, Magdalena. "Watching Films in the Ruins: Cinema-going in Early Post-war Berlin." *Participations: Journal of Audience & Reception Studies* 12, no. 1 (May 2015): 762–82.

Saryusz-Wolska, Magdalena, and Anna Labentz, *Bilder der Normalisierung: Gesundheit, Ernährung und Haushalt in der visuellen Kultur.* Bielefeld: transcript, 2016.

Schallie, Charlotte. "Fashion Disappears from Germany." In *Broken Threads: The Destruction of the Fashion Industry in Germany and Austria*, edited by Roberta S. Kremer, 98–108. Oxford: Berg, 2007.

Schenk, Ralf. "Zwischen den Zonen: 'Ehe im Schatten' und andere Filme zwischen Ost und West." *film-dienst*, no. 21 (1997).

Scherpe, Klaus, ed. *In Deutschland unterwegs: Reportagen, Skizzen, Berichte 1945–1948.* ed. Klaus R. Scherpe. Stuttgart: Reclam, 1982.

Schittly, Dagmar. *Zwischen Regie und Regime: Die Filmpolitik der SED im Spiegel der DEFA-Produktionen.* Berlin: Christoph Links Verlag, 2002.

Schivelbusch, Wolfgang. *In a Cold Crater: Cultural and Intellectual Life in Berlin 1945–1948.* Translated by Kelly Barry. Berkeley: University of California Press, 1998.

Schmidt, Martin. "Raub an allen Fronten." In *Glanz und Grauen: Mode im 'Dritten Reich.' Begleitbroschüre zur Sonderausstellung*, edited by Claudia Gottfried. Ratlingen: LVR Industriemuseum, 2012.

Schmidt-Herzbach, Ingrid, and Thomas Wald. "Rettet die Kinder." In *Weiterleben nach dem Krieg: Schöneberg/Friedenau 1945–46*, edited by Susanne zur Nieden, Helga Schönknecht, and Eberhard Schönknecht, 59–66. Berlin: Bezirksamt Schöneberg, 1992.

Schmidt-Herzbach, Ingrid, and Renate Genth. "Die Frauenausschüsse: Das halb gewollte, halb verordnete Netz." In *Frauenpolitik und politisches Wirken von Frauen im Berlin der Nachkriegszeit 1945–1949*, edited by Renathe Genth et al., 47–74. Berlin: trafo, 1996.

Schmitt, Malwi. "Die strahlenden Jahre: Berliner Modegeschichte 1945–1961." In *Kleider Machen viele Leute*, edited by Katja Aschke, 246–54. Reinbek/Hamburg: Rororo, 1989.

Schnurre, Wolfdietrich. "Sammelrezension." In *Wolfdietrich Schnurre: Kritiker*, edited by Rolf Aurich, Jörg Becker, and Wolfgang Jacobsen, 168–73. Munich: edition text + kritik and Deutsche Kinemathek, 2010.

Schröder, Christian. *"Mir sollen sämtliche Wunder begegnen": Hildegard Knef, Biographie.* Berlin: Aufbau, 2004.

Schubert, Doris. *Frauen in der Nachkriegszeit. Band 1: Frauenarbeit 1945–1949, Quellen und Materialien.* Düsseldorf: Schwann, 1984.

Schütz, Sabine. "Vom Zuckersack zum Traummodell: die Entwicklung der Nachkriegsmode in Westdeutschland." In *Aus den Trümmern—Neubeginn und Kontinuität: Kunst und Kultur im Rheinland und Westfalen 1945–1952*, edited by Klauf Honnef and Hans M. Schmidt, 177–83. Cologne: Rheinland-Verlag, 1985.

Schwarz, Uta. "Der blockübergreifende Charme dokumentarischer Bilder: Tradition, Ideologie und Geschlecht in der Repräsentationsordnung der bundesdeutschen und DDR-Wochenschau der 1950er Jahre." In *Massenmedien im Kalten Krieg: Akteure, Bilder, Resonanzen*, edited by Thomas Lindenberger, 203–34. Cologne: Böhlau, 2006.

———. *Wochenschau, westdeutsche Identität und Geschlecht in den fünfziger Jahren.* Frankfurt am Main: Campus Verlag, 2002.

Selheim, Claudia. "Kleidung und Mode in Bayerisch-Schwaben zwischen 1945 und 1960." In *Beiträge zur Nachkriegsgeschichte von Bayerisch-Schwaben 1945–1970*, edited by Peter Fassl, 291–309. Augsburg: Bezirksheimatpflege, 2011.

Shandley, Robert R. *Rubble Films: German Cinema in the Shadows of the Third Reich.* Philadelphia: Temple University Press, 2001.

———. "The Truth Value of Cinema—German Rubble Films and Historiography." *Tel Aviver Jahrbuch für deutsche Geschichte* 31, Special Issue "Medien—Politik—Geschichte" (2003): 92–102.

Siebenbrodt, Michael, and Lutz Schöbe, eds. *Bauhaus 1919–1933: Weimar–Dessau–Berlin.* New York: Parkstone, 2009.

Sieglohr, Ulrike. "Hildegard Knef: From Rubble Woman to Fallen Woman." In *Heroines without Heroes: Reconstructing Female and National Identities in European Cinema 1945–51*, edited by Ulrike Sieglohr, 112–27, London: Cassell, 2000.

Sobotka, Jens Uwe. *Die Filmwunderkinder: Die Filmaufbau GmbH Göttingen.* Düsseldorf, Universitätsverlag: 1999.

Sridhar, Naveen. *Candlelight in a Storm: Born to be a Berliner.* Bloomington, IN: AuthorHouse 2015.

Stacey, Jackie. *Star Gazing: Hollywood Cinema and Female Spectatorship.* London and New York: Routledge, 1994.

Steege, Paul. *Black Market, Cold War: Everyday Life in Berlin 1946–1949.* New York: Cambridge University Press, 2007.

Stitziel, Judd. *Fashioning Socialism: Clothing, Politics, and Consumer Culture in East Germany.* Oxford: Berg, 2005.

Strate, Ursula. "Kleider machen Stars—Stars machen Kleider: Schnittstellen zwischen Mode, Musik und Film." In *MusikSpektakelFilm: Musiktheater und Tanzkultur im deutschen Film 1922–1937*, edited by Katja Uhlenbrok, 148–59. Munich: edition text + kritik, 1998.

Strauß, Annette. *Frauen im deutschen Film*. Frankfurt am Main: Peter Lang, 1996.

Street, Sarah. *Costume and Cinema: Dress Codes in Popular Film*. London: Wallflower, 2001.

Strehl-Firle, Hela. *Und danach war alles anders*. Düsseldorf, Econ-Verlag, 1965.

Sultano, Gloria. *Wie geistiges Kokain . . .: Mode unterm Hakenkreuz*. Vienna: Verlag für Gesellschaftskritik, 1995.

Swett, Pamela E. *Selling under the Swastika: Advertising and Commercial Culture in Nazi Germany*. Stanford, CA: Stanford University Press, 2014.

Sywottek, Arnold. "Zwei Wege in die 'Konsumgesellschaft.'" In *Modernisierung im Wiederaufbau: Die westdeutsche Gesellschaft der 50er Jahre*, edited by Axel Schildt and Arnold Sywottek, 269–74. Bonn: Dietz, 1998.

Sywottek, Jutta. *'Darf man jetzt von Mode sprechen?' Bekleidungsindustrie und Textilwirtschaft im Nachkriegsdeutschland*. Hildesheim: Arete, 2014.

Szepansky, Gerda. *"Blitzmädel" "Heldenmutter," "Kriegerwitwe": Frauenleben im Zweiten Weltkrieg*. Frankfurt am Main: Fischer, 1986.

Taylor, Lou. "The Work and Function of the Paris Couture Industry during the German Occupation of 1940–1944." *Dress*, no. 22 (2005): 34–44.

Tremper, Will. *Meine wilden Jahre*. Berlin: Ullstein, 1993.

Trimborn, Jürgen. *Hildegard Knef: Das Glück kennt nur Minuten*. Munich: Deutsche Verlags-Anstalt, 2005.

Veillon, Dominique. *Fashion under the Occupation*. Translated by Miriam Kochan. New York: Berg, 2002.

Vogt, Guntram. *Die Stadt im Kino: Deutsche Spielfilme, 1900–2000*. Marburg: Schüren, 2001.

Volz, Gunther. "Trümmermode und New Look: Kleidung und Mode in München 1945–1949." In *Trümmerzeit in München: Kultur und Gesellschaft einer deutschen Großstatt im Aufbruch 1945–1949*, edited by Friedrich Prinz, 301–11. Munich: Beck, 1984.

von Kardoff, Ursula. "Vier Frauenbildnisse von heute." In *In Deutschland unterwegs: Reportagen, Skizzen, Berichte 1945–1948*, edited by Klaus R. Scherpe, 51–56. Stuttgart: Reclam, 1982.

von Moltke, Johannes. *No Place like Home: Locations of Heimat in German Cinema*. Berkeley: University of California Press, 2005.

von Moltke, Johannes, and Hans-J. Wulff. "Trümmer-Diva: Hildegard Knef." In *Idole des deutschen Films: Eine Galerie von Schlüsselfiguren*, edited by Thomas Koerbner, 304–16, Munich: edition text + kritik, 1997.

Wagner, Gretel. "Das Deutsche Mode-Institut 1933–1941." *Waffen- und Kostümkunde* 39, nos. 1/2, 1997, 84–98.

———. "Everyone Is Talking about Dior: Media Response in German Magazines and Books." In *Christian Dior and Germany: 1947 to 1957*, edited by Adelheid Rasche with Christina Thomson, 230–47. Stuttgart: Arnoldsche, 2007.

———. "Die Mode in Berlin nach 1945." In *Berlin en Vogue: Berliner Mode in der Photographie*, edited by F. C. Gundlach and Uli Richter, 130–46. Berlin: Wasmuth, 1993.

Waidenschlager, Christine, ed. *Heinz Oestergaard: Mode für Millionen.* Berlin: Wasmuth, 1992.

———. "Modefürsten, Modekönige, Modezaren an der Spree." In *Die schöne Rheinländerin: 40 Jahre Mode im Rheinland. Eine Ausstellung im deutschen Textilmuseum Krefeld*, 20–23, Krefeld: Textilmuseum, 1989.

Walford, Jonathan. *Forties Fashion: From the Siren Suits to the New Look.* London: Thames & Hudson, 2008.

Warth, Eva-Maria. "The Reconceptualization of Women's Roles in Wartime National Socialism: An Analysis of 'Die Frau meiner Träume.'" In *The Nazification of Art: Art, Design, Music, Architecture and Film in the Third Reich*, edited by Brandon Taylor and Wilfried van der Will, 219–30. Winchester, Ontario: Winchester Press, 1990.

Weckel, Ulrike. *"Die Mörder sind unter uns*, oder: vom Verschwinden der Opfer." *WerkstattGeschichte* 9, no. 25 (2000): 105–15.

Wette, Wolfram, Ricarda Bremer, and Detlef Vogel, eds. *Das letzte halbe Jahr: Stimmungsberichte der Wehrmachtpropaganda 1944/45.* Essen: Klartext, 2001.

Werner, Ilse. *So wird's nie wieder sein . . . Ein Leben mit Pfiff.* Kiel: Michael Jung, 1991.

Werner, Wolfgang Franz. *"Bleib übrig!" Deutsche Arbeiter in der nationalsozialistischen Kriegswirtschaft.* Düsseldorf: Schwann, 1983.

Westphal, Uwe. *Berliner Konfektion und Mode, 1836–1939: Die Zerstörung einer Tradition.* 2nd ed. Berlin: Edition Hentrich, 1992.

Wiesen, S. Jonathan. *West German Industry and the Challenge of the Nazi Past 1945–1955.* Chapel Hill: University of North Carolina Press, 2001.

Wildt, Michael. "Changes in Consumption as Social Practice in West Germany during the 1950s." In *Getting and Spending: European and American Consumer Societies in the Twentieth Century*, edited by Susan Strasser, Charles McGovern, and Matthias Judt, 301–16. Cambridge, UK: Cambridge University Press, 1998.

Wortig, Kurt. *Ihre Hoheit Lieschen Müller: Hof- und Hinterhofgespräche um Film und Fernsehen.* Munich: Kreisselmeier, 1961.

Zierenberg, Malte. "The Trading City: Black Markets in Berlin during World War II." In *Endangered Cities: Military Power and Urban Societies in the Era of the World Wars*, edited by Marcus Funck and Roger Chickering, 145–58. Boston: Brill Academic Publishers, 2004.

Züchner, Eva. *Der verbrannte Koffer: Eine jüdische Familie in Berlin.* Berlin: Berlin Verlag, 2012.

Index

Page numbers for the illustrations are in bold face

Printed in the United States
by Baker & Taylor Publisher Services